With the benefit of hindsight

Valedictory reflections from departmental secretaries, 2004–11

With the benefit of hindsight

Valedictory reflections from departmental secretaries, 2004–11

Edited by John Wanna • Sam Vincent • Andrew Podger

Australian National University

E PRESS

Published by ANU E Press
The Australian National University
Canberra ACT 0200, Australia
Email: anuepress@anu.edu.au
This title is also available online at http://epress.anu.edu.au

---

National Library of Australia Cataloguing-in-Publication entry

Title:	With the benefit of hindsight : valedictory reflections from departmental secretaries, 2004-11/ edited by John Wanna, Sam Vincent, Andrew Podger.
ISBN:	9781921862731 (pbk.) 9781921862748 (ebook)
Subjects:	Civil service--Australia--Anecdotes. Australia--Officials and employees--Anecdotes.

Other Authors/Contributors:
Wanna, John.
Vincent, Sam.
Podger, A. S. (Andrew Stuart)

Dewey Number: 351.94

Cover design and layout by ANU E Press

Printed by Griffin Press

Contents

2012 Valedictory Series Foreword

The Valedictory Series, first published in November 2006,[1] affords the public service the opportunity to honour some of our most distinguished leaders, retiring Secretaries and agency heads.

Like previous publications this edition contains words of wisdom from a diverse group of people with a range of different styles. Without doubt all sixteen papers provide a thought-provoking experience for the reader and an insight into the views of some highly effective leaders and communicators about public service craft – leadership stories, career reflections and their ideas for the future.

This publication, prepared in partnership with ANZSOG, compiles edited versions of the Valedictory Lectures delivered as part of this series, complemented by essays from other former colleagues.

As Andrew Podger noted in his essay:

> ...the APS has a history of which we should all be proud, and that pride should be fostered as an important means of reinforcing confidence in our role and capability today.

Roger Beale, in his essay, mentions that while analytical and emotional intelligence, together with education and drive are all of importance, a certain degree of toughness and moral independence is part of every successful secretary's personality.

Ric Smith emphasises the value of collaboration, a theme woven throughout *Ahead of the Game: Blueprint for Reform of Australian Government Administration:*

> The best times have had this in common: they have been those occasions in which public servants from many different agencies have come together to work as one team to deliver a clear result. Ironically, I saw this at its best in the aftermath of the Bali bombing...

Leadership is, not surprisingly, a difficult business. Often there are no right answers and a leader cannot be the font of all knowledge – although some are remarkably well-gifted in this sphere.

Perhaps, fundamentally, and most importantly for the success of the Service, a Secretary's commitment to upholding the APS Values and Code of Conduct is

---

1 Most of these lectures were published at the time as commemorative pamphlets and placed on the APSC's website (under the 'Forum Speeches' link).

a mirror of their ability. After all as past Public Service Commissioner, Lynelle Briggs, observed in her lecture, Secretaries are the leaders of the APS and their behaviour is watched and modelled:

> Studies have shown that people will do what they see a leader do; even when that leader tells them behaving that way is unacceptable.

I trust that my foreword will whet your appetite to delve into the words of some thoughtful and committed former public servants.

I have been fortunate to work alongside almost all of them over the years and, to varying degrees, enjoyed a shared, and sometimes fraught, commitment to serving the public.

Steve Sedgwick
Public Service Commissioner

Introduction

Andrew Podger and John Wanna

Secretaries of government departments in Australia are the bureaucratic leaders of their generation. They are ambitious, highly-talented executives who have risen to the very pinnacle of their chosen vocation – public service to the Australian nation – usually after having spent most, if not all, of their professional careers dedicated to the public service. They serve governments as their top advisers and in policy terms are often some of the most important decision-makers in the country.

As bureaucratic leaders they also sit atop a very large pyramid. At any point in time no more than twenty individuals hold these esteemed positions out of a federal public service of some 165,000 employees, some 245,000 in Commonwealth government employment, and a population of around 22 million. The departments they run are some of the largest organisations in society, much larger in terms of the number of employees and number of functions than their equivalents in the private or non-government sectors.

In this collection we have assembled the valedictory speeches from a departing echelon of secretaries (and one or two other equivalent agency heads) who left the Australian Public Service between 2004 and 2011. Over this period of time, among the Canberra mandarinate, it became accepted and, indeed, expected that departing secretaries and heads of significant agencies would present a valedictory address given to their peers at some public farewell function. The first two in this collection of speeches were initiated by the secretaries themselves and given at functions organised by their agencies. Perhaps because of their substance, or their notoriety, it was decided in late 2005 to formalise the process with the Australian Public Service Commission acting as host and organiser (records of around seven of these ten formal valedictories were internally published by the APSC between 2005 and 2010).

Peter Shergold, then Secretary of the Department of the Prime Minister and Cabinet, had read the valedictory address given in July 2005 by the head of the UK civil service, Sir Andrew Turnbull, and was impressed and believed we in Australia should do something similar. A number of departing secretaries chose not to deliver a valedictory at the time, or felt uncomfortable proffering commentary on the eve of their departure, or were just too busy with other things to devote the necessary time to the speech. We invited each of these to make a contribution to our compilation, albeit sometime after their departure.

Most agreed, so that the sixteen former secretaries (13 men and three women) in this collection include most who left the APS over this period. On our count we are still missing four who ceased to be a secretary in this period.

The speeches roam across the terrain chosen by the speaker. There was no set format or template that had to be followed. The content and robustness of the speeches was entirely up to the presenter either at the time of their departure or in response to our invitation. Accordingly, they contain reflections, commentaries, occasional fond memories or key turning-points in their careers, critiques of changes that have occurred or trends they feel are not for the best, and some pay particular attention to the remaining challenges their successors, the public administrators of tomorrow, will face. Some discuss how they manage their private and public lives, while others steer clear of this and focus on public administration more decisively.

Significantly, most of these former secretaries started their working lives as graduates in agencies with strong internal cultures emphasising rigorous training, analysis and making a difference. When they started out they were one of many hopefuls aspiring to leadership positions in national administration. Of course, each year thousands start out on a public service career path; of these no doubt many have ambitions to climb up the ladder, but few can ever reach the top. Gradually each intake is whittled down by departures, transfers, resignations, even illness or incapacity; some leave the public service due to a loss of interest or commitment, perhaps because they are unsuited in temperament, or are insufficiently talented or motivated.

The original intakes are gradually narrowed at senior levels until only the exceptionally talented stayers remain. In most cases secretaries are internal appointments with considerable experience, selected by invitation rather than by outside advertisement. Most were clearly Canberra insiders who had spent their careers in the national capital in Commonwealth bodies, but some were total outsiders, coming from public sector experience in the states. So, not only are these gifted practitioners the most capable of their generation, they are also the survivors and victors of the 'greasy pole' inside government that rubs administration against politics. If it is too much to claim that they actually embody the state, they certainly occupy the fulcrum between government and the community, and between our political and administrative systems.

Some of the former secretaries contributing to this collection managed to hold the office for around a decade serving multiple governments and working with various ministers; others served a much shorter term perhaps with just one minister in one government. Three served as the Australian Public Service Commissioner besides heading departments and agencies (Peter Shergold, Andrew Podger and Lynelle Briggs). As a group of executives their trajectories differ according to the contingencies and circumstances they faced. Most left office at their choosing, announcing their intention of resigning perhaps to retire or to take up some other career or job offer. A few felt pushed from their posts and were terminated before they would themselves have chosen to go. Some have gone on to enjoy glittering careers in other professional spheres after their stint as secretary; most are still making a contribution in the broader public interest; a very few simply retired after they left the job. One or two have begun (or continued) to write, making public contributions to public administration or policy analysis and deliberation, policy and administrative reviews, or to teaching and training.

As a group of relatively experienced secretaries, they fulfilled many roles depending on circumstance and the requirements of the government of the day. Included in our group were former central agency coordinators and fix-it operatives; some had earned a reputation as strategic policy advisers who had progressed by intellectual prowess, others headed large and complex policy portfolios, some ran delivery agencies or specialist functional units. At least ten straddled both line and central agency responsibilities in their time as public service leaders, employing the lessons and experiences from one set of functions to the other.

Interestingly for students of public administration, their backgrounds are diverse and contrasting. Unlike in some other countries (and particularly the UK and France) there is no natural elite or aristocratic cadre who occupy the posts almost by entitlement or social standing and who have been schooled and socialised through elite tertiary institutions such as Oxbridge or studied at the *Grandes Écoles*. By contrast, Australian secretaries come from all walks of life: some of their families were engaged in timber-gathering, ran share farms or country banks; one's father was a politician, others' fathers include a local doctor, an accountant and a state government engineer; some had mothers who had professional careers of their own in teaching or health services, while others' mothers played a more traditional role. Many came from small towns or rural backgrounds. They earned scholarships to their local universities often before going on to undertake higher degrees, with some choosing to study overseas. Despite this diversity, they are mostly men with an English-speaking background, and only one had a disability.

As these speeches illustrate, these secretaries are also human beings coping with the pressures of managing careers and personal lives. They try to manage work-family balances despite the onerous demands of the job. At times in their careers they were sometimes fortunate, lucky, exasperated, disappointed, proud of their achievements, worried things are getting away from them or becoming harder to manage. Each one has a different personality and took different approaches to crafting their reflections in the speeches.

So what do they tell us about the nature of public service and government administration, about leading public institutions, and about the state of public policy more generally? From the outset it is clear that there is no uniform message, no single narrative levelled either in praise or in criticism, other than pride in the public service and strong belief in the contribution it makes to the Australian community. They have their own personal 'takes' on how the public service looks to them, on its performance and on the challenges confronting public administration into the future. Most spend some time looking back, reflecting on the extent of change that has occurred over the length of their careers; but equally importantly they look forward, anticipating future policy dilemmas and capacity challenges.

Several strongly dispute the notion that there was ever a 'golden age' of the APS from which some subsequent fall from grace has occurred. Roger Beale notes in his 2004 speech that for every great man of the past there were others holding back reform, and that 'those great men of the post-war public service were also great haters and great players of time-wasting, self-indulgent bureaucratic games'. 'The system had to change – and it did', he says. Others also are comfortable with the influential speech given by Peter Shergold (see AJPA 63(4) 2004) when he was Secretary of PM&C originally entitled 'Once was Camelot in Canberra?', which poured scorn on the 'golden age' affliction. Ric Smith and David Borthwick refer to the more collegiate approach in the modern era. But equally secretaries are not complacent and consider it essential (and prudent) to enhance the critical capacities of the public service and its abilities to analytically scrutinise or challenge ideas inside government in the pursuit of good public policy. They are also conscious of increased accountabilities applying to today's secretaries that were far less onerous for their predecessors prior to the 1970s. According to these more recent secretaries, their distant predecessors had an easier set of tasks to perform and accountabilities to meet, and a more leisurely pace at which to do it.

There is a general agreement about the important challenge of managing the relationship with ministers, making it work, finding ways to ensure ministers get the advice they need to hear. Ministers are important partners and gatekeepers in their public service endeavours – whether identifying priorities, providing policy advice, appraising risk, or delivering services to the public. Ministers bring the all-important political dimension to the table without which many decisions or actions would not be taken. As politicians they may be a little distant or wary, constantly time-poor and at times motivated by different concerns, but finding ways to work with ministers is crucial to the secretary's own performance and that of their agency. Shergold highlights the nuances of the relationship, observing how closely he worked with each of his ministers: 'yet not one minister was my friend'.

Unlike many in the general populace, secretaries almost universally have a high level of respect for ministers and the roles they perform. But managing the minister in a constantly changing political environment is not easy and requires a constant prudential balance; and these former secretaries display some divergence of views about the balance between being responsive to the political realm (the minister and cabinet) and the degree of independence needed to present alternatives, cautions or even warnings to gung-ho ministers. In his 2005 valedictory Andrew Podger writes: 'I doubt there are many today who would argue that the APS needs to shift the balance further towards responsiveness'. On the other hand, Michael L'Estrange, writing in 2011, well after the public debate between Podger and Shergold over secretary employment arrangements, states: 'I share Peter Shergold's view that the provision of frank and sometimes unwelcome advice by secretaries to ministers is a question of character, not of contract'.

Some secretaries highlight the increasing numbers of ministerial advisers and the roles they are charged to undertake in the minister's name, and the impact this has on relationships with ministers. Ric Smith notes that 'we now have a whole new layer or level of government'. Like others, Smith comments about this trend not with any sense of antagonism or nostalgia for the day when advisers were not around, but expresses concern about the impact on the respective accountabilities of ministers and secretaries. Patricia Scott writing in 2011 says there has been real progress in clarifying the role of ministerial advisers since their code of conduct was introduced, but remains concerned about 'the all-too-common experience of the adviser that is exclusively a political operative with little policy experience, overflowing confidence in their ability to discern policy on the basis of a quick Google search and an unrelenting focus on the short-term political imperatives'. She prefers having senior people with both policy expertise and the confidence of the minister. She also advocates having senior departmental officers playing key roles in ministerial offices.

Several secretaries highlight the importance of longer-term strategic policy analysis and advice (perhaps even contingency planning and strategic thinking), and a focus on the public interest notwithstanding the role of ministers to determine policy. David Borthwick speaks about advising on policy 'as if for a thousand years', and suggests some measures to address the pressures from increasingly savvy specific interest groups and governments being more reactive to the intense pressure of the 24-hour news cycle. He argues that 'today there is a much stronger focus on developing public policy that is genuinely in the national interest and, consequently, there is a much stronger focus on working together'.

A few highlight particular policy fields and exhort continued effort and analysis. Ken Henry focuses on the central responsibility of economic management and on the challenges facing governments in enhancing national economic wellbeing. Instead of reflecting back on his own career, he chooses to 'look ahead at the economic landscape upon which future Treasury secretaries will be developing policy advice'. Mark Sullivan calls for continued boldness in addressing Indigenous disadvantage, noting the need to get the support of Aboriginal community leaders and to remember the 'wonderful positives that come from embracing Aboriginal and Torres Strait Islander culture and practice'.

While most of these former secretaries did not mention much about their relations with the Prime Minister, or prime ministerial styles – which varied substantially from Keating to Howard, to Rudd to Gillard – several express concern about weakening cabinet processes and moves towards presidential styles of government. Several would also like to see further improvements to collegiality across government (between executives from different agencies and between different agencies) and strengthening of the links with the coordinating agencies at the centre to better coordinate and integrated whole-of-government policy responses.

Not surprisingly, many of the former APS leaders highlight the management issues and the importance of implementation, some providing considerable detail on specific management challenges including IT management, performance pay, recruitment and development. Lynelle Briggs highlights the scale of the change management task facing those in the Human Services portfolio, while Dennis Trewin describes the changing world faced by one of our oldest agencies, the Australian Bureau of Statistics. Given that management is one of the essential functions of a secretary, it is perhaps puzzling that more of these former secretaries did not say more about management or mention management dilemmas at all. Allan Hawke is an exception, using his essay to take a firm stand against performance pay which was the order of the day when he was a secretary, citing a wide range of evidence in support of his argument. While Hawke notes his failure to win the argument against the orthodoxy in the early 2000s, no-one here argues for performance pay (though Michael L'Estrange considers that it 'has never fulfilled the best hopes of its champions or the worst fears of its detractors').

Given the era in which they spent their senior careers (the 1990s), most are conscious of the tension between consolidation or centralisation and decentralisation or devolution. There is a divergence of views about the merits of devolution, Peter Shergold perhaps reflecting the majority view worrying that it may have gone too far while Peter Boxall extolling its virtues and doubting the merits of some of the more recent attempts at re-centralisation.

Few refer to their relations with the Parliament, although the occasional grilling particularly from senators at Senate Estimates hearings is certainly burnt into their consciousness. The theatre of parliament is a forum in which their ministers play, and something to be wary about, but not sufficiently contentious or onerous for secretaries to warrant much comment in these speeches. Ken Matthews asks if APS leaders have 'become [too] docile and unassertive' in Senate Estimates and other forums, both public and private. Most believe in informing parliament genuinely about what is being undertaken; although many seem to express a preference for a greater level of independence from the parliamentary realm than they are granted. But this view is not universal and traditionalists remain comfortable with being ultimately accountable to parliament conventions.

Of increasingly more importance to today's leaders are relations with the public and of good two-way communication. These externalrelations are highlighted in several speeches, partly out of concerns to improve the effectiveness of policy implementation but also to advance the agenda for what is now more described as 'citizen-centred services' or 'citizen engagement'. Briggs believes a 'transformational change' is taking place in the way public services are delivered, based on an 'outside-in' approach instead of 'the more traditional internally driven 'tell you' model', describing the work she led in Human Services. Trewin emphasises the growing importance to the ABS of user engagement to handle the growth in demand and the dramatic changes in the way users access statistics.

Similarly, the difficulties in managing media relations are frequently identified as an important part of the job of a secretary (and a risk to be managed because of the potential downsides of negative coverage). Matthews applauds Ken Henry's regular public economic and reform contributions, saying senior public servants 'have a responsibility to be more active on the conference circuit'. L'Estrange seems more circumspect; while referring to the personal confidences that are entered into by secretaries which need to 'be respected in both the short and longer term', he says 'this ongoing responsibility is of a different order to that applying to elected decision-makers'. The two are referring to different issues, of course, but one perhaps reflects a more traditional approach inclined to public service anonymity while the other reflects a desire for more open public engagement. Podger raises another aspect of this difficult issue in his valedictory of 2005, suggesting that constraints on public access to information and controls on government communications may not reflect the public interest but partisan interests.

Relations between the Commonwealth and state or territory governments are highlighted directly by two contributors and indirectly by others. Borthwick says the trend towards greater control by the Commonwealth is unlikely to be reversed. 'The Commonwealth is absolutely capable of developing strategies for managing complex projects at a local level, and delivering services across Australia which cater to the different needs of different communities', he argues, while stating that 'the acquisition of new responsibilities does bring with it new challenges'. Matthews focuses on the 'new paradigm' of priority for regional Australia highlighting challenges for 'the city-based Australian Public Service'. *Promoting the APS Values* is not mentioned directly by many, but there is frequent reference to the critical role of the public service, reflected in the titles chosen by Shergold ('In the national interest') and Borthwick ('As if for a thousand years...'). These secretaries all took their APS leadership responsibilities seriously.

Finally, and naturally enough, the vagaries of negotiating personal career paths and development are mentioned by nearly all. They recount how at certain junctures significant mentors were important to their careers and the choices they thereafter made; who recruited them for significant jobs or who they followed into challenging managerial or policy roles; and who helped shape their career path. Much of this genuflexion is highly personal and included by way of public appreciation. In giving their valedictory, speakers would typically cite lists of names of the many with whom they worked, or who helped their careers along, but who would not be familiar to today's readership. We have taken the liberty of editing out much of this personalised expression of gratitude from the publication. Nevertheless, it is interesting to note the similarities of patterns in their progression through the ranks and through different policy and organisational challenges. There was once some commonality to the making of a secretary.

Yet as L'Estrange predicts, probably accurately, the career paths of secretaries in the future are likely to be much more varied and dissimilar in their composition and experiences – a development he applauds. Robert Cornall represents one of those with a more varied career path including both private sector and state government experience. In identifying the lessons he learned in the APS after working for the Victorian government, he makes the interesting point that it 'was like moving from the under 15s to the seniors over night'. The adjustment was not just to the size and scale of the Commonwealth but also to the breadth of responsibilities including the international dimension. While the males often thanked spouses, partners and families for their support, as Joanna Hewitt mentions, it is often still very difficult for women in relationships where both partners occupy senior professional appointments to deal with the work-family balance over time, especially when significant distance separates the family.

These speeches provide an important contribution to understanding the challenges of public administration in the modern era as seen from the top of the service. There are differences of opinion on some issues, partly reflecting the different times when the speeches were made, but also reflecting some healthy debates within the APS that deserve more public exposure. The different aspects of the responsibilities of secretaries that these former mandarins decided to focus upon also reflect the breadth of the challenges in the job. All are thoughtful, and all demonstrate a commitment to the role of the APS and a concern to see its capability to be able contribute to the Australian community continue and grow.

1. Yes, minister—the privileged position of secretaries[1]

Roger Beale

In March 2004 Roger Beale retired from the Australian Public Service after 8 years as Secretary of the Department of Environment and Heritage and nearly 20 years in departmental head and equivalent posts, including in the departments of Transport and Prime Minister and Cabinet. Much of Beale's public service career involved microeconomic reform, including work with the states and Commonwealth on National Competition Policy; establishing the National Heritage Trust; and setting a framework for measuring carbon pollution in Australia and participating on the Australian team negotiating the Kyoto Protocol.

Departmental secretaries

Early in my career I was lucky to be taken under Sir Frederick Wheeler's wing as one of his 'young people' when he was Chairman of the Public Service Board. As a result I was privileged to observe in action many of the great post-war figures of Australian public service – Wheeler himself, Wilson, Crawford, Randall, Tange, Bunting – as well as some lesser-lights such as Donald Anderson, Lenox Hewitt, Crisp and so on. Coombs I only saw at a distance.

I have met every secretary over the last thirty years or so, and worked with many of them. Against this background I wish to comment on some of the currently fashionable criticisms they attract – that today's secretaries are just a shadow of the post-war greats and that as a result of the changes in tenure that started in 1984 and were sharpened in the mid 90s we have become politically supine and led our departments down the same path.

In reality we have all heard these criticisms on and off for nearly twenty years now. Of course the great men – sadly no women – of the post-war period (Wilson, Wheeler, Tange and their ilk) were formidably bright, tough as old boots and firm in their dealings with ministers. But we forget a few things. First, for every Alf Rattigan at the Tariff Board courageously trying to open up the Australian economy there were senior public servants in industry, trade, agriculture and labour trying to perpetuate the web of protective tariffs, centralised employment

---

1   This speech was delivered in March 2004 at a function organised by the Department of Environment and Heritage.

arrangements and regulations and subsidies; for every Wheeler trying to get a better deal for women and promote the entry of graduates in the public service there were senior colleagues trying to hang onto the preference for returned soldiers, the limits on the proportions of graduate entrants and to oppose the lifting of the marriage bar.

Second, while it is true that many secretaries exercised a great deal of personal power, this was often done in a way that was imperious rather than democratic. It is not surprising that first Whitlam and then Fraser believed that some key parts of the bureaucracy failed to engage with policies for which the Prime Minister had a clear democratic mandate. Both parties demanded greater policy responsiveness from the public service – but this should not be confused with being supine. As Sir William Cole put it, 'It is your duty to argue – once is essential, twice if the issue is important, but three times or beyond it begins to sound like nagging.'

Finally, I would suggest that those great men of the post-war public service were also great haters and great players of time-wasting, self-indulgent bureaucratic games. Inter-departmental warfare was rife and personal feuds carried out over decades abounded. Anyone who drafted letters for Wheeler or Hewitt would have understood the disregard they felt for each other and the way that it was allowed to spill over into public administration. And they were not alone. John Stone was a late and particularly bizarre manifestation of this weakness.

The system had to change – and it did. We should honour the great men of the past. But let us keep this in perspective. The current and immediately past generation of secretaries and agency heads, which at last contains a share of talented women, is undoubtedly on the whole better educated, harder working, much more inclined to take a whole-of-government view of issues rather than a narrowly departmental one and are far more interested and capable in management than many of their illustrious predecessors.

On the question of politicisation of advice as a result of tenure shifts, I think this too has been overemphasised. In the areas I have worked in – the economic, industry and environmental – I have been impressed not just at the quality of the advice provided by secretaries but also their willingness to provide it even when it would not be welcomed. That has not changed over the years.

While analytical and emotional intelligence, together with education and drive are all of importance, a certain degree of toughness and moral independence is part of every successful secretary's personality. These are not people to easily push around. People try – senior colleagues, lobby groups, some ministers and even prime ministers at times. But from my observation this is little different now from over the past 30 years, and the success rate is not, from my observation, any higher.

In some senses secretaries and their senior departmental colleagues are in a privileged position. Their advice is provided in private, sometimes orally, and their views are not usually referred to as justifying government policy decisions – and any sane government wants to get plain, unvarnished advice in camera, even if it decides to ignore it. The corollary is that secretaries have to be very careful about their public presentation – they need not to be seen as either advocates of government policy, nor of course to inadvertently or otherwise criticise it.

Over the years, the biggest risk to the provision of straightforward advice has always arisen not from fear but from the desire to be liked by our political masters, loved by an external constituency or to push a personally preferred policy line. Those have always been, and always will be, temptations for those advising the powerful.

Economic modelling

One issue does worry me however, and that is the way in which economic modelling is sometimes commissioned and used. From a professional economist's viewpoint, the almost mythic power ascribed to economic models in public policy discourse is puzzling. Even good models are only as useful as the input assumptions allow them to be – and sometimes I have seen these used to distort rather than illuminate public policy debate.

Models should play an important role in thought experiments about policy choices and alternative instruments. But far too often in public debate they are used as weapons of offence and defence – usually, not by those who produce them, and often by those who do not really understand them.

The focus is placed on a single number – the cost or gain to GDP – on a single set of assumptions. This is 'dumbing down' of the public policy debate. This problem is not restricted to economic modelling as anyone who has followed the climate change science debate or that on genetically manipulated organisms will understand – it is very easy to fall into the trap of failing to mention uncertainties and assumptions that are often clearly spelled out in the source papers, or to confuse scenarios and projections with forecasts.

Expert advisers should always set out clearly and prominently their assumptions and their sources so their reasonableness can be judged, as well as any inherent error margins in the analytic techniques used and the sensitivity of results to all of these. This should be very explicit in the executive summaries of the advice so that it is not easy to 'cherry pick' the conclusions that are preferred without being equally aware of the cautions and limitations.

Ministerial responsibility and the tenure of secretaries

These problems are not new or particularly associated with secretaries, or even necessarily the public sector. They certainly do not flow from the changes in tenure at the top. But the reduction in tenure and the increase in personal accountability for secretaries does have its downsides. There is a real risk that the old myth of strict ministerial responsibility for egregious administrative and policy blunders is in the process of being replaced by an actual strict secretarial liability for departmental error.

This is perhaps more pronounced at the state level than the Commonwealth, but the progressive decline in the time in office of secretaries over the last 30 years is worrying – particularly if the focus is on the time which a secretary is given in an individual department. You simply cannot provide the longer-term planning, staff development, budgeting and change management that are critical to high performance if you are only chief executive for two to three years – five to seven is often needed. Perhaps we ought to be thinking of five years being the normal term, and more ordered and deliberate processes for considering the removal of secretaries perceived to be underperforming.

Ministers

But enough about secretaries. Ministers get a raw deal from the press and the public; an unjust deal, in most cases at least. I have worked directly to 25 ministers and one prime minister. The vast majority of these have been talented, hard working and decent. Some have lacked one or other of these qualities – but there is only one I can think of who lacked all three, and I am not going to disclose who he was!

Of course it wasn't Robert Hill or David Kemp. In different ways I have had a relationship with both Robert and David that I have treasured – just as I did in earlier times with Bob Collins and John Dawkins. I thank all the ministers I have assisted in the past for the privilege of working to support you in this great democratic adventure.

Wheeler versus Westerman

Wheeler, when Chairman of the Public Service Board, had a long running dispute with Sir Alan Westerman, Secretary of the Department of Trade and

Industry (and by implication with Black Jack McEwen the Deputy Prime Minister and leader of the Country Party) over whether the Department of Trade should get an additional special high level staffing position. Eventually Menzies wrote to Wheeler asking him to attend a cabinet meeting to explain the Board's refusal to provide it – noting that Westerman, Bunting and Randall would be present. Wheeler refused Menzies' invitation to attend cabinet on the grounds that it would be improper for the board to appear to be 'hauled' before cabinet in the presence of its secretary peers and suggested that the Prime Minister might instead care to call on the board instead. This was the last folio on the file and Trade did not get its high level position – much to the satisfaction of the Treasury.

Secretaries and democracy

Speaking of which – there is nothing more democratic than accompanying your minister on a visit to a key part of the department's constituency. We used to do that more often in the days before MoPs' act staff. For example when I was running the growth centres program under Kevin Newman I went with him to Albury-Wodonga to open the Uncle Ben's Pet Food Factory. That was fine. Then we went to the Boomerang Hotel where he was going to give a speech I had written to the Chamber of Commerce. Air conditioning hadn't reached that far yet – they just had big fans and open windows – with gentle breezes blowing from the abattoir holding pen across the road.

Anyway he got up to speak. He didn't trip, clearly pulled the right speech from his pocket and was well away. I had a carafe of red wine and relaxed. In fact I drifted off to the gentle drone of the blowies and the buzz of the minister. Then I woke up with a feeling that something was terribly wrong. The speech was going on for far too long. Then I realized that somehow he had started again from about page two. And just after that he realised what he had done. He began to stammer, thump the table and say things like 'as I say again for emphasis' while he worked out how to bring it to an end. Kevin in fury was a horrible sight – puce face, straining buttons, froth on the lips – and he came across, pointed and said 'this is your fault – you should put 'THE END' at the end.' 'Yes, Minister', was my reply.

Finally, if I were a young person would I do it all over again? Unequivocally yes. It is not an easy life, but it is immensely rewarding. There are frustrations, there is scrutiny, there is more competition for the ear of ministers – but it is still a huge privilege to be part of our national democratic life.

2. My fortunate career and some parting remarks[1]

Andrew Podger

Andrew Podger is currently professor of public policy at The Australian National University and adjunct professor at Griffith University and Xi'an Jiao Tong University. Originally a mathematician, he joined the Australian Public Service as a cadet with the Australian Bureau of Statistics in 1978. He served as Secretary to the Departments of Health and Aged Care, Housing and Regional Development, and Administrative Services before becoming Public Service Commissioner in 2002. His last role as a public servant was to chair a task force for the Prime Minister on the delivery of health services in Australia.

I have indeed been blessed with a fortunate career in the Australian Public Service. From my beginnings at the Bureau of Statistics to the departments that immediately followed − the Social Welfare Commission, the Department of the Prime Minister and Cabinet, the Department of Social Security (my first SES job and the most enjoyable period of my career) − I serendipitously worked in a series of remarkable teams.

My good fortune continued when I joined the Department of Finance in 1982 under the stewardship of enormously strong financial reformers including Mike Keating, Tony Harris, Pat Barrett, Tony Blunn, Malcolm Holmes, Neil Johnston, David Rosalky and Alan Briggs.

At the Department of Defence I not only worked with fine civil servants but also military leaders of great skill and integrity such as Peter Gration, Alan Beaumont and John Baker.

My period at the Department of Housing and Regional Development would have been a huge success, but it ran out of time. While the likes of Jeff Harmer, Jeff Whalan, Lyndsay Neilson, Mark Johnston, Alan Evans and Christianna Cobbold were not always easy to marshal, our department was a happy one. I remain bemused that the public housing micro-economic reforms that were even approved by COAG disappeared in 1996, and that our cooperative approach to city and regional infrastructure of national importance seems only now to again be getting the attention it deserves.

---

1 This speech was delivered in June 2005 at a farewell function organised by the Department of Prime Minister and Cabinet and the Australian Public Service Commission, before the system of formal valedictory speeches was introduced.

Being appointed Secretary of the Department of Health was my greatest challenge, as I had the task of revitalising a department and portfolio that, while talented, was low on morale and high on cynicism. And yet, some changes in structure and personnel led to me working with a good group of CEOs heading up HIC, Medibank Private, the Food Authority, ARPANSA, the PSR, CRS and AIHW. The team in the department also coalesced with Judith Whitworth and Dick Smallwood to give us the credibility we needed within the medical profession, while David Borthwick added to our economic credibility. Mary Murnane, my saviour during the Aged Care crisis, provided the essential continuity and corporate knowledge for the executive. Moreover, the division heads were as strong a group as you will find anywhere, most having been in the health and community services field for a long time, but now working much more as a team rather than as robber barons.

The APS Commission was an altogether different proposition, having been well managed by my predecessor Helen Williams. Moreover, while in the job I received able support from Lynne Tacy and Jeff Lamond in particular. We faced some turnover in the SES, but I know I left my successor Lynelle Briggs with a strong team comprising a mixture of human resources expertise and exceptional analytical talent.

I was also fortunate to have worked closely with ministers and parliamentary secretaries from both sides of politics who, in nearly all cases, were enormously hard working, intelligent and genuinely concerned for the welfare of Australians. Well before I became a departmental secretary I had the privilege of working closely with not only Dame Margaret Guilfoyle, but also Fred Chaney, John Dawkins, Peter Walsh, Robert Ray and John Faulkner. As secretary I worked briefly with Bob McMullan and then with Brian Howe for two years when he was Deputy Prime Minister; this was followed by Michael Wooldridge for six years and his junior ministers and parliamentary secretaries such as Judi Moylan, Warwick Smith, Trish Worth and Grant Tambling. In the Commission I worked with Tony Abbott and Kevin Andrews; many different personalities and styles, and quite different political philosophies, but from close up I can say firmly that familiarity does not breed contempt. I also worked with some excellent and dedicated advisers such as Rod Kemp, Jenny Macklin and Barbara Carney.

Some parting remarks on the Australian Public Service

When Roger Beale retired as Secretary of the Department of the Environment and Heritage in 2004, he questioned the popular assumption that the 'golden age' of the Australian Public Service was in the 1950s and 1960s and that today's APS and its leadership are somehow of a lesser quality. I too question the veracity of this notion. One need only look at the remarkable contributions of recent leaders such as Tony Ayers, Mike Keating and Ian Castles, all of whom I believe have left legacies that will stand the test of time. Helen Williams will also be recognised as a great pioneer for women in the service, and a champion of our profession. But in doing so, I do not want to denigrate the exceptional characters of earlier eras: Robert Garran and Duncan McLachlan at the beginning of the twentieth century; Melville and Giblin in the 1930s; the 'Seven Dwarves' of the 1950s of whom Sir Roland Wilson remains amongst our most brilliant stars; Fred Wheeler in the 1970s with his emphasis on due process; and Bill Cole.

But the fact is, the APS has a history of which we should all be proud, and that pride should be fostered as an important means of reinforcing confidence in our role and capability today. During celebrations marking the centenary of the APS in 2001, it was noteworthy how much pride and morale today's public servants took from the various studies undertaken on the history of the service to mark the occasion.

Peter Shergold, like Roger Beale, has also highlighted that it is wrong to judge today's service against the context in which it operated in the past. We are subject to much more scrutiny than were our predecessors, and there are many more players on the stage with whom we must compete, and share power and authority. In fact, in sheer terms of overall expertise and education, today's Australian Public Service is far more capable than it ever was in the past.

And yet, the credibility of today's leadership is not enhanced if it does not acknowledge our current challenges, weaknesses and occasional failures. Let me now focus on that perennial challenge for the service: balancing our responsibility to be responsive with our duties to remain apolitical, impartial and professional.

Like all such balances, the proverbial pendulum swings back and forth over time, and it is dangerous to assume that there was ever a period of equilibrium when an exact balance was achieved. Ian Hancock's 2003 book *The V.I.P. Affair*, for example, demonstrates that some of our acclaimed leaders of the past overstepped the mark in giving ministers what they wanted and not giving the parliament the facts it legitimately sought. On the other hand, one of the reasons

I so admire Sir Roland Wilson is because of his firm understanding of the need to be responsive as well as apolitical and impartial. 'I hope,' said Wilson, 'that I shall never be guilty of ignoring the voice of the people. In fact I feel that some of our public service administrators have been altogether too much infatuated with their own crackpot views and the sooner I subject my own thinking to the supervision of my political masters the better we shall get on.'

There was bipartisan consensus in the 1970s and 1980s that the service was too independent and not as responsive to the elected government as it ought to be. As a consequence, while the changes enacted in the 1980s and early 1990s to rectify this problem did generate some debate, they have generally been accepted by both sides of politics. For example, Prime Minister John Howard observed in 1996 that the APS was working more cooperatively with ministers and ministerial staff than had been his experience when Treasurer in the Fraser government. Howard would of course build on those earlier changes by for example introducing performance pay for secretaries.

I doubt there are many today, however, who would argue that the APS needs to shift the balance further towards responsiveness. The more serious questions for contemporary public servants concern our professionalism, our impartiality, and whether our clear obligation to be responsive has occasionally caused some of us to be too concerned to please.

What were the lessons for the APS from the Children Overboard affair of 2001? Much has been said about the poor record-keeping, the unclear lines of accountability, the role of ministerial advisers, the passing on of information without adequate caveats about its authority, and the failure to correct inaccurate advice. I have covered these issues, particularly about ministerial advisers, before. But I also remain uneasy about public servants trying to hide their legal authority and responsibility and to refuse to hear requests for asylum they would have had to consider; and about senior public servants and military officers continuing to maintain in the Parliament the possibility that children were thrown overboard many weeks after Air Vice Marshall Houston's advice [that children were not thrown overboard] was given and known to have been given.

Now I know from bitter experience with the MRI affair the way hindsight can highlight mistakes with no appreciation of the circumstances and the real choices faced at the time. Consequently, I have always been reluctant to point the finger at people who were under enormous pressure at the time. But my concern is to ensure we learn the lessons from such experiences and, for me, the lessons from this case relate to giving more emphasis to our obligations of professionalism, impartiality, being apolitical and complying at all times with the law – the obligations that imply a degree of independence notwithstanding our need to be responsive.

Much has been said about 'frank and fearless' advice. I have rarely found it particularly challenging to offer policy advice that was not welcome. Rather, where courage was needed was when advising on due process, on releasing documents under FOI, on making corrections in the Parliament, on tender processes, on publishing performance data in the Annual Report, on giving an individual or an organisation opposed to the government fair treatment, and not giving favoured treatment to advisers seeking jobs in the department.

The elected government certainly has the authority to determine the public interest when it comes to matters of policy, and as Mike Keating said when he was Secretary of the Department of Prime Minister and Cabinet, it would be arrogant of public servants to assume they have greater understanding of the public interest. But the public service does have particular responsibility for the public interest in ensuring due process: fair treatment of those affected by government decisions, transparency of decision-making, careful and diligent management of programs and compliance at all times with the law.

Let me now highlight one area that is very difficult, but has been causing me increasing concern in recent years. It relates to communications and to freedom of information and has implications for the long-term capability of the service as well as its obligations of impartiality and professionalism.

Communications are at the heart of politics, and the enormous increase in the power of the media has required a sophisticated response by politicians – particularly by those in government. This includes careful control to ensure consistency and to influence the agenda, as well as to present the government, the government party and the key politicians in the best possible light. In turn, the media has, I believe, become more cynical and more determined to find the information that might challenge the official position, and then to sensationalise it. We thus have a spiral, and the public service, ever obedient to the elected government, has had its links with the media and the public subject to much closer control.

It is hard to deny the right of the elected government to issue instructions about communications by public servants. Moreover, public servants are rightly prohibited from leaking confidential information which, apart from any specific security concern, does untold damage to the trust of ministers in the public service.

But let me raise some examples to illustrate my unease. There is widespread concern in both government and the senior echelons of the APS that FOI has so widened access to information that countermeasures are needed. Examples could include fewer file notes, diaries being destroyed regularly, and documents being given security classifications at higher levels than are strictly required and handled to minimise the chances of FOI access. Given recent concerns expressed by the Auditor-General and others about record-keeping, most senior public servants recognise that these countermeasures must not hide the decision-making trail. But the trail that is left is often now just a skeleton without any sign of the flesh and blood of the real process, and even the skeleton is only visible to those with a need to know.

Now what is being protected here? The public interest, or the partisan interest of the government of the day? Maybe the liberal interpretation of FOI legislation by the courts has undervalued the public interest in allowing the government to deliberate on issues without constant public glare that tends to promote special interests and a short-term view. But there must be strong suspicion that partisan interests are often the main consideration, and public servants desiring to be responsive may be encouraged to give more weight to the concerns of ministers than to the public interest in due process, and the implicit and explicit requirements of administrative law.

The FOI Act explicitly requires that it be interpreted to further the object of extending as far as possible the right of the Australian community to access information held by the government, and that any discretions conferred by the Act are to be exercised as far as possible to facilitate and promote, promptly and at the lowest reasonable cost, the disclosure of information. Is that really our approach?

While I lack any statistical evidence, my impression is that departments are not only publishing less policy research, but are also conducting less. Some of the slack is being picked up by specialist agencies like the Productivity Commission and the Australian Institute for Health and Welfare, and by external bodies including universities. But the public service has a substantial share of the nation's expertise in many fields, and exposing that expertise in public forums is important for the public and also for fostering that expertise and capacity into the future by allowing our work to be externally tested from time to time.

There is also a tendency to require all contacts with the media to be managed through the minister's office. I would hardly suggest public servants disobey lawful directions by ministers, but there are many circumstances where the public interest would be better served by direct access to officials. For example, in crises where the public expects to hear from the professional experts – the Chief Medical Officer, or the Head of the Fire Service or the Chief of the Defence Force. I think it is also good practice for the official holding a legal delegation to publicly give reasons for a sensitive decision – as I insisted upon in the case of the licence for the Riverside Nursing Home. While open accountability is one of the APS Values and is explicitly within the system of ministerial responsibility, in my view it is best met in these sorts of cases by direct communication by the public service with the public. Apart from anything else, it tends to place the emphasis back onto due process, the requirements of procedural fairness and the specific provisions of program legislation.

Returning to Children Overboard, I wonder if the problems were exacerbated, rather than contained, by the severe constraints on the Navy officers from speaking publicly about operational matters. An inaccurate statement by an official can be corrected by that official without much fanfare if done promptly. Statements by ministers are far harder to correct, particularly during an election.

But as I previously said, these things are difficult. And yet, I would like to see more discussion of what is good practice and, if it is the case that the FOI Act is undermining public interest in particular situations, then let's see the Parliament debate the matter and amend the legislation we are bound by. I am probably showing my naiveté, but it would also be nice to think the media could be more responsible in its approach, taking seriously some of the suggestions recently made by Michelle Grattan on the matter.

3. Performance management and the performance pay paradox[1]

Allan Hawke

Allan Hawke enjoyed a distinguished career as a senior public servant and diplomat. He was Chief of Staff to Prime Minister Paul Keating (August 1993-February 1994), Secretary of the Department of Veterans' Affairs (1994-1996), Secretary of the Department of Transport and Regional Services (1996-1999) and Secretary of the Department of Defence (1999-2002). Hawke next served as High Commissioner to New Zealand from 2003-2005 before serving as Chancellor of The Australian National University (2006-2009). Allan Hawke currently serves on the board of the Canberra Raiders NRL club.

Leaders often define themselves by the issues on which they take a stand. My seven-and-a-half years as a secretary in three departments of state spanned an era when performance-based pay became the order of the day — a fashion I resisted for the reasons outlined in this chapter. The essence of my argument is that:

- performance pay is at odds with public service culture;
- performance pay ignores the complexity of how the public service actually works;
- performance pay is bad for morale and teamwork; and
- performance pay gives senior leaders an excuse to avoid real leadership.

My experience suggests a better way to facilitate the admirable aim of a high performing organisation; this framework is set out towards the end of the paper.

During my public service, I came to appreciate the importance of rituals, symbols and words. So it may come as no surprise that I believe the term 'human resources' indicates a mindset that treats people as human capital, assets, units of production etc with inherent control connotations. The term should be outlawed in favour of the more positive notions of people and performance.

---

1 Paper provided by Allan Hawke to the editors in 2011 in lieu of a formal valedictory upon his retirement in 2005. It draws upon material he presented in 2001 for an SES breakfast on Defence's performance framework.

The performance pay paradox

In my view, performance based pay experiments in the Australian Public Service have all been abject failures in the eyes of the people affected by them. Given the complexity of much of the public service, success or failure are mostly shared outcomes — that's because responsibility for meaningful bundles of work can rarely be made coincident with individual responsibility. This factor alone bedevils performance pay. Performance appraisal and pay assumptions usually include that:

- evaluation covers performance over a (normally) 12 month cycle, not just the period of recent memory;
- evaluators are consistent with one another or equilibrated through a moderation process;
- evaluators apply a consistent 'objective' standard between employees; and,
- individual employee contributions can be distinguished from the contributions of other managers and workers.[2]

These beliefs usually arise from the command and control school of management.

Douglas McGregor[3] developed Theory X and Theory Y in the 1960s to describe what he discerned to be two very different approaches to workforce motivation. Importantly, Theory X and Y are not different ends of a continuum as commonly thought.

Based on traditional views of direction and control, Theory X asserts that:

- the average person has an inherent dislike of work and will avoid it if they can;
- most people must be coerced to contribute toward organisational objectives; and
- most people prefer to be directed, wish to avoid responsibility, have relatively little ambition, and want security above all.

Theory X managers see their job as being to 'motivate' their employees, believing carrots and sticks are the only effective way to get things done. Herzberg proved

---

2   Kohn, Alfie, 'Punished by Rewards: the trouble with gold stars, incentive plans, A's, praise and other bribes' (Boston: Houghton Mifflin Co., 1993).

3   Douglas McGregor of the MIT Sloan School of Management developed his Theory X and Theory Y explanations of human motivation in the 1960s. He is cited as creator of the 'human resources' term, influenced the way performance reviews are conducted and shaped the idea of pay for performance in the private sector. Although his theories are rarely referred to nowadays, they underpin many modern day management philosophies, including the 'hard' versus 'soft' schools.

30 years ago that motivation is an internal construct and you can't actually motivate others to do much of anything other than what they want to do, or what they perceive to be in their self interest.[4]

This might be illustrated by how supervisors respond when an employee approaches them about a stuff-up. The carrot and stick school tend to shoot the messenger, assign blame and punish. So employees learn not to confess further errors, potentially leading to disastrous consequences. Those with a more positive view thank their staff for drawing attention to the problem and work with them to fix it. They get told of future problems as they emerge and have the opportunity to resolve them before things get too far out of hand.

I believe the vast majority of Australian Public Service (APS) staff would not see performance pay as being in their self interest. The rewards (even for secretaries) are relatively small, the ranking system rankles because many good performers not given the top rating think they have been short changed, and the system is not regarded as fair. Leadership and management policies and practices provide an insight into how leaders regard their employees; 'Punished by Rewards'[5] argues the case against the carrot and stick approach.

Performance pay acolytes (usually in an unstated or unrecognised manner) consider that a reservoir of withheld effort must be coaxed or coerced out of people. This is the underlying premise for incentive pay programs and/or a manager's efforts to motivate and control their workforce.[6]

The reality is that there are not many bad people in the workplace. What's interesting is that so many executives shy away from dealing directly with poor performance and unacceptable conduct in the workplace, especially given the way those affected by these inappropriate behaviours feel about it. One might therefore expect this aspect to feature in performance pay regimes, but even there it seems to be the exception rather than the rule.

---

4   Herzberg, Frederick – 'One More Time: How Do You Motivate Employees?' Harvard Business Review, September-October, 1987.

5   Scholtes, Peter R – 'Reward and Incentive Programs are Ineffective - Even Harmful' and his other articles and books, particularly 'The Leader's Handbook'.

6   During the late 1980s I was seconded to work with Tony Ayers in the Efficiency Scrutiny Unit. Each time we got 12 scrutinies together, I would sit in on a three day course with the Scrutineers called 'Managing and Consulting' run by Ross Begbie. After attending six of these courses, I was well and truly hooked on the approach and lessons. It was retitled 'Results through People' following a comment by David Block and I used that term and the course (modernised from time to time to include the latest relevant research findings) and Ross Begbie wherever I went after that to very good effect. A healthy cadre of Victor and Victoria Stone graduates are applying the lessons learnt, while Ross and his team are still teaching new people what leadership and management is all about.

Most APS performance based pay programs follow a three step process:

- determining the approach — what's to be done, by when and to what standard;
- the performance period — normally the calendar or financial year; and
- the performance review — the boss undertaking an 'objective' evaluation of the subordinate's performance.

Typically, evaluation involves a boss/subordinate discussion followed by the assignment of a numerical rating, sometimes with forced rankings according to the classic bell-shaped normal distribution curve. (Defence's system, by contrast, was based on incremental advancement up the pay scale, without forced rankings). The outcome usually has a remuneration implication covering pay at risk, merit pay, bonuses and judgments about contenders for promotion. Responses to 'why do it?' usually say:

- as a basis for differential pay/reward for outstanding performers;
- to provide performance feedback to individual employees;
- to identify candidates for promotion;
- to foster communication between supervisors and subordinates; and/or
- to motivate employees.

As I recall it, performance pay was introduced as a back door way of lifting remuneration for senior staff. That could not be achieved through the Industrial Relations Commission because of the very restrictive rules applying to pay increases at that time which the government had advocated to the Commission and felt bound to adhere to. It was argued that since employees contribute at different levels of effectiveness and effort, this could be recognised through introduction of a performance pay regime. The fact that that rationale no longer applies seems lost with the effluxion of time, although some departments and agencies have now done away with performance-based pay.

Nevertheless, the practice remains widespread in the APS because so many managers believe in it. They believe it works without consciously and critically analysing the assumptions behind the practice.[7] And they believe in it, despite the fact that 90 per cent of managers consider the approach to be unsuccessful.[8]

---

7 'Driving Performance and Retention through Employee Engagement' by Lloyd Morgan of the Corporate Leadership Council.

8 Defence has kindly kept most of my speeches on their website — see in particular, 'People Power' address to the International Seminar of RUSI Australia on 17 November 2000; 'A Public Sector Performance Framework — the Defence Model' (which avoided the trap of relative rankings and performance pay outcomes) address to PSMPC Breakfast 18 April 2001; and "Putting People First" — keynote address to AHRI 21 August 2001.

Some commentators argue that the practice continues despite evidence to the contrary because it relates to the manager's need to maintain control – or the illusion of control. Peter Scholtes, who has researched and written extensively about performance, appraisal and pay, argues that such a performance 'management' regime is inherently the wrong thing to do because three faults are common to all variations on the theme:

- it doesn't work;
- it's wrong to focus only on individuals or groups, because most opportunities for improvement involve systems, processes and technology; and
- performance 'management' is judgment, not feedback; it's a hierarchical dynamic.

Even when well intended ratings are judgmental and related to control of the person being evaluated based on the presumption that the person's inadequate contribution is separable from any systemic origin of poor performance. Where such schemes are in operation, most individuals or groups will work towards optimising their performance, regardless of its impact on the system. Creative accounting, goal displacement, withholding information, reduced quality at the expense of more output, individual visibility which discourages co-operation and other gaming strategies are the perverse results of such a perverse system. The inherent contradiction of proselytising individual performance pay assessments while simultaneously exhorting teamwork escapes the zealots.

The method, criteria and philosophy of evaluation differs between one evaluator and another. People are subjective and they are not at all objective about their subjectivity. Numerous factors affect favourable or unfavourable bias – including age, family and educational background, physical appearance etc. None of these are job-related, but they do influence the outcome of performance evaluation. Where these discriminatory practices are pointed out, the people concerned deny they exist.

Performance pay can lead to patronage, subordinate sycophancy, playing and paying favourites, oiling the squeaky wheel and other inappropriate practices. Imagine the consequences if ministers wanted to be involved in the process and decisions below secretary level.

A former secretary once commented that he had assessed his SES as all being in the top five to ten per cent! Let's assume for the purpose of illustration that there is a truly unbiased performance pay system in a typical Gaussian distribution. Half of your people will learn that they are below average – a statistical inevitability. Some may accept their fate; others will view this as proof that their manager is incompetent. Some will redouble their efforts to prove the judgment and system wrong – that may be noticed, and they may be lucky enough to be ranked above average next time — if so, someone above average last time will fill their below average slot this time. All of this must do wonders for morale and superior workplace performance.

Then there's the case where people are told their rating by their direct supervisor before it disappears into the black box of moderation and comes out at a lower level — apart from the lack of transparency, the recipient's perception is one of unfairness and it's deeply demotivating. Those that invoke 'science' in moderating people's scores to a decimal point are kidding.

The Orwellian named 'efficiency dividend' has had particular effects on some small agencies (particularly those where most of their budget comprises staff costs), leading to very significant differences in pay rates for people doing jobs classified at the same level. The reality is that how well or badly people are paid in these circumstances often depends on how well their organisation has done in the budget bidding process. As well as the equity argument, this works against mobility and a unified APS. The Moran blueprint's analysis of what's happened since devolution of bargaining in 1997 is spot-on as are the accompanying recommendations. I think there is a compelling case to abolish performance pay and return to centralised pay fixing, perhaps under the auspices of the Australian Public Service Commission.

Secretaries

How did I rationalise these views with the performance pay regime for secretaries? In my day, the Prime Minister determined, on advice of the Remuneration Tribunal, that secretaries would be eligible for an annual 10 per cent bonus of total remuneration for superior performance, or 15 per cent for outstanding performance. Every 12 months, each secretary wrote a self assessment based on criteria which included:

- meeting government objectives;
- management;
- strategic, high quality, frank and timely advice to ministers;
- leadership; and
- professional and personal integrity and adherence to the APS Values/Code of Conduct.

Other aspects were covered from time to time, including what was being done about IT outsourcing when that ideology was popular.

The self assessment, which formed the basis of a discussion between the secretary and portfolio minister, was copied to the Secretary of PM&C and Public Service Commissioner. They, in turn, discussed the secretary's performance with the portfolio minister and reported to the Prime Minister who decided the outcome.

The Remuneration Tribunal's guidelines said that performance-based remuneration was not a device to provide salary supplementation to office holders and should not be applied or administered in that way. Rather, it was a way of recognising performance over and above what was reasonably expected of the office holder performing their duties competently. I could never believe that secretaries would work harder or differently just because of the possibility of an additional 10 or 15 per cent before tax.

The key question that arose in my time was whether the system of appointing and removing secretaries caused politicisation of the APS. The issue was complicated by the differential use of three and five year appointments and the implied message in who got those 'contracts'. However you answered these questions, there was the potential for a perception issue.

The portfolio minister obviously expressed satisfaction or dissatisfaction with a secretary's performance in discussion with the Secretary of PM&C and Public Service Commissioner. One danger was the inference that the subsequent award (or non-award) of performance pay meant that the secretary had satisfied (or not) the minister's partisan political demands. In the case of the term of office, people drew conclusions about the Prime Minister's view by reference to whether the appointment was for three or five years. I argued without success to do away with performance pay and fold it into base salaries, although that did subsequently occur for secretaries when Prime Minister Rudd came to office.

The discussion on goals, priorities and the nature of the minister/secretary relationship is a very positive step, as is the annual self-assessment report from the secretary and associated interaction with the portfolio minister. Cabinet ministers were wary that their performance and judgments were also being assessed and reported to the Prime Minister by the Secretary of PM&C and may have tailored their comments accordingly.

Performance-based pay conclusion

To sum up, I believe that performance bonuses, performance appraisal linked to pay outcomes, and other performance management schemes which involve a 'proportion of pay at risk' lead to distorted results and raise issues of equity, ratings moderation and forced distribution. I am aware of the argument that performance pay works in some organisations where rewards constitute a significant part of total remuneration, and where judgments about performance are based on things under the direct control of the individual being assessed and people are satisfied that the assessments and mechanisms used are fair and reasonable. None of those preconditions can be assured in the APS.

To me, a 1996 *Human Resources Management* article quote captures it nicely:

'From several perspectives, merit pay schemes do seem desirable; yet, in spite of this, merit pay often brings about results precisely the opposite from those desired: dissatisfaction, discouragement and decreased performance.'

I tried to influence the Management Advisory Committee's paper on performance management to no avail against the prevailing orthodoxy. Some years later the Australian National Audit Office (ANAO) carried out an audit on performance management in the APS which should have been enough to convince the diehards to abolish performance pay, but the practice continues today with the same problems and unintended consequences. The conclusion may be that most APS agency heads are still disciples of and wedded to Theory X practices.

Results through people

The great mentor, Tony Ayers, once sat patiently listening while I explained at some length why something wouldn't work. When I finished, he said 'I hear what you are against, now tell me what you are for'. It's to that end that I now turn.

'Results through people' was my credo, a refrain familiar to those in Veterans' Affairs; Transport and Regional Services; and Defence when I worked there. Eight years after serving a three year term as Secretary of Defence, the following brief overview enunciates what I stood for in terms of a performance framework and as context for what I took a stand against. My foundation belief was that people want to do a good job and make a genuine contribution – to their team, their organisation, and their nation. The leaders' task is to create an enabling culture and to facilitate that end through:

- sharpening the focus on the results that the organisation (or team) is there to achieve;
- putting in place governance processes where accountability for achieving results is clear; and
- fostering a climate where people can give their best and strive towards their potential, through regular performance feedback and support for learning.

These three elements sound simple. Yet anyone who has tried to achieve sustained organisational improvement will know that getting them right is much harder in practice. What's hard about the first theme — focusing on results — is that even after the agency head has opened up a dialogue with the minister to clarify requirements, a lot of thinking work needs to be done by senior executives in order to translate the overall direction into specific, measurable results. That is, turning agreed high level goals into language that is comprehensible and meaningful, so that they can be absorbed, understood and acted on by staff.

Then comes the task which senior executives often underestimate — the sheer repetition of communicating the messages required so that people know what is expected of them in order to make an effective contribution. Saying it once or twice has negligible impact in my experience; by the fiftieth time when you are thoroughly sick and tired of saying it people begin to think you might just be serious about it.

What's hard about the second theme — developing robust governance processes — is that most people find 'the hot seat of accountability' an uncomfortable place to be. A proliferation of 'governance committees' is a likely consequence. Defining how responsibilities, roles and accountabilities differ between executives at each level is another very tough ask. Given the tendency to micro-manage, the agency head must be vigilant to ensure that senior executives are taking a real leadership role rather than simply meddling in technical aspects of the task, for which someone in their team is actually responsible. It is, of course, vitally important to set out the contributions expected of individuals for specific and more broadly described results in such a way that people can see for themselves how what they do fits in and allows the effectiveness of their contribution to be assessed. We tried to do that through our Plan on a Page approach (see Attachment 1).

What's hard about the third theme — fostering the climate where people can give their best — is that it calls for 'soft skills', the very skills that are the hardest to get right and easiest to get wrong. People need to be properly informed of what is expected of them and how those tasks are to be performed; a necessary pre-condition for feedback and individual improvement. Judicious use of feedback and a commitment to support people to improve their performance and to learn are also essential elements. But most of all, there must be a willingness to be judged on the extent to which leadership rhetoric is matched by day-to-day behaviour in the workplace.

People will give you a fair day's work if they receive what they consider to be a fair day's pay. Their expectations here are principally affected by what they see other people who do similar work are getting. That's one reason why Defence's pay scales (for SES and non-SES) were transparent to everyone in the organisation.

We positioned Defence in the top quartile of APS remuneration, recognising that that position would erode over time as others increased their pay rates. That is to say, we took a broadly fair and reasonably competitive position and adjusted our position in the light of market movement each bargaining round. To complement that approach, we developed a People Leadership Framework (see Attachment 2).

Research by the Corporate Leadership Council suggests that employees stay with an organisation when they believe it is in their self interest, which they define as 'rational' commitment. This is all about financial, developmental and professional rewards. The second side of this coin is emotional commitment, which involves the extent to which employees derive pride, enjoyment, inspiration or meaning from something or someone within their organisation. Emotional commitment is regarded as more valuable in driving employee effort than rational commitment. Indeed, employees are more likely to exert discretionary effort when emotionally committed – when they believe in the value of their job, their team or their organisation. Further detail about the above issues is available in an article in the March 2003 Canberra Bulletin of Public Administration and from the Department of Defence's website.

Attachment 1(a)

Plan on a Page

The intention underlying 'performance management' schemes is well founded where it:

- clarifies individual responsibilities;
- links those to the work of their areas;
- provides a means of regular performance feedback;
- improves openness, transparency and fairness.

We took a different approach from most other departments and agencies. Our approach (based on the government's workplace relations guidelines) endeavours to build performance through a feedback and development focus – without scores and ratings. The military has, of course, had a longstanding performance appraisal system which plays an important role in the promotion and placement of service personnel in a highly planned career management system.

Our 'Plan on a Page' involves each supervisor and team member agreeing on what needs to be done and what support is required to do this. It establishes the five to seven (no more than nine) objectives that the team member will work towards.

The results-focussed 'Plan on a Page' also identifies learning and development needs. It's important that senior leaders demonstrate their commitment to growth and improvement – to model the way for others.

Australians don't like to fail and they hate letting down anyone they like. So explicit agreement about the learning and development required to get results is a key to 'people power'. It is also about treating people as individuals and helping them work towards their aspirations and potential – to be the best that they can be. The essential question is whether you are learning and growing – whether you're a better person today than last week – rather than how you compare with others.

Supervisors and team members meet quarterly in a two-way feedback process which also reviews progress towards the results and discusses how the team member is developing/improving their performance. If, at the end of the twelve months, the team member has failed to meet their objectives, that also reflects adversely on the supervisor's performance as the coach.

The Chief of the Defence Force and I focussed very hard on the Senior Leadership Group. Our organisational renewal strategy rested on getting involvement and ownership by this group. Unless they themselves changed their day-to-day behaviour, there would always be a rhetoric – reality gap that undermined our efforts to pave the way to real organisational improvement. Behaviour change is hard to achieve, as anyone who has tried to kick a habit knows only too well. The motivation to change behaviour has to come from within – which is why senior leaders who didn't fully 'own' the renewal agenda found it increasingly hard to survive the scrutiny that the Chief of the Defence Force and I were placing on them.

Many Defence leaders were open to feedback, and were working hard at changing their behaviour in an endeavour to treat people as more than just 'human resources'. We were committed to holding our senior leaders just as accountable for stewardship of their people as for delivering the results they are responsible for.

The results of these 'Performance Exchanges' for civilians are linked to remuneration through increment-based advancement until individuals reach the maximum pay point in their pay band.

The upper limit of the pay band gets adjusted every two years or so when we review our Certified Agreement and Australian Workplace Agreements, having regard to equivalent rates on offer elsewhere in the APS. (The SES AWAs and Certified Agreements were important vehicles for increasing productivity and facilitating the cultural change we were seeking.) Some people argue that this approach penalises the high flyers, because they don't get financial recognition of their superior contribution to the organisation. My retort to this claim is that they are the very people most likely to benefit from accelerated promotion in open merit-based competition.

Money matters, of course. But money does not matter enough to outweigh workplace culture issues. We believe that people want to be paid a fair day's pay for a fair day's work. If people don't feel they're fairly paid, they become dissatisfied. If they do consider they're fairly paid, then we believe they look for other things in the workplace.

The research of an Army Reservist, Brigadier Nick Jans, shows that job satisfaction is a strong predictor of career commitment and the decision to stay in Defence. Leaders can influence job satisfaction through:

- role clarity and focus (do individuals know what they have to do and the contribution they can make?);
- empowerment (do people have the skills, authority and freedom to act while still held responsible for results?);
- teamwork (do others co-operate with and back each other up?);
- learning (can people innovate, learn from doing, take calculated risks and still be supported?).

These factors underpin a high performance culture. They create a work environment where everyone wants to – and can – make a real contribution.

Attachment 1(b)

SES Plan on a Page

Employee's Name:		Supervisor's Name:	For the forward period:
PART A: Key Expected Results (KERs)		**PART C: Review notes (in terms of KERS, Values and SES Leadership Capabilities)**	
1. Adheres to Defence Values, demonstrates behaviours consistent with those values and with Australian Public Service Values			
PART B: Learning and development needs and actions		**PART D: Learning and development activities undertaken and their effectiveness**	
Employee's Signature:	Date:	Employee's Signature:	Date:
Employee's Signature:	Date:	Employee's Signature:	Date:

Attachment 2

Defence people leadership framework

To be an effective senior leader in Defence it is implicit that the following Defence Values are upheld and promoted: Professionalism, Loyalty, Innovation, Courage, Integrity, Teamwork			
PERFORMANCE PRINCIPLE			
Challenge	People like a challenge and new set performance standards	when	they are clear about our purpose and understand where their contribution fits in.
Elbow-room	People are responsible, accountable, exercise self-direction and self-control	when	their supervisor involves them in decisions affecting their workplace and allows them to do their job.
Feedback	People exercise imagination, and creativity to solve problems	when	they get constructive feedback on their ideas and are confident that communication lines are open.
Self-esteem	People who feel good about themselves do good work	when	their supervisor recognises a job well done – praise from supervisors does wonders for self esteem.
Pride	People are proud of the job they do and the organisation they work for	when	the organisation is making a meaningful contribution to society, engendering trust and mutual respect.

LEADERSHIP CAPABILITY Defence leaders:	LEADERSHIP BEHAVIOUR Defence leaders:
Set the standard for performance	1. Articulate and communicate performance expectations 2. Explain where people's contribution fits in 3. Exemplify the standard and encourage/assist others to perform to the standard 4. Measure performance and reward/sanction appropriately
Give meaningful direction	1. Involve people in decision-making 2. Communicate the objective with clarity 3. Link direction to corporate goals 4. Ensure people have what they need to get the job done, within resources allocated
Make communication a priority	1. Tell it as it is 2. Make sure messages are understood 3. Listen and respond 4. Actively create a trusting environment
Create the climate for success	1. Take an interest in people as individuals 2. Explain people's roles the organisational direction 3. Value and acknowledge people's contribution 4. Recognise people by name
Persist until the job's well and truly done	1. Celebrate the team's achievements 2. Continually review progress and adjust priorities 3. Help people understand why the job is important 4. Understand the resources necessary to complete the tasks

4. Thirty-eight years toiling in the vineyard of public service[1]

Ric Smith

After a brief career in the West Australian secondary school system, Ric Smith joined the Department of External Affairs in 1969. In that department — and its successor, the Department of Foreign Affairs and Trade — he held numerous important positions, including postings in New Delhi, Tel Aviv, Manila and Honolulu. In 1992 Smith was appointed Deputy Secretary in DFAT with responsibility for Australia's relations with Asia. He acted as Secretary of DFAT for much of the period from December 1992 to May 1993. From March 1994 to the end of 1995, Ric Smith served on secondment to the Department of Defence as Deputy Secretary, Strategy and Intelligence, before being appointed as Australian Ambassador to China in February 1996. He served there, and as non-resident Ambassador to Mongolia, until February 2000. From January 2001 to October 2002, he served as Australia's Ambassador to Indonesia. During this time, Bali was bombed and he, along with many others, played a major role in the recovery and repatriation of Australians. Ric Smith returned to Canberra in November 2002 to commence his role as Secretary of the Department of Defence, from which he retired in November 2006.

I am honoured to be the first retiring Australian public servant to have been invited to give a valedictory address. Many more distinguished colleagues have retired without such an opportunity. Let me start with a disclaimer. In preparing for this occasion I have been conscious that in other realms, and perhaps especially the United Kingdom, there is something of a tradition on occasions such as this of great oratory built around grand visions of the civil service as an institution; visions in the UK case conceptualised around the triumph that was Trevelyan and the wonder that is Westminster. If you were looking forward to anything so grand — to a laying out of great wisdom and intellectual riches about the Australian Public Service; where it has been and whither it is bound, then you will be disappointed. Instead I wish to present the reflections of one who has toiled in the vineyard of the Australian Public Service these past 38 years more as a tradesman than a philosopher — much less an artist or a visionary. It will be in large part a narrative tale, with a few thoughts born of long experience of the Westminster-with-Canberra-characteristics system we now have. My time in the APS has been fun, practical, sometimes quite hard — even painful — but always worthwhile and fulfilling.

---

1   This was the first of the formal valedictory speeches delivered at a function organised by the Australian Public Service Commission in November 2006.

The beginnings

I was not destined to work in the Australian Public Service. Within my own extended family, over three generations that preceded me, there was only one public servant – an uncle who, so far as I could tell, had joined the service to support a gambling habit. Yet my first paid employment, at the end of my fifth year in high school, was as a postman, delivering the greeting cards which people sent to each other to mark Christmas 1961. I had an Australia Post-issued red bike and a cap, and when I got the chance to deliver the mail in my own suburb on one 40-degree-day I fully expected my mother to turn the neighbours out to watch me pedal down our own street on her majesty's service. For once – probably the only time – she let me down.

I did not return to the post office the next year, but while at university a few years later I found myself working over the Christmas holidays as a yardman at the Department of Supply at Karrakatta. If this first intrusion into the defence empire was not a sufficient augury, more portentous was my special assignment – to repaint some steel 'bailey bridges' which had been destined as an aid project in Indonesia but withheld because of the Indonesia-Malaysia confrontation of 1962-1966. I was told 'the bosses' believed they might soon begin to rust. So in a sandy paddock in Perth's blistering Christmas heat, I painted them from 7am until 10am each morning, then hung around the workshop for the rest of the day contributing little but learning much – if not about the public service, then about life. Years later as I crossed one 'bailey bridge' after another while being driven through Sumatra as Ambassador to Indonesia, I wondered whether these were the ones I had painted. Strangely, decades in the monsoonal climate had not rusted them. I must have painted them well.

It was through teaching that I made my first formal entry into public service. For the four years of my teacher training I was paid seven pounds two and ten pence a fortnight, without which going to university would have been more difficult. Teaching scholarships or bursaries were wonderful vehicles of social mobility in the 1960s. I taught for three years in rural and regional Australia, an experience which did more for me and my understanding of people than another ten years at university would have achieved. But rich as the teaching experience had been, there was plenty else on offer for the 15 per cent of us school leavers who completed university in the 1960s. In 1968, I applied for what we now call the 'graduate intake' in the Department of External Affairs and, to my mother's pride and my father's astonishment, was accepted.

Canberra in 1969

Twenty-four of us joined External Affairs in 1969 at the end of what we remain confident was the only decade last century worth a damn. Most had tertiary qualifications that put mine in the shade: some had won prestigious scholarships; many spoke foreign languages and some, most amazing of all — to me at least — had travelled and even studied overseas. My starting salary was $3,820. Honours graduates got more. The only woman in our group was paid a little less. I should not speak for the others, but I think I am right in saying that most of us were motivated to join External Affairs not by any interest in the public service as such, nor even any noble interest in serving the public, but rather by our own personal interest in international politics and foreign affairs.

Indeed, I do not think I had even heard the term 'public administration', and it was probably not until the 1980s that I first heard the term 'public policy'. And yet, this did not matter because in 1969 I did not appreciate that I had become involved in either. In the first year we did the usual three rotations in the department — which then occupied just the easternmost wing of what was called the 'Admin Building', now named after the Prime Minister of our day, John Gorton. My first rotation was in the aid branch (the whole of the Colombo Plan was run from one branch); my second in the conditions of service section. With most of my 'intake' colleagues assigned to high policy sections, it seemed to me that I had been picked from the start as a tradesman rather than a serious policy type. But I did learn a few tricks from some wily colleagues which stood me in good stead later, and I also got paid overtime which was acceptable to claim in the administrative areas of the department but not in the policy areas.

Canberra was then a town of some 122,000 people, ending geographically at Woden and Aranda. We lived in hostels — the Kurrajong and Lawley House I recall well. Social life centered on places like the Burns Club, the Italian Club, the Rugby Union Club and the Eastlake Football Club. We watched the moon landing in July 1969 in our offices — on black and white television. It was said later that if Goulburn had the big merino and various towns in Queensland their big bananas and pineapples, then Canberra deserved the big grey cardigan. But those who took that view risked overlooking the colour that really did exist in the mix of larger-than-life characters from the press, Parliament House and parts of the public service which was at its best at the Wellington Hotel on Friday nights.

The 20,000 or so public servants whom we joined in Canberra in 1969 constituted fewer than 10 per cent of all Commonwealth public servants. The workforce we joined was of course overwhelmingly male. It was only after 1966 that women could remain in the public service after they married, and the idea still had not caught on very well. Equal pay for women in the service was not mandated until 1969 with its implementation phased in through to 1973, and paid maternity leave was not available until 1973. But there were some powerful women in the workplace – they were in the typing pools and had our careers in their hands, or were pushing tea trolleys and purveying gossip vital to our futures. It was a workforce in which age and position went together because promotion was underpinned by seniority.

It was also a time in which accountability, by today's standards, was slight. Indeed, the word itself did not come into use for many years. There was no administrative law as we now know it – no ombudsman, no Administrative Decisions Judicial Review Act, no Administrative Appeals Tribunal, and no Freedom of Information Act. Parliamentary committee hearings were few – there were no Senate estimates hearings before 1970. As far as I have been able to find out, Sir Arthur Tange, that most eminent predecessor of mine, only ever attended two parliamentary committee hearings – the first was to present a Defence submission to the Public Works Committee in 1978; the second an appearance before the Privileges Committee on a personnel matter after he retired. Departmental secretaries were then 'permanent heads' and remained so until 1994. They certainly did not see themselves as CEOs. The word 'responsive' first entered the APS argot in the 1980s, when Peter Wilenski gave it some respectable philosophical underpinnings, but it was only in 1999 that it became enshrined in the Public Service Act. It was a time of great central authority.

The Australian Public Service environment was dominated by a monster called the Public Service Board. A Stalinist institution populated by people who knew little but their own arcane business, it had a veto over virtually everything that happened in the Public Service – the creation of positions, promotions and appointments (through the appeals system), conditions of service and organisational structures. You could not scratch yourself without consulting 'the Board'. In addition, there was an interdepartmental committee called the Overseas Visits Committee which vetted all proposals for overseas travel by public officials and often rejected agencies' bids or reduced their delegations.

Probity, thoroughness and good record-keeping were among the great strengths of the APS of the time, but it was also a service characterised by caste divisions and turf warfare. The castes existed formally in the form of four 'divisions': a fourth division existed for clerical and registry staff, typists and so on, and a third division for other non SES but nevertheless higher status officers. Informally, casteism was sustained more subtly through unofficial distinctions in some departments between 'professional' officers and 'administrative' officers. These distinctions were maintained in internal promotions and job preferment, and manifested among other places in tensions between relevant unions.

As for the turf wars between departments, they were tough and real. Differences in policy, or – more often – over who had the right to advise on policy in particular areas, were fiercely fought in meetings at all levels and in vitriolic correspondence that often went to ministerial levels and were only ever partially settled at the Commonwealth Club. The ones of which I was most aware were those between the resource and primary industry departments, and between the foreign affairs and trade departments, in their various and changing names, but there were many others. They generated not just paper-based hostility but in many cases lasting personal enmities, some of which can still be found in relationships between people whose names remain well known in this town. The term 'whole of government' which we hear so much about today was then, I think, unknown. It was all sadly wasteful of energy and effort.

By offering this sketch of the APS as it was then, I have indicated some of the ways it has changed over these 38 years. The changes have been driven by a range of factors, some from within the service and successive governments, some from the changing nature of society and our economy and the wider world of which we have increasingly become a part. Many of the changes were driven by the Coombs Royal Commission of 1975-77 which had an enormous impact on the APS over the next two decades. A raft of internal and structural changes followed, together with the administrative law provisions which now shape so much of the way we work. After a series of further reviews, the 1980s and especially the 1990s saw more reforms, many in the areas of people and financial management and also in further decentralisation. This culminated in the enactment in 1999 of the new Public Service Act which gave agency heads clear responsibility for managing their staff in ways that would maximise agency performance.

Through all of this, as a result of both legislative and social change and of course market demand, women have become a significant part of the service in both numbers and influence. In 1969, 21 per cent of Commonwealth public servants were women; today, the figure is 56 per cent. And I cannot forget the smoking. The effectiveness and speed with which it was turned off in the workplace was remarkable. By December 1988, when the wife of a government minister reportedly left an item of underwear in an ashtray on his desk after a late night visit to his office, most of us were surprised only by the fact that he still had an ashtray in his office. It was not just attitudes to smoking that had changed! Consider now some of these principal changes.

Public service change: the numbers

In talking about public service change in the broadest sense, it is hard to go further without talking about numbers. In 1969, there were nearly 219,000 Commonwealth public servants. That number continued to grow, reaching its zenith in 1975 with a figure of some 277,500. It then declined steadily, reaching 143,000 in 1996 and 113,500 in 2000. Today it stands at about 146,500, of whom some 52,000 – or about 36 per cent – are in Canberra. This contrasts with the fewer than ten per cent who were Canberra-based in 1969. In reflecting on these numbers it is necessary of course to take account of the enormous structural changes that lie behind them. The big numbers of the 1970s included government-owned businesses like the PMG and the shipyards and munitions factories which have long since been divested.

Even the more recent apparent growth reflects changes of a structural kind, such as the inclusion for the first time this year of around 5000 employees from Medicare. So in effect the raw numbers reflect how often and how significantly the definition of what is the business of government has changed over these years.

The information revolution

If the numbers have been affected by what the public service does, they have also been affected by technology, especially information technology. Computerisation, to use an old-fashioned term, ranks with the employment of women as the biggest change in the public service workplace in my working life. From manual typewriters to electric typewriters to word processors to whatever we call them today; from 'man-drolically' typed telegrams encoded with 'one-time-pads' to automatically encrypted e-mails, the change has truly been a revolution because it has affected not only the tools of our work but what we do, how we approach it and what is expected of us.

Interestingly, when computers were introduced into the public service they were seen as a means by which staff savings could be achieved, euphemistically called 'productivity gains'. It took a long time for us to realise that the true significance of IT went beyond the tools of our trade; that we were in fact caught up in an information revolution that was changing the volume, pace and nature of all that we did and the way we related to each other. Partly because we were slow to realise this, successive governments underestimated the scale of the investment required, and at various stages were panicked into new or more radical ways of providing and managing the essential ingredients of the revolution. If IT has been the biggest change factor in my time in the public service, it has also – partly for that reason – been the most difficult issue to manage.

Nor is its management getting any easier. We now better understand both the nature and scale of the investment needed and have plenty of good advice about ensuring that our business drives our IT needs, not the reverse. But we are faced with managing the cultural and other consequences of the sheer volume of our transactions. As an illustration, each day my own organisation generates on average some 1.7 million e-mails and receives 680,000 e-mails from external sources – of which 470,000 (or almost 80 per cent) are spam. I see few greater challenges for the public service of the future than managing its IT. The issues will include those of costs, of project managing in an environment of rapid technological change, and of network security – as well of course as that already sorely taxing matter, records management.

Ministers' offices and staff

While the role and number of women in the service and the information revolution have been two of the great internal changes of the past 38 years, the third great change to the way the government is run and by whom has been the growth in ministerial staff and the role of ministerial offices. It has been fashionable among older public servants to lament this change. That is not my purpose here. Rather, it is to note the reasons for it and its significance. Nor are my comments in any sense partisan. The growth has in fact been bipartisan.

While the figures for 1969 are not available, I understand that in 1972 there were 150 people employed in ministers' offices. By 1983 the number stood at 207, and today there are 415, including those in the offices of the parliamentary secretaries. From personal observation, I know there were four staff in the Canberra office of our first Foreign Minister, Billy McMahon, in 1970. All were public servants on some sort of secondment. Their role was to manage his paperwork and his diary, and not to give policy advice. Today, most ministers have six to eight advisers in addition to a number of other support staff. Some of the staff concerned are of course departmental liaison officers employed under the Public Service Act who do a great job in moving paper between ministers and their departments, but most are now employed under the MOPS Act.

The numbers have not been the only thing to change. More importantly, the work done by staffers has changed, and over the years has extended much beyond paper and diary management to include advising on the full range of a minister's responsibilities. In effect, by comparison with 1969, we now have a whole new layer or level of government. Why have these changes occurred? The move to the new Parliament House in 1988 is of course a part of the answer. Indeed, the new House did much more than just facilitate larger ministerial offices; it also created a completely new physical environment for the doing of government business. Consequently, ministers go to their departments much less often – indeed, only rarely. And the Wellington Hotel – or the Hotel Canberra back bar, or the rose garden – are no longer places of business with ministers: Parliament House is a complete village, and provides all the venues needed.

That said, there have been other more profound reasons for the growth in the numbers and roles of ministerial staff. They include the information revolution, and what I call democratisation. The information revolution has not only generated greater volumes of data which needs to be known to and processed by ministers, but it has also dramatically changed the velocity and timeliness of business. Government has become a '24 by seven' business, and information has become instant and global in its origins. Government departments and agencies, proceeding at their more stately paces and necessarily placing a high premium on thoroughness and clearly traceable lines of accountability, have been unable to meet all of their ministers' needs.

Departments have also struggled in their responses to the democratisation process. By this I mean three things. The first is the increased need of ministers to be able to respond to and participate in what we sometimes rather grandly call the 'public debate'. This means principally the media and parliament itself, but also other forums in which the business of government is scrutinised, the number, reach and expectations of which have grown with the information revolution. Second, ministers in this communications-rich environment are anxious to shape the presentation of their business to suit their electoral needs, and this is an area into which public servants cannot and should not cross.

And third, the information revolution – and globalisation more generally – together with greatly increased demands for accountability, have required ministers to know about, be involved in and make decisions on a wider and deeper range of issues than ever. Ministerial staff are thus critical to the identification of issues for ministers and to managing the enormous volume of material which consequently comes to them.

All of this results in an unmistakably different policy advising and management environment and a different set of relationships between ministers and their departments than existed 30 years previously. There are a number of consequences of this situation that secretaries and other senior public servants need to be aware of. One is that there is another layer of government, and another source of advice to ministers, not always transparent to the department itself. Another is that dealing with ministers' offices is a critical job-skill for many public service positions: the days are long gone when a departmental secretary could refuse to take a call from a staffer in what was then called the 'private office'.

Further, experience in a ministerial office is increasingly regarded as a significant career enhancer. These are fairly self-evident consequences of the growth of ministerial offices, but there are more profound aspects of the subject and the process of democratisation that it reflects. One of these is that ministers have acquired the resources and capacity to reach further into the management of their agencies, and for reasons of perceived accountability, want to do so. But as a former senior colleague once put it, this risks their becoming the effective CEO, and secretaries becoming in effect their Chief Operating Officers. If that becomes the case, then the respective accountabilities of ministers and secretaries may have to be changed in areas affected not only by convention but also by legislation. The obverse of this issue is the need for secretaries – and indeed public officials generally – to understand that many more of their decisions and actions today are likely to have a policy or even political impact than was the case in the past.

There are no simple responses or formulae for managing these issues. They are all part of what ministers and their secretaries deal with. But if we were looking for steps that could be taken to improve working relationships and the understanding of accountabilities, I would offer the suggestion that newly-appointed ministers and possibly aspiring back-benchers and newly-appointed secretaries or agency heads might be given the opportunity to attend workshops or seminars on the respective roles and responsibilities of ministers, secretaries and other departmental officers under our Westminster-with-Canberra system. This would include addressing their respective roles and responsibilities under the Public Service Act, the FMA Act, the FOI Act, and other relevant legislation. It would also embrace the less formal conventions that support the ministerial-public service relationship. Lest this be thought to be an unduly radical suggestion, I should hasten to say that something like it now runs in the UK.

The matter of a code of conduct for ministerial staff has of course been raised by others in the past. I believe the APS has benefited from its code, not just as a statement of values and an instrument of accountability, but also – as I can attest from experience – as a valuable tool of personnel management. It would not be easy to draft such a code for ministerial staff, involving as it probably would the very contentious question of who would enforce it and possibly also the need to define where ministers' offices end and departments or agencies begin. I suspect the debate on this issue has some distance to run.

I referred earlier to the increasing volume of material going to ministers in the form of briefs, submissions and so on. My own department is a case in point, and from what I hear, not unique. In 2000-01, we sent 2111 briefs or submissions to the minister; by 2005-06, the number had reached 5958. In 2000-01, we put forward 45 Cabinet submissions; in 2005-06, the number was 89. In a positive sense, this tells us that government is working as it should and that ministers are making the real decisions, as they should. But it also risks overwhelming ministers, and that cannot make for good government. This too is a significant issue which requires a clear understanding between ministers and secretaries about what is wanted, and is certainly not an easy matter to resolve.

Risk in the public service

One further issue on which I would like to venture a view is the growth in compliance requirements, both 'hard' and 'soft'. By 'hard' compliance requirements I mean the clearly legislated requirements, like the FMA Act or audit requirements, or those which are established by government policy. By 'soft' requirements I mean the plethora of directives, guidelines, procedural criteria and so on that we are required to have to deal with in a host of situations that may arise in the course of our work. These compliance requirements are often driven by fear of criticism and of litigation and compensation claims. They are often put in place in response to an administrative error or a breakdown in decision making or advising of ministers. They often substitute for, and indeed limit the scope for, common sense, values-based judgements. And in minimising the scope for reasonable risk-taking behaviour, rules and guidelines, they limit public service creativity and effectiveness.

Tony Blair recently commented very pertinently on this subject. In a speech on 26 May 2005 he argued that 'we are in danger of having a wholly disproportionate attitude to the risks we should expect to run as a normal part of life. This is putting pressure on public policy-making…to act to eliminate risk in a way that is out of all proportion to the potential damage…We cannot respond to every accident by trying to guarantee ever more tiny margins of safety. We cannot eliminate risk. We have to live with it, manage it. Sometimes we have to accept: no-one is to blame.' This too is a debate worth having.

Changes in the international environment

Let me divert from the public service for a few moments to say something about changes over these 38 years in the international environment, which has of course been the subject of my professional interest. In 1969, the Cold War was the defining feature or 'organising principle' in world affairs. The decolonisation process was yet incomplete, the pursuit of independence was a strong theme, and the notion of sovereignty as a precious commodity was being nourished by the strength, rhetorically at least, of the recently decolonised nations in the United Nations. Apartheid ruled in South Africa, and anti-racism was a persistent theme in international affairs. Terrorism existed, but was arguably less global, and global security was defined almost exclusively by the interests of nation-states. Australia in 1969 was at war in Vietnam, and we regarded Taiwan as China. We were still adjusting to the UK's admission to the European Economic Community. We were a colonial power in the South Pacific, embarrassed unduly by that but optimistic about what an independent Papua New Guinea might make of itself. Like most other countries, we were highly protectionist. Our defence force then numbered nearly 89,000, with a civilian defence workforce of just over 39,000, and in 1969-70 we spent 1.16 billion dollars or 3.2 per cent of our GDP on defence.

Our world today is defined by the word 'globalisation'. In 1969, the word itself was unknown, at least to me. We were aware of something called automatic data processing and of early generation computers, and we welcomed jumbo jets when they first flew commercially in 1970. But I do not think many of us picked these events then for what they were: the harbingers of globalisation. Australia did pick up on the trend by the 1980s though, and thereafter responded well to the new world with the result that we are now among the most globalised nations.

Looking back on these 38 years, four events stand out in my mind for their significance in shaping world affairs. Three – the rise of China, the end of the Cold War and the events of 9/11 – will not surprise you, but the fourth might: the fall of the Shah of Iran. This is not the place to try to add to all that has been said and written about the meaning and consequences of each of these events, but I would just proffer the view – consistent with the main subject of this address – that 9/11 was probably one of the more significant contributing factors to the rediscovery of the role and importance of government in Western societies after the 'smaller government' fetish of the 1990s. If I may offer a view on the most significant Australian government decision of these 38 years in the realm of foreign and international security policy, it could only be the decision to intervene in East Timor in 1999. As to defence, since 1999 we have deployed some 90,000 personnel overseas on more than 30 operations. Our defence capabilities have truly come to make an important contribution to Australia's international standing. This we do with 51,000 ADF members, 18,000 civilian employees and 1.9 percent of GDP.

Conclusion

In addition to my first experience of war, my first overseas posting (in India for three years) gave me a keener understanding of government and how it was done. While I had long been interested in politics, to see another government at work – even one that looked like ours with a federal system, two houses of parliament and a robust public service – and to try to understand it and work with it, was a valuable learning experience about the nature of government. In the approximately thirty years since then, I have sustained that interest. In later postings in Israel, the Philippines, the United States, China and Indonesia, and in visiting and working in scores of other countries, I have always taken a close interest in how their governments work, and why some work better than others. In all of this one thing has been manifestly clear to me: whatever the constitution, the structure of government, the party system or the quality of political leadership, in the end little can be achieved without robust public institutions and an effective public service.

And a corollary of this is that, even in those countries which have had weak public institutions, the key to getting things done – for political leaders and foreign diplomats alike – is to find the best of the public servants available and try to work through them. They will invariably be overworked and much harried individuals, but I have seen whole governments virtually dependent upon a bare handful of them. From all of this I have become convinced that our own public service is one of the best. Others have reached the same conclusion, but my view is based on much experience watching and working with governments in many countries, and often trying to help struggling or even failing governments function. Frustrating, ponderous, and sometimes overweight: whatever their undoubted misgivings, our public servants are always there, always steady, generally very hard working and honest to a high degree. In short, the Australian Public Service is a national asset, and significantly under-recognised for the contributions it makes.

And yet, challenges nevertheless remain for our public service. I have already referred to IT management issues. Beyond that, I believe most of the challenges are in the personnel area. From talking to other secretaries, I know that many of us now are hard-pressed to recruit adequately for all the jobs we offer, and I know that a number of us have vacant SES positions for which we cannot identify suitably qualified applicants. Much is made in the defence world of the challenge of recruiting to the ADF; in truth, the public service is facing many similar challenges. In broad terms, we need to think more about the sort of people we want to replace us, and how we are going to recruit and train them, and do that much more deliberately.

More specifically, in the area of skills I believe that historically we have given corporate support and service delivery skills too little attention in the Australian Public Service. Traditionally, in part reflecting the old caste divisions I referred to earlier, we have attached greater weight to policy work than to service delivery and corporate work. This has been reflected among other ways in the allocation of SES positions. But it is contrary to the current trend in public sector management, which places increasing weight on accountability in spending money, managing assets and delivering services, and on project and contract management. I do believe we need to redress that imbalance. I referred earlier to toiling for 38 years in this vineyard. I did so, as I said, as a tradesman rather than a philosopher or a visionary. Beyond my normal competitive instincts and a desire to do the best I could, I also did it without any particular ambitions. I did not apply for my first two promotions, nor for my last. I simply kept turning up every day, and they kept doing it to me. I am glad they did, whoever they were. It has been a privilege to be able to serve 12 Foreign Ministers, seven Trade Ministers and three Defence Ministers.

It was also a privilege to have represented Australia abroad – in each of the world's four most populous countries as well as in places like Micronesia, the Marshall Islands, Palau and Mongolia. It was an honour to be appointed as the secretary of the government's largest organisation, the Department of Defence, and a privilege to serve alongside this generation's finest military leaders – in particular my 'co-diarchists' General Peter Cosgrove and Air Chief Marshal Angus Houston. The best times have had this in common: they have been those occasions in which public servants from many different agencies have come together to work as one team to deliver a clear result. Ironically, I saw this at its best in the aftermath of the Bali bombing, where incidentally I also saw some wonderful volunteer work by Australians. In a less dramatic but nevertheless gratifying way, I saw it as ambassador in Beijing from 1996 to 2000, where the embassy came together as one Australian team with the Australian business community to deliver some terrific results for Australia. And I saw it again in the strongly committed multi-departmental team I had in Jakarta in 2001 and 2002.

5. The last count — the importance of official statistics to the democratic process[1]

Dennis Trewin

Dennis Trewin joined the Australian Bureau of Statistics (ABS) in 1966 as a statistics cadet and was Australian Statistician from 2000 to 2006. Prior to that he was Deputy Australian Statistician responsible for economic statistics and a Deputy Government Statistician in New Zealand. Other appointments he held include Australian Electoral Commissioner, Chairman of the World Bank Board on the International Comparison Program, a member of the Committee responsible for preparing the 2006 report on the State of the Environment and Adjunct Professor at Swinburne University of Technology, Melbourne. Dennis Trewin is a past President of the International Statistical Institute, International Association of Survey Statisticians and the Statistical Society of Australia. He is currently Chair of the Policy and Advocacy Committee of the Academy of Social Sciences Australia

In this valedictory address I will reflect on the Australian Bureau of Statistics (ABS) — both past and future — before making a few comments on the APS more generally.

The Australian Bureau of Statistics

I started work in the ABS in December 1965 as a vacation student and then as a statistics cadet before starting work full-time in 1968. At that time, the ABS was actually the Commonwealth Bureau of Census and Statistics and a Branch of Treasury rather than a statutory authority (but largely independent except for budget considerations). The Australian Statistician was referred to as the Commonwealth Statistician. Four out of the last five Statisticians had been Tasmanians as a consequence of their early signing of an Integration Agreement with the Commonwealth government. Core outputs were publications full of statistical tables and few words. Also there was no seasonal adjustment or summary of main features and as a consequence relatively little media reporting of official statistics.

---

1   This speech was delivered in December 2006 at a function organised by the Australian Public Service Commission.

Moreover, social statistics were based on the Census or administrative systems (e.g. births, deaths, migration cards). Household surveys had just started. These were quarterly labour force surveys. The first social supplementary survey was conducted in 1968 – a survey of chronic illness in NSW. Official labour force statistics were based on registered unemployed and were very unreliable. Monthly labour force surveys were not introduced until 1978, and Statistics cadets were our main source of graduates; it was difficult to otherwise persuade graduates to come to Canberra.

But there were more things in common than different. Our core purpose has not changed: we remain the provider of official statistics for the government and the community. There has always been a strong emphasis on the quality and integrity of outputs, and professionalism – our core values have not changed. Similarly, confidentiality was always regarded as paramount. The Census and Statistics Act is still recognisable from that period, indeed from when it was first created in 1905. We have had the support of governments throughout my time at the ABS.

ABS staff numbers over this period have been up and down: 10 staff in 1905 not including those working in the state statistical offices; 2500 in 1968; 3500 in 1975 to 2900 now. But productivity has improved substantially. Although staff numbers have declined since the mid 1970s, outputs have increased substantially, including the number of statistical collections. Technology and methodology developments have been key contributors. Close alignment between the technology and methodology areas and the business areas has been a key factor and one which I will return to shortly.

During my time as Australian Statistician, I have tried to:

- maintain the quality and integrity of statistical outputs, particularly core statistics like population, national accounts and prices, and extend our outputs to new areas of policy interest. Such new areas have included environment (water), social policy and innovation;
- improve productivity (as required by the Certified Agreement) by redesigning business processes, utilising our technology/methodology capabilities;
- improve user engagement by listening, explaining and acting instead of just listening (we were always fine at listening but not at the follow-up);
- in recognition of the increasing demand for detailed statistics, increase access to data and more generally improve usefulness of data for analytical purposes, particularly by improving access to microdata. Free data on the web has been a positive and well received step;
- make the ABS website the core way of accessing our outputs, including regular publications;

- be media friendly and accessible, not just myself, but specialist staff throughout the ABS (most Australians probably find out about official statistics through the media);

- keep compliance cost to a reasonable level (the number of complaints has declined substantially). Access to taxation data has been of great assistance in reducing the compliance cost on business. Compliance cost on all business, particularly small business, has reduced by more than 40 per cent since the Small Business Deregulation Task Force reported in 1996.

The way users access statistics has changed dramatically over the last six years. The following table is indicative of this trend.

Table 1: Demand for different forms of statistical output

	1999-2000	2005-2006
Website		
Pages viewed	14.9m	78.0m
Products downloaded	26,795	1.9m
Telephone inquiry service	17,600	68,000
Publications – revenue	$3.0m	$0.3m
Confidentialised Unit record files – applications processed	214	252

As the table shows, website access has increased fivefold. Products downloaded are now 70 times greater than what they were six years ago [the year 2000]. Not surprisingly, the demand on our printed publications has reduced substantially (although phone inquiries have increased). This is a good outcome. We prefer as many users as possible to be able to 'self-help'.

Although use of Confidentialised Unit Record Files (CURFs) have not increased that much over this period, you didn't have to go back much further to find their use was almost negligible. The increase of CURFs increased considerably as a result of a special agreement with the Australian Vice Chancellor's Committee. Statistical leadership across all providers of statistics is another area where I have tried to put more focus but progress has not been as great as hoped. But I think the direction is correct.

I am fortunate that I inherited an organisation that was in very good shape and had a strong reputation. There was no need for major change. We could afford a continuous improvement strategy reacting to new demands, the changes in our environment and new opportunities that arose.

There are four key challenges for the ABS for the future that I would like to mention:

- improving the national statistical system;

- making greater use of administrative and transactional data bases;
- improving the user experience;
- enhancing the international comparability of statistics.

I will discuss each in turn. The first challenge is improving the National Statistical System (NSS). Clearly the ABS has some technical skills in statistics that might be of use to others. And increasingly our information management skills are being recognised as being particularly strong.

Our involvement in NSS work recognises that the ABS is not the only provider of statistics. There are advantages to both producers and users of statistics if we can work in a more coherent way. Government agencies increasingly need to work in a 'connected' way. This will only happen if they are prepared to share information, including statistical information. It is important that this information be coherent – for this we need to be using the same concepts and definitions to the extent possible. This requires leadership on standards and classifications, a role which the ABS is well suited to play. It is also important that the range of statistics be of good quality – not perfect but based on sound statistical methods. Again the ABS has a constructive role to play.

Key NSS activities might include: developing and promoting standard classifications and coding tools; developing and promulgating statistical frameworks, standards and definitions for general use; providing access to statistical infrastructure such as our business register; promoting good practice (e.g. through training); maintaining networks of statistical practitioners; and possibly over-recruiting statisticians recognising that some might move to other agencies. Another thing we are doing is developing statistical centres of expertise that have knowledge of all relevant statistics not just those of the ABS (e.g. environment statistics).

From our perspective, the NSS will be considered successful if more good quality statistics become publicly available, something that is good for both democracy and effective policy. For example, macro-economic statistics/policy is very dependent on transparent and trusted statistics. This is also true for other fields of statistics. It is good for government, particularly if things are going well – better to have policy debate focussed on facts rather than advocacy or anecdote. And yet, there is reluctance by some to make information publicly available in case it might embarrass the minister (at both Commonwealth and state levels). It will occasionally, but I would argue that in most cases it is better for governments if debate was based on trusted facts rather than the alternatives.

The second challenge is greater use of administrative and transactional data bases for statistics, something that is presently underutilised. These are beneficial because:

- they can reduce compliance cost (e.g. ABS use of taxation data has been a major reason for the 40 per cent reduction in compliance cost);
- they can provide more detailed data than from sample surveys because you effectively have a census of the population in scope of the administrative system (e.g. regions or small populations);
- they often have an in-built longitudinal element which enables you to better understand the dynamics of the population.

Of course, there are privacy issues associated with this issue that have to be carefully managed, but we should not be scared off by them.

Australia is well behind many other countries in its use of administrative data for statistical purposes. The use is most prevalent in Scandinavia with their register systems. But Canada, which has a lot of cultural similarities to Australia, also has a history of record linkage for statistical purposes. It is not controversial.

The ABS could act as custodian of these data bases for statistical purposes (as we do for births and deaths, immigration cards, customs and taxation) or could act as statistical and information management advisers to agencies who prefer to retain custodianship. In many cases we are finding access to administrative data more difficult than in the past. There are a variety of reasons such as privacy, statistical support not being core business and, in some cases, concern about information becoming public.

The third challenge is to improve the user experience. The website is crucial: our strategy is one of continuous improvement with occasional leaps in the improvement of the design of the website. But we will be continually improving usability, increasing content, developing new graphical presentation tools and developing better links to related websites. The establishment of a National Data Network as a single source to all statistics in particular fields (e.g. environment statistics) is another related initiative, as while custodianship will not change but awareness, coherence, access and usability of statistics can improve.

We will also continue to improve access to microdata through remote access facilities (e.g. through the Remote Access Data Laboratory and Table Builder system to access 2001 and 2006 Census data) and by setting up collaborative arrangements with other government agencies that are consistent with our legislation.

Another means of improving the user experience is to develop linked data sets that can be used for research and analysis purposes, particularly understanding the interconnection between different social outcomes. We have started by establishing the first round of a longitudinal link of population census records. It proved to be non-controversial during the 2006 Census.

The fourth challenge is improving international comparability of statistics. Official statistics are being used more extensively for international comparisons, perhaps with the assistance of international organisations like the OECD. Comparing statistics for Australia with those from other countries provide a context for Australian figures. Differences can be illuminating in evaluating the effectiveness of current policy or for assessing alternative policy options. This is one of the main reasons why the ABS is an active contributor internationally, particularly to the development of international statistical standards to support comparability of data.

I am often asked why the ABS is so well regarded, particularly internationally. There is a combination of factors of course but top of the list is core values. Our core values are integrity, professionalism, a focus of service, relevance, trust of data providers and access for all. They are widely accepted and understood. More importantly, they reflect the behaviour of staff at all levels and in all offices. That certainty makes my job much easier.

The Australian Public Service

Now turning to the APS more generally, I wish to make four quick points. First, I want to emphasise the importance of a close alignment between IT providers and the business areas. This needs to work in two directions (whether there is an internal provider of IT or it is outsourced). IT is a great enabler and source for innovation but only if there is alignment with business areas. Furthermore, developments must be treated as business projects rather than technology projects. They should be driven by the desired business outcomes. This may involve redesign of business processes. This is often necessary to get full benefits from the investment. Finally, you should ensure good project management arrangements are in place.

Second, I want to recall the words of Drucker: 'good leaders don't make many decisions'. This may seem counterintuitive but it implies that good leaders provide the authorities, policies, procedures to enable others to make sound decisions. A question public servants – and perhaps some ministers – should ask themselves is whether they get involved in too many micro decisions. And yet, I realise it is easier for an organisation like the ABS which is not subject to day to day involvement with ministers to set up the authorities, etc to enable effective delegation.

Third, I think we have to assume that new graduates are capable of some difficult work very early in their career. We just can't rely on the recently retired to undertake the more difficult or complex tasks or the APSC will not develop at the rate it should. Our young staff want to be tested – this is the consistent feedback I received from the annual ABS Youth Forum. I think I was fortunate in being thrown in the deep end early in my career. Furthermore, turnover is high among our younger staff so it doesn't make sense to make a high investment in their formal training in their early years. Also, work experience can be the most effective way of learning. That was certainly my experience.

Fourth, I want to discuss how to manage errors – something that is inevitable if only because of volume of work. They also tend to be more public now than what they were even ten years ago. The ABS does make errors but fortunately not too many. The ABS approach is to (a) admit error and subsequently apologise; (b) don't seek blame but try to learn from it particularly and assess whether there are systemic problems; and (c) undertake an independent review if necessary. This generally works well for us but only if we make relatively few errors. Such an approach may have more general applicability.

In conclusion, it has been a great privilege to be Australian Statistician during such an interesting period, and I also greatly appreciated support from government. It has provided us with an adequate budget, but perhaps more importantly it has shown an excellent understanding of the importance of the integrity of official statistics to the democratic process. This is not true for all countries.

6. Balancing Life at Home and Away in the Australian Public Service[1]

Joanna Hewitt

The daughter of a bank manager, Joanna Hewitt was educated in Perth and 'nearly every little town in Western Australia'. She joined the Department of Foreign Affairs in 1972 after completing an economics degree, but later took time off and went to the London School of Economics to undertake a masters degree. She rose through the ranks in Foreign Affairs to become Ambassador to the European Union and Belgium in 2000 before being named Secretary of the Department of Agriculture, Fisheries and Forestry (DAFF) in October 2004. Joanna Hewitt has faced several hurdles blocking her path, including a delayed posting to Stockholm in the mid-1970s because of her gender, and the challenges of balancing motherhood with a career as a senior public servant.

It is a special honour for me to speak today, close to my point of departure from the Australian Public Service and my departure from Australia for the next three years.

My resignation takes effect a little earlier than I had expected, a few months short of my three-year term as Secretary of the Department of Agriculture, Fisheries and Forestry (DAFF).

As some of you will know, I will be leaving with my fifteen-year-old son, Tom (and our golden retriever, Stella), to join my husband, Mark, who has been in Washington, DC, on posting since the beginning of this year.

It's a complicated business in any family to manage two careers and the needs of children (in our case, three) but it's even more complicated if overseas postings are part of the story. Having said that, I would add that complexity is not all bad. With a little bit of juggling, we have had wonderful opportunities to serve Australia in fascinating places as well as in the policy hub of Canberra.

In Mark's case, before we were married, he served in Canada and Israel. My early posting was in Sweden and I managed a detour through the United Kingdom after that to do my masters degree at the London School of Economics (LSE).

We both spent quite a few years in Canberra after those early postings and our marriage in 1987, then managed three and a half years in Paris when Mark

---

1 This valedictory address was presented at a function organised by the Australian Public Service Commission in April 2007.

was at the embassy and I had a superb job in the Organisation for Economic Cooperation and Development's Agriculture Directorate. Later, when I was appointed Ambassador in Brussels, Mark spent a couple of years as deputy at our embassy in Berlin. We commuted by plane every weekend, except one, in that time. But to return to the reason for my departure now from a job I have relished, as DAFF Secretary, the bottom line is that the commute across the Pacific is a far cry from a flit across Western Europe and four months apart is about all we are prepared to manage.

So, as I wrap up a career that started when I joined the then Department of Foreign Affairs (DFAT) as a trainee in 1972, I thought I would pick out a few of the issues and experiences that stand out for me. I will try to spare you the blow-by-blow career story. It would be long and tortuous and it's also quite unorthodox so in no way stands as a model for the aspirant secretaries in the audience. Also, a sage former DFAT boss of mine once told me the essence of a good speech was that it should end before the audience dares hope it might.

I will start, though, by telling you that I grew up in a family of four girls in rural Western Australia. Our dad worked in one of the big banks and we moved around the countryside regularly. It might have boosted my credibility as Secretary of the Agricultural Department to have been born in Denmark and lived in Harvey, Manjimup, Northam, Three Springs and Kojonup as well as Perth, but it certainly confused the Nordics when I was posted to Stockholm and my passport showed I was born in Denmark.

With hindsight, the rhythm of upping sticks every two or three years must have imprinted itself quite deeply when I think about the way I have changed jobs and continents.

In fact, I stumbled into international work. I did an economics honours degree at the University of Western Australia and had been thinking of a career in journalism. I was working part-time for the *West Australian* in my final two years at university but almost by accident I ran across the Department of Foreign Affairs' campus recruitment. After the rounds of testing and interviews, I was offered a place as a diplomatic trainee. I knew then it was exactly what I wanted to do.

As an aside, I would note that campus recruitment remains a hugely valuable part of our efforts to nurture and sustain the APS. At DFAT and DAFF, I have been thrilled and relieved every year to welcome fresh graduate recruits with stunning qualifications and impressive skills. In DAFF we have doubled the number of graduates we recruit since I have been Secretary and the results have been excellent.

I joined Foreign Affairs as one of 42 trainees, of whom eight were women. There was a bit of fuss about the fact that I was a married woman trainee and I was mortified after agreeing to do an interview with *The Australian* newspaper about this bold move by the department's management to see 'Joanna sets pace at Foreign Affairs' as the front-page headline the next day. (I note that at the time I was wearing what looks like a hippie headband and a long Indian cotton skirt for the photograph. There were none of the black tailored suits worn by today's smart women grads. The men in our day were also more creative dressers. Does anyone remember pastel safari suits?)

It took me a year longer to get out on my first posting than almost all of the other trainees because the *Public Service Act* had to be changed to allow 'an officer and his or her spouse' to be posted rather than 'an officer and his wife'. It seems almost incomprehensible today that the system could have been so inflexible but at the time I was not really upset or surprised. More extraordinarily, one of the other women trainees from my year was in the process of being divorced. The rather forceful head of management services of the day insisted that she not be posted until the divorce was final so that 'a woman of dubious marital status' was not representing Australia abroad. Even at the time, this seemed absurd, and if equal application of the policy to existing male staff of the department were made it would have made a serious dent in our overseas representation.

In any case, the posting was great at a time when Australia was rather enthralled by 'the Swedish model' in many policy fields, but perhaps especially at that time, in industrial relations. It was pretty obvious to me that a lot of the Swedish experience could not be readily translated directly to our more adversarial culture but I learned a lot and loved it, apart from the cold and dark.

I took a bit of time out after Stockholm to go to the LSE and finished my thesis two weeks before my first daughter, Francesca, was born. I was a bit anxious about returning to work a year later but once I was comfortable with the childcare arrangement, I found it worked pretty well. I do recall one of my women colleagues at DFAT about that time suggesting we lobby for a childcare centre to be set up in the department. I was so busy just managing the work and home stuff that I did not feel I had much time to spare on what I thought was a lost cause. I knew the climate would be hostile to the idea and to my shame I said I did not think it was worth wasting our energies. My colleague was on the right track and the childcare centre DFAT introduced about 20 years later has been a huge asset for the department as well as the staff who use it. But I suspect I was right about our slim prospects of success in the mid-1970s.

Just before my second daughter, Olivia, was born in 1979, I decided to leave the service for family reasons and resumed academic work, lecturing and writing at Griffith University in Queensland. I even embarked on a PhD but came to the conclusion part-way through that I was not really cut out for life as a scholar. The pull of public policy was strong.

I returned to Canberra in 1983—incidentally as a recently separated single mother, when my two girls were three and six years old. I could not go back to Foreign Affairs because it was possible to enter the department's policy ranks only as a trainee. I was offered re-entry at base level but I chose instead to join the Office of National Assessments (ONA) in the equivalent of an EL1 job. Again, this inflexibility seems bizarre in retrospect but proved to be a blessing in disguise.

I had some wonderful years after ONA at the Department of the Prime Minister and Cabinet (running the parliamentary briefing unit and speech writing) and later as Private Secretary in the Office of the Minister for Trade. I went on to my first SES job in the Industry Department and later moved to the Department of Trade. In these jobs, I grew hugely in my understanding of our system of government, the parliamentary and cabinet processes and the media. I had fabulous role models and mentors and a great sense that I could play a part in the contribution of the Public Service to national life. Big policy shifts like the floating of the dollar, important steps in tariff reform and the establishment of the Cairns Group made it a heady time to be working on trade and industry policy. There was a very lively sense that we were in a marketplace for ideas and I revelled in it all. I also seem to recall that in quiet weeks (and there were some then) we occasionally indulged in longer lunches than we could begin to imagine today.

I ended up back in my old home when the departments of Foreign Affairs and Trade were merged in the 1987 machinery-of-government changes. I think I was the only member of staff to have worked in both former departments and spent a certain amount of time as an interpreter across the divide. We talk today about the culture of organisations but, frankly, in the first year after the merger, DFAT was suffused with some bitter culture wars.

It was worth persisting. I am convinced that our combined foreign and trade policy arrangements give us a real edge internationally through national interest-focused diplomacy. Australia's extensive (and expensive) diplomatic network is geared up to push hard for our economic as well as our political and security interests in the world. A lot of the debilitating turf warfare of the past has been abandoned while we get on with the job. This is not common in foreign services, some of which in my experience are poorly equipped even to understand the interests of the countries they purport to represent. And although a lot of skilled diplomacy was conducted for Australia in the years before the merger, I clearly recall being present during a ministerial visit to a small European post in the mid-1980s when the ambassador declined to answer a basic question from my boss, the Trade Minister of the day, John Dawkins, about the local economy. At full ambassadorial height (and pomposity), he declared that 'we don't do that sort of thing on the fifth floor of the embassy'. Fortunately for us all, the minister decided to be amused rather than infuriated. It simply could not happen today.

At the risk of breaking my own rule about brevity, I will say a bit about what later turned out to be the closer road to my DFAT appointment.

I was lured to the then Department of Primary Industries and Energy (DPIE) from DFAT in 1988. At the time, for family reasons, it seemed unlikely that postings were going to work and an opening came up as head of the Livestock and Pastoral Division in DPIE. Again, this was a great experience for me. I soaked up a lot of practical industry policy and industry politics and headed three separate divisions over my time there, dealing with issues as diverse as dismantling of the wool reserve price scheme, the establishment of Landcare and the early years of the Uruguay Round of trade negotiations. Geoff Miller was the Secretary and set pretty exacting standards for 'first best' policy analysis. There was a comfortable, open atmosphere in the department and I had some wonderful colleagues, many of whom I have been working with again in DAFF.

It wasn't all beer and skittles. The worst part of that period was my work on forestry policy at the height of the battles between the environment movement and the forestry industry. It is hard to describe just how brutal and personal the politics of forestry were within the government itself and between interest groups. It was extremely difficult to do good work when the government was divided on the issues, and I seemed to spend some pretty unproductive hours just trying to keep to within striking distance of good practice. There was not a lot of interest in objective, evidence-based advice. On one of the worst days I remember having to listen politely to complaints from a wilderness group about the fact that jet trails could be seen in the sky over a national park in Western Australia while we were worrying about how many of the displaced forestry workers could really get jobs in eco-tourism. Relationships between the players in the departments, ministerial offices and the industry and environment groups were personalised and bitter and there was a lot more heat than light.

I had my work cut out for me persuading staff in my own division that it was worth persisting with good policy and practice. I would often get to a Friday evening and be able to think of nothing positive we had achieved except helping to prevent the worst from happening. We have made huge progress in these areas of our work now and the excellent rapport in today's DAFF/DEW joint team, which advises both ministers on natural resource management issues, is a model I could only have dreamed about in the late 1980s.

It was a relief to move to DPIE's Corporate Policy Division in 1990 to handle the agricultural trade negotiations and broad industry policy advising. I loved my return to one of Australia's great battles—to bring agricultural trade squarely into the multilateral rules framework and to fight for access to the world's protected agricultural markets. It is an argument that has been under way for 50 years (since the Treaty of Rome and the inception of Europe's Common Agricultural Policy) and though we have made some strides that need to be acknowledged, including the Uruguay Round Agreement on Agriculture and some reform in Europe, the pace has been dismal and over the past few years the debate in important developed and developing counties seems to have drifted dangerously. It is disturbing to hear a new wave of protectionist prescriptions just as misguided as the old being dressed up in euphemistic language, such as calls for 'policy space' for countries to manage the pace of change associated with globalisation.

This is not a fight Australia can afford to lose. We export two-thirds of our agricultural production and agriculture still represents nearly one-quarter of our total export profit. We understand that reform is a hard road through our experience at home. We have invested heavily in analysing the costs and benefits; indeed, analysts in DAFF, our Bureau of Agriculture and Resource Economics (ABARE) and DFAT know as much about the distorting farm programs of other countries as their own analysts. But in representational democracy you need enlightened leadership from governments and influential groups in industry and the media to make headway against vested interests. So it's back to the marketplace for ideas. And when we are trying to persuade governments and citizens in other countries that change of the sort we have been through would also be good for them, we really have our diplomatic work cut out for us.

I did a lot of this work at the Organisation for Economic Cooperation and Development (OECD) in the mid-1990s and later as Ambassador to Brussels. Sometimes, though, I despaired about the tone of Australian advocacy on agricultural policy reform. We are rightly enraged about the unfairness of distortions we face in world markets and we want to see big change, and quickly. It is important to remember when you are trying to persuade another party to do something they are reluctant to do—even if you can show them that it's good for us all—that you need to put a bit of effort into the tone and pitch of your message.

We can come across as blunt and blustering as well as passionate. I am sure this has been said of me as well as of lots of my colleagues. It's understandable, but not always effective. So while we continue to fight the good fight, we need to remind ourselves that the same basic truths apply in diplomacy whether you are right or wrong, whether your cause is just or not. We need to be clever, to articulate our good arguments credibly and to understand and operate well in the context (or, as the trade negotiators say, the authorising environment) in which the debate has to be won.

After my stint at the OECD I was thrilled to be appointed Deputy Secretary at DFAT in 1996. I straddled work in lots of different areas over the next five years including the rather familiar trade policy and work in the United Nations on climate change and regional diplomacy. This included my role as Asia Pacific Economic Cooperation (APEC) Ambassador through the Asian financial crisis, difficulties in our relations with Malaysia during its year as APEC host following the imprisonment of Anwar Ibrahim and the diplomacy in the margins of the Auckland APEC Leaders' meeting to get agreement to the Interfet force in East Timor. Another highlight of those years during a visit to Rangoon was the opportunity to meet and speak at some length with Burma's Democratic Party leader, Aung San Suu Kyi, under house arrest at her home. Sadly, not much has changed there.

For the first time in my career, I also took on responsibilities on the corporate side of the house, handling DFAT's staffing and finances during a tough period of budget cuts and downsizing. I led negotiations for the first two collective agreements and helped introduce more modern management arrangements. A little bit to my surprise, I found I also loved the management role and the positive rewards that came from working directly with colleagues to improve the way our department was run.

I sought out my ambassadorial appointment in Brussels, which also met all my expectations. It is a somewhat under-appreciated city and, despite the weather and reputation for bureaucracy, is a fascinating global capital abuzz with the activity of Europe's institutions and all those who seek to influence them. The weather is awful but the restaurants superb. The work was a mix of the familiar trade and agricultural policy along with broader foreign and security policy work as the European institutions expanded their reach into new fields. It was a stimulating professional environment and, despite the inward preoccupations of the day, particularly the focus on the enlargement of the European Union and attempts at negotiation of a new European Constitution, I found I could always get access to have Australian concerns heard, even if we could not always get the responses we were seeking. My work with NATO was also very interesting around the time of the commitment of troops to Iraq.

While it has not had a lot of attention at home, I was impressed by the achievement of the European Union's enlargement, which unfolded on my watch. I suspect the rest of the world has not really given due credit to the architects of this huge geopolitical move that has guaranteed the people of half a continent personal freedoms, the rule of law and a real prospect of prosperity after more than 50 years of authoritarian communist rule. If we could only see such bold and visionary steps in European agricultural reform!

My first assignment after returning from Brussels was to take over the World Trade Organisation (WTO) lead negotiator role at the failed WTO conference in Cancun. This was hardly propitious timing but I take some comfort from what we achieved in a WTO Framework Agreement in mid-2004. It cost me a large number of days in transit between Canberra and Geneva and at times I felt I was spending more time with my counterpart negotiators in the small group of countries at the heart of the process than with family or colleagues at home. I have every reason to keep a close eye on progress with the conclusion of the Doha Round.

My appointment as DAFF Secretary in October 2004 was a wonderful surprise. The portfolio suited my experience well and I was lucky already to know a good number of my colleagues and industry figures from my DPIE and trade policy days. I was rearing to have a go at leading one of the great departments and it has been a marvellous experience.

For the sector over this time, Dorothea Mackellar says it all. The drought has set a very harsh backdrop for Australian farmers and their resilience and grit in the face of the past five or six severe dry years deserve our respect. There will be tough times ahead even when we get rain because water storages are at such precariously low levels. But flooding rains have also been part of the story as Cyclone Larry showed. Climate variability is an inescapable feature of our continent and the emerging scientific consensus suggests we will have to cope with even more of it. The work we have already begun on developing better predictive and management tools for farmers will need to be taken much further.

It is true, as the Prime Minister has said, that agriculture is in the Australian psyche. But its important place in the Australian economy has been maintained through hard work and innovation, not sentiment alone. We know that the care of much of our landscape is in the hands of farmers and that the survival of vibrant rural Australian communities depends heavily on the fortunes of agricultural industries. It is also true that this cannot be guaranteed through policies of cosseting and protection that have failed everywhere they have been tried. Australia needs to retain its competitive focus and smart approach to agriculture. Without that eye to the markets we would be left with the museum agriculture of many OECD countries and that would not support our farm families or our export performance.

That's the end of my Agriculture Policy 101 snippet. These ideas have been at the centre of bipartisan agricultural policy in Australia for decades. We have been lucky on the whole to have had thoughtful and responsible leadership in our farm organisations to help us avoid some of the policy pitfalls. Our approach is not always popular with the industries, and the constitutional split of responsibilities between federal and state governments has encouraged some unprepossessing politicking at times. On the whole, though, there has been a clear-eyed focus on what serves us best.

As Secretary, I have tried to nurture some of the great strengths of our service. In DAFF we have an extraordinary line-up of specialist talent ranging from plant biologists to veterinarians, from economists to ecologists and from generalist policy advisors to the Australian Quarantine Inspection Service (AQIS) operational staff at the front line. There's a great sense of purpose in the portfolio and a real empathy with our stakeholders, even on the occasions when our advice does not support farm industry proposals.

In this job, as in all the work I have done in the APS, I have been really grateful for the opportunity to be heard on the policy issues in play. Some of them have been difficult, as a scan of any week's rural media would confirm. Just think about wheat marketing or apple imports. It has always seemed to me that our system, which gives public servants a good chance to present arguments and engage with ministers, is about as good as it gets. I am deeply committed to the Westminster principles, which leave decision making to the elected government, except in specialist, technical areas where governments have chosen to vest authority in expert statutory bodies. It has sometimes been necessary for me to remind staff, especially some of our highly qualified expert colleagues, that in our democratic system the only right decision is the one the government takes. That does not mean we cannot present views and make recommendations. It does mean that we respect and implement as effectively as we can the decision that is made.

Forging relationships of trust with ministers is at the heart of effective government in Australia. In Canberra's tight environment we do have a great opportunity to do that. In my work, with lots of long international flights and exhausting all-night negotiating sessions, I have had more opportunity than many. I am grateful for this.

I will say a final word from a woman's perspective about life in Australia's Public Service. First, it was a real delight to be appointed Secretary in the talented company of the October 2004 group of Lynelle Briggs, Lisa Paul and Patricia Scott, joining the 'dean of the women secretaries group', Helen Williams, as well as Jane Halton.

I have been a bit stunned by recent debate about whether it really is possible to have both a career and a family and enjoy it all. I know I have been lucky. My three children have all been happy and healthy and have taken pleasure in our life overseas as well as at home. They seem to have coped well with all our juggling and work-related travel. I have sometimes wondered whether this is just my impression but my daughters cannot have thought it all bad. In fact, from the day we arrived in Paris when they were teenagers and made their first foray out onto the Champs Élysées, they have been committed internationalists as well as committed Australians. They have also chosen to work in public policy—both of them in international organisations, based in Jakarta and Geneva.

I owe much to my husband, Mark, who has been brilliant at sharing the load and making life outside work so much fun. This is even more obvious to me as I've managed more or less as a single parent again over these past few months. I will also owe a debt of gratitude to my sister, Ricky, who lived in Canberra when my girls were small and gave me wonderful support and companionship as well as being a very special aunt.

I also know that flexible work arrangements can help a lot. The public sector has led the wider economy in this area and has benefited greatly as a result in the quality and continuity of its staff. Not everyone approves but I hope we take a few more measured steps. It simply does not seem to me to be sensible, sustainable or necessary for women, or indeed parents, to have to choose between their children and their work.

I expect to be spending a bit more of my time on the home front with my son when I get to Washington. My daughters, incidentally, warn me that the idea of spending more quality time with mother is not necessarily appealing for a boy who is about to turn sixteen!

I leave my job with a sense of optimism about our service and the future of our country.

Australians have an instinct for directness and innovation that serves us well in government as in the wider society and economy. We are generally ready to look at the evidence on an issue and, when the case for change is clear, to face up to it. We are part of the 'new world' rather than the old.

I will be following the cut and thrust of Australian life from the other side of the Pacific with close interest. I'll really miss working with you. My colleagues in DAFF have been a wonderful and talented bunch. My secretary colleagues have been a great source of collegiality and professionalism, working across the dividing lines of portfolios in a constructive way wherever they can. I'll also miss the people in the farm organisations, the rural community groups and those who work with a passion for the rural environment. Thank you all for joining me this afternoon.

7. In the national interest[1]

Peter Shergold

Peter Shergold emigrated to Australia from the UK in 1972 to take up a lectureship at the University of New South Wales, becoming head of the university's Department of Economic History in 1985. Having worked closely with non-government organisations in the area of ethnic affairs during his academic career, Dr Shergold was invited to establish the Office of Multicultural Affairs in 1987. For the next twenty years he held several prominent positions in the Australian Public Service, including head of the Aboriginal and Torres Strait Islander Commission (ATSIC; 1991-94); Public Service Commissioner (1995-98); Secretary of the Department of Employment, Workplace Relations and Small Business (1998-2002); and Secretary of the Department of Education, Science and Training (2002-03). From 2003 until 2008, Peter Shergold was Secretary of the Department of the Prime Minister and Cabinet, Australia's most senior public administration position. On leaving the APS he established the cross-university Centre for Social Impact of which he is the Macquarie Group Foundation Professor. He is also Chancellor of the University of Western Sydney. He chairs the National Centre for Vocational Education Research and the New South Wales Public Service Commission Advisory Board. He also serves on the boards of private sector companies (AMP, Corrs Chambers Westgarth) and non-profit organisations (National Centre of Indigenous Excellence, General Sir John Monash Foundation and the Sydney Writers' Festival).

I was born in Crawley New Town, England. For an idea of its repute, one need look no further than the interestingly titled tourist guide, *Crap Towns: The 50 Worst Places to Live in the UK*. Most of my childhood and adolescence was spent there. My dad being in the Royal Navy, many of his postings were around Portsmouth. According to the guide, visitors 'sit glassy-eyed…staring out at the grey horizon and wondering, presumably, how to end their lives.' If that doesn't sound bad enough, my wife Carol and I went to university in Hull, which was actually ranked worst town in Britain. According to one correspondent, 'Hull did teach me one valuable lesson. No matter what happens to me in later life, no matter where I live, or how bad things are, I will know that it can never, ever be as bad as living in Hull.'

Perhaps that explains why in July 1972 I seized the chance to come to Australia. On no more than the trusted word of my doctoral supervisor (without submitting a job application, let alone attending an interview), I was recruited as a lecturer

---

1   This is an edited version of a speech delivered at a valedictory function organised by the Australian Public Service Commission in February 2008.

at the University of New South Wales. Promised $6280 a year and a return economy air ticket, it was too good an opportunity for a poor and pallid student from the London School of Economics to knock back. It seemed to offer, at the least, three years of paid employment, cold beer and sunshine. It became a great deal more.

Fifteen years later, on 2 March 1987, I was offered a position in the Australian Public Service. I had long since decided that Australia was my country, but the attraction of academia had started to wane. I had risen to become the head of the Department of Economic History just at the point at which the discipline was in precipitous decline. I had written a well-reviewed scholarly treatise which was 'highly recommended' to readers by *Choice* – to little effect, it transpired. After 30 years it has now sold 1,976 copies (for anyone interested, 24 copies remain in a Pittsburgh warehouse). I faced the prospect, yet again, of delivering first-year lectures three times a day to reluctant students. They not unreasonably failed to understand why a major in accountancy, marketing or human resource management required an understanding of the Industrial Revolution.

In part because of my interest in the role of ethnicity in Australian history, but also to raise my flagging spirits, I had begun to work pro bono as a consultant to non-government organisations, particularly ethnic communities' councils. So when in 1987 the Hawke government decided to establish an Office of Multicultural Affairs in the Department of Prime Minister and Cabinet I was approached and invited to apply. I did not know the job existed and I'm fairly sure that I never did submit my statement of qualifications against the required criteria.

The reasons why I was head-hunted remain to this day obscure. Indeed I suspect that my appointment undermines my oft-espoused support for the importance of the merit principle in the APS. I was offered a position as a first assistant secretary. It sounded important. I had no clear ideas what responsibilities were conveyed by such a grand title (and indeed spent my early weeks in a bemused state trying to locate the second and third assistant secretaries). Nevertheless I was confident that the Australian Public Service would, at the least, offer two years' reprieve from university management (I write, of course, oxymoronically).

Once again I hopelessly underestimated the extraordinary turn of fortune that serendipity had thrust upon me. I have now enjoyed a wonderful 20 years – intellectually fulfilling, administratively demanding, full of interest and rich with opportunities to learn. Not always successfully, I have been given the chance to do a job founded on social responsibility and – although I admit this only at my moment of valediction – moral purpose. It is surely no small thing to work in an occupation that takes 'national interest' and 'public good' as its reference points.

I am honoured to have the chance to reflect on my APS career. Although it has been touched with singular good luck, I have a strong sense that my sentiments are shared in varying degree by thousands of retiring public servants when they stand as guests of honour at their final afternoon tea. While I have on many occasions talked with vigour (and evoked no little controversy) on the quality and character of the Australian Public Service, instead, in this valedictory I will reflect on my own experiences. Nonetheless, I hope I can recount my story in a manner that says something truthful about the vocation of public service.

Since 1987 I have worked directly to 3 prime ministers and 9 ministers. In chronological order they have been Bob Hawke, Robert Tickner, Gary Johns, David Kemp, Peter Reith, Tony Abbott, Ian Macfarlane, Mal Brough, Brendan Nelson, Peter McGauran, John Howard and Kevin Rudd. They have ranged across all points of the political spectrum and all quadrants of the Myer-Briggs personality profile. Yet beyond the particularities of their character, competence and ideological persuasion all those I have served have sought to make a difference.

All were generous in the respect they accorded my views. More remarkably, all bore and accepted what Prime Minister Howard described (with kindly if weary forbearance) as my childlike enthusiasm. Verona Burgess, perhaps more accurately, suggested I am prone to excitability. On a good day that quality comes across as passion. On a bad day it's tiring, even to myself.

I have worked closely with each of these ministers and sometimes come to know their spouses and family. I have had high regard for them. I have learned to recognise their interests, concerns and individual quirkiness for – as any senior public servant soon discovers – an understanding of such matters is central to the ability to influence. In many cases, I have come to enjoy a level of intimacy in which confidences have been shared beyond the public policy at hand.

Yet not one minister was my friend. I say this with care, knowing it can be so readily misinterpreted, but in my experience it is of the utmost significance to understanding the role of a senior public servant. Indeed, in 20 years I have very rarely called my minister by first name, even in private. This may seem archaic, even quaint. It reflects my deep-seated judgement that, whatever public servants think of the ability of their ministers, it is vital that they always recognise the importance of the position that ministers hold (and the responsibilities they bear). Formality is, for me, a statement of respect for the framework of democratic governance within which ministers and secretaries operate.

Equally important, formality bears testimony to my experience that however cordial and close the relationship between a public servant and minister, and however founded in mutual trust, there will inevitably come moments when it is necessary to provide advice that is uncomfortably frank; to convey (and share with others) information which is unwelcome and even – on legal or administrative grounds – to conclude that one is unable to do what a minister would prefer. When such circumstances arise, often unexpectedly, it helps that both parties fully understand their respective roles. It is on such occasions that the distinction between public servant and political appointee needs to be clearly comprehended: the former serves a position, the latter a person.

I have been extraordinarily fortunate always to serve prime ministers, ministers – and, indeed, their personal staff – whose work ethic, capacity and political commitment I respected. That has allowed me the opportunity to contribute to some of the great issues of public policy. As head of the Office of Multicultural Affairs from 1987 to 1990 I was able to prepare the National Agenda for a Multicultural Australia. Launched in a spirit of bipartisanship by Prime Minister Hawke and NSW Premier Greiner, the Agenda offered a careful statement of the rights and responsibilities of Australians of diverse origins set within a distinctively Australian institutional framework. Unfortunately this balance was not always sufficiently understood or espoused by those who saw multiculturalism – a noun I always eschewed – as the ideological vanguard for cultural relativism.

As CEO of ATSIC between 1991 and 1994 I grappled with the wickedly difficult political response to the Mabo High Court decision and how to negotiate and legislate recognition of native title. I held meetings of Indigenous leaders to garner their views; one, discerning my English accent, responded that it would have been nice if I'd asked 200 years earlier.

As Public Service Commissioner from 1995 to 1998, I worked with successive governments to modernise the legislative framework of public service management. Those efforts bore fruit, after I had moved on, in a new Public Service Act. Enacted with opposition support, it placed a greater emphasis on the distinctive values and ethical conduct that underpin public service. To a significant extent the Act stripped away the prescriptive controls that had accreted over three-quarters of a century. It provided legislative support for the devolution of management authority to the agency level.

Asked to move to the Department of Employment and Workplace Rleations (DEWR) to bed down the new workplace relations legislation, I arrived just in time to administer the government's approach to the 1998 waterfront dispute. It was a testing time. In something of an understatement I noted in the department's Annual Report that it 'was a matter of disappointment to me that on occasions the vigour of political debate was personalised into an attack on the integrity of public servants doing their job.' Then, as on many other occasions, I came to recognise how an environment of fierce political contest brings a particularly challenging – dare I say exciting – character to public sector management. Public service partisanship lies, very often, in the eye of the beholder.

In 2002 in the Department of Education, Science and Training (DEST) I had the opportunity to regalvanise the process of reform of higher education. The policies that emerged recognised the imperative to provide universities with greater public funding, enhanced their capability to bolster their own financial resources and actively promoted greater diversity of teaching and research. Finally, during my five years at the Department of Prime Minister and Cabinet (PM&C), I have been able to engage myself in issues as varied as welfare-to-work reform, counter-terrorism, Indigenous disadvantage, vocational education and, most recently, the role of emissions trading in managing the risks associated with climate change.

It would be a dull public servant who would not be stimulated by such a cornucopia. For me, however, it is not only the development of public policy that has afforded satisfaction. I have spent two-thirds of my APS career in line and operational agencies delivering programs in areas as diverse as Indigenous services, workers' compensation, small business, workplace relations, education, employment and training.

It is this line agency experience, I suspect, that helps to explain why I have arrived so firmly at the conclusion that the implementation of government policy is just as important to good public administration as its formulation. A public service should be held to account for the extent to which it can deliver the changing policy directions of governments on time, on budget and to their expectations. That is why, in 2005, I established a Cabinet Implementation Unit within PM&C. That is why, too, I have enjoyed talking as often as possible to the Australian public servants who work in hundreds of state and regional offices and call centres across the country. The challenges they face in directly delivering government policy – both entitlements and obligations – are significant.

I think few Australians appreciate the extent to which public servants in quite junior positions wield extraordinary power over the lives of individuals. They deliver welfare payments and health benefits, identify labour market opportunities, issue passports, scrutinise tax returns and decide on migration visas. They administer grants and award contracts. Every day they make decisions that affect the hopes of citizens. They deserve not only better training but greater influence. The more I have been willing to listen to their experiences, the better has been my capacity to design the policies and establish the administrative guidelines of the services that are implemented on behalf of government.

Over two decades I have learned the scale and diversity of the nation served by the APS. I have always believed it necessary to see at first hand the administrative operation of the programs oversighted by my departments. I have spent many happy hours talking both with those organisations who deliver them and those individuals who (sometimes reluctantly) participate in them. Over the years I've visited Job Network members, Work-for-the-Dole schemes, small business incubators, group training companies, science laboratories, parents and citizens groups, rehabilitation providers and a myriad diversity of community organisations.

I have also visited scores of remote Aboriginal towns and outstations from Wiluna to Bamaga, from Hopevale to Ernabella, from Yirrkala to Tikjikala. Often I despair at the abject failure of well-intentioned policies to make a substantive difference to the appalling conditions in which too many Indigenous Australians live. Yet not infrequently I am uplifted by the transformative power of individual community leaders able to achieve small victories in the face of overwhelming odds.

The hierarchy of officialdom can often fail to recognise the experience and commonsense of the field officer. Yet there are characteristics of public service that transcend differences of situational authority. The Secretary of PM&C and the customer liaison officer in Centrelink share this: that neither can say, 'I alone was responsible for the development or delivery of a particular government policy'. In this profound sense the public servant really is a bureaucrat, integrated into a vertically and horizontally structured organisation that has been designed to plan, administer, implement and evaluate the millions of daily transactions that Australian governments manifest to their citizens.

General practitioners and nurses can know the patients they have healed or comforted. Teachers can watch the progress of the students who have learned from them. Architects can see their legacy in the buildings they have designed. Even now, more than twenty years on, I – if no one else – can read the scholarly articles that I wrote as an academic and see my name attached to their arguments. It is a form of posterity.

Not so for the public servant, and for two good reasons. First, public policy is, by the nature of political dynamics, almost always transitory. Policies, or at least the specific programs and particular initiatives that give them shape, come and go. I struggled hard between 1991 and 1994 to mould the organisational dysfunctionalities of ATSIC into an effective vehicle for Indigenous self-determination. A few years later I contributed to ATSIC's abolition and the creation of new organisational and political approaches to the public administration of Aboriginal and Torres Strait Islander affairs.

That difficult experience in many ways typifies the challenges faced by professional public servants serving successive governments with equal commitment. It is the hard uncompromising edge of non-partisanship. It is the point at which frank and fearless advice, given in confidence, appropriately concedes to the will of elected government. Public service is not a job for everyone. It requires a toughness and fortitude that, without good leadership, can descend into employee cynicism about the cyclical nature of change.

Second, it is unusual indeed that a political leader (still less a public servant) can say with honest assurance that 'this policy is mine'. Whether born after a long intellectual gestation, or conceived hurriedly in response to unexpected crisis, political initiative rarely has a single parent. The intersection of public debate, political discourse and media commentary – and the increasing range of individual and institutional advocates able to exert influence – mean that policy formulation is nearly always an iterative process marked by collective deliberation and political compromise. At most, looking back, I can boast that I was given opportunity to suggest new approaches, to comment on the ideas of others and to exert some influence on the shape of the final outcome – and, of course, nearly always in a manner that was hidden from public gaze. The power I had was the power to persuade. A public servant does not leave monuments behind.

Yet public service has its own rewards. I have been part of the discussion on matters that have the power to transform; I have participated in moments of intense political debate; I have had the power to wield together groups of bright young women and men and charge them with bringing strategic coherence to an ill-formed but exciting new idea. These may seem the aspects of public service life that are unexceptional but they are, in a sense, the lifeblood of senior public service. Perhaps it is for that reason we forget that they are nevertheless special. Meetings and briefs are the means by which public servants put their fingerprints on the evolution of a nation.

Admittedly, I have had occasions available to few others. I have sat in on meetings of prime ministers and presidents, seeking to quiet my fears that it is only a matter of time before I am exposed as an impostor. I have enjoyed breakfast at No. 10 Downing Street, lunch at Chequers, a barbecue at the Western White House and a state dinner at the White House – and can report that on each occasion the company was more memorable than the food. I have never taken such opportunities for granted nor pretended that they are the due of a senior public servant.

I have appreciated my good fortune. Carol, my wife, joshes that I am the one always smiling at the camera when the photos are taken. Perhaps. Certainly while I have focused on the content of leadership discussions I have always taken time to examine the surroundings, read the body language and absorb the atmosphere. Details are important. I have wanted to remember clearly such occasions for the time, now arrived, when I would no longer be invited to attend.

I am keen to avoid sentimentality in my farewell remarks. Yet there have been moments of such emotional potency in my public service career that they will forever remain vivid: being with the Prime Minister at the beginning of a New York Yankees baseball game when the coaches and players stepped out of their dugouts to salute the Australian national anthem; flying by helicopter across the breath-taking grandeur of the Himalayas after the devastation of earthquake and seeing at first hand our young reservists ministering to the needs of desperate survivors; being present at a working lunch between prime ministers Howard and Blair when a harried official had to interrupt with news of an attempted terrorist attack on the London Underground; going out to Government House on an idyllic Canberra morning to discuss, with Peter Hollingworth and his unwell wife, how sadly his term would end – these are the times imbued with such poignancy that they bring richness to the experience of public service.

Even the most mundane incident, remembered in the light of what followed, can be seared on the memory. I can recall vividly Carol and I being walked around the block by our dog on Boxing Day in 2004 when I received a call on my mobile telephone. It was to alert me that there had been an earthquake off Indonesia and that early reports were coming in of a tsunami. 'I'm not sure,' I said to Carol, 'but I think we might have to change our plan to go on holiday tomorrow.'

We did and I am forever grateful. Instead of two weeks on the NSW South Coast I had the chance to work with an extraordinary team of ADF personnel, police and public servants from a dozen agencies, brought together by a moment of unanticipated crisis. To have seen the speed and the efficiency with which aid was planned and delivered; to have played a part in the conception and development of an unprecedentedly bold reconstruction package and, within days, to have flown with the Prime Minister to Jakarta to announce it was an opportunity given to few. It bore testimony not only to government vision but – as the Prime Minister noted at the time in a national address – to the capacity, commitment and camaraderie of Australian public servants able to give it effect.

The APS is not a career that is suited to everyone. It offers the opportunity to work from the inside but always in a manner that is responsive to the directions set by government. Within that framework one has the chance – indeed, the obligation – to present policy advice that is strongly argued and unvarnished, to set forward a range of alternatives, to establish and interpret the facts as objectively as possible and to ensure that the consequences of actions are foreseen. But professional public servants can only exercise influence.

However frank, robust and compelling their advice, it must always be the government they serve which makes the political decisions. It is for elected ministers, individually and collectively, to establish their view of the public interest and to be held responsible for it at the ballot box. Public servants who come to believe, intellectually or ethically, that they have a view of the national interest superior to that of the elected government need to leave and enjoy the freedom of pursuing policy goals from the outside. Being on the inside has its constraints as well as its opportunities.

In some ways the value of professional public service is fully appreciated only at the moments of transition when prime ministers, or governments, change. In November 2007 Australians took pride in the manner in which John Howard conceded defeat and Kevin Rudd accepted victory. Most were pleased that John and Janette Howard, on their final day in the Lodge, showed Kevin Rudd and Therese Rein around. There was a dignity in the handover of power which symbolised the resilience of Australian democratic process.

Equally impressive was the extraordinary seamlessness of change. Throughout the pre-election caretaker period teams of public servants, in every Commonwealth agency, prepared briefs to serve an incoming government of either persuasion. It's an experience I've been through seven times. The plans were in place. Late on the evening of November 24 the Prime Minister announced that he had lost power. At 9.00am on the morning of November 25 I flew to Brisbane with Barbara Belcher to brief the Prime Minister elect.

The essence of public service is often unseen by the public. As an illustration, let me continue my account of the 2007 election. On November 28 Prime Minister Howard came to farewell the department who had served him for almost 12 years and received an outstanding ovation. On December 18 Prime Minister Rudd came to speak to his department about his expectations of them. He received similarly enthusiastic applause. It was clear that those who worked in the Department of the Prime Minister and Cabinet, no matter what political views they held in private, fully understood that they served the Prime Minister of Australia. I was proud to lead them.

The warmth of my valedictory may suggest a naïve optimism about the state of the APS. I hope not. It is true that I am buoyed by the ability of the public service to continue to recruit the best and brightest from our universities and by the fact that the Commonwealth's public sector agencies remain employers of choice for large number of graduates. I am cheered, too, by the large proportion of respondents to the annual *State of the Service* report who report satisfaction in their employment: last year 84 per cent agreed that they felt motivated by their job, 79 per cent were proud to work in the APS and 81 per cent would recommend the APS to others. Clearly I am not alone in the regard I have for public service.

Of course there are challenges. I worry that the devolution of the APS, which has undoubtedly improved the management of agencies, may have gone a little too far. It is not just the economic inefficiencies or systems dysfunctionalities that concern me. I fear that the values that underpin public service, and the cooperation necessary to ensure the best interest of the whole of government, may be undermined by the reassertion of bureaucratic territorially. In my experience the whole of the APS is much greater than the sum of its parts.

I regret that there have been administrative failures on my watch as notional head of the APS. The Palmer and Comrie enquiries into the unlawful detention of Australian residents, and the findings of the Cole Royal Commission into the behaviour (in particular) of the Australian Wheat Board in breaching UN sanctions, exposed significant organisational weaknesses – inadequate channels of communication, structural demarcations, insufficient quality control and poor reporting systems. Yet the willingness of agencies to acknowledge their failings and, more importantly, to set in place mechanisms to address them in a strategic way, suggest a public service with the capacity to continually address performance. The APS can and will continue to make itself over.

I have not found these challenges easy. Indeed, although it may not be apparent from my gregarious nature, I have found leadership of the APS a lonely job. There have been few days when I have not found something to worry about and, when they have occurred, someone else can generally be relied upon to have found it for me. In the nature of the job many of the matters that I have struggled with are not ones that can be widely discussed. Not infrequently have I found it necessary to rely on my own counsel, and ask, among others, the following questions: How hard and persistently should I continue to debate policy? How soon should I concede that I have lost the argument? These are the dilemmas that lurk beneath the cliché of 'frank and fearless advice'.

What has made my job easier – and conversely, what makes my final hour in the APS so wrenching – is the collegiality and goodwill I have received from so many public servants in so many agencies in so many circumstances. My career has been smoothed – on occasions protected – by having deputies and executive assistants who have looked out for my interests. They are, in my view, the two positions upon which a leader utterly depends.

I have always felt supported, too, by the senior executives of the APS, and in particular by the secretaries and agency heads with whom I share collective leadership. I rarely say it, and fear I don't always exhibit it, but it is their advice, goodwill and loyalty which has sustained me when things have got tough. I am delighted to have this public opportunity to recognise them. The APS is in very good hands.

The decision to leave the APS has not been easy. I was honoured that Mr Rudd asked me to stay on and strongly tempted to agree. This is not a political statement but an acknowledgment that a change agenda always offers extraordinary opportunities and fresh challenges to a public servant. But, for the first time in my life (at the age of 60) I thought it sensible to plan my career. I decided that whatever the outcome of the [2007] federal election I would step down at the end of my contract.

Five years seems to me the right time to do a job like this – indeed it represents the longest period I have been in any public service position. In the public sector, just as in the private, organisational invigoration is often stimulated by leadership renewal. Equally relevant for me, personal fulfilment often comes from taking on new ventures. That is why, while you have all been toiling to meet the new government's ambitious timetable, I decided to learn downhill skiing. I hope I will be better at my new job.

It may seem odd, given previous comments on my earlier academic life, that I have decided to return to university. In truth, the chance to establish a Centre for Social Impact was irresistible. Whilst I love the making of public policy, and I believe that the APS contributes mightily to that effort in extraordinarily beneficial ways, I am increasingly persuaded that it is far too important to be left to governments and public services.

Over the years I have come to the view that it is the voluntary efforts of hundreds of thousands of individuals, and the support and advocacy of not-for-profit organisations that gives Australian democracy its vibrancy. To an increasing extent community-based (and often faith-based) organisations not only lobby governments for change but contract with governments (and public services) to deliver their program and services. In a variety of ways they are forging new partnerships with the private sector to make concrete the corporate commitments they make on social responsibility. The 'third sector' builds the social capital that makes us a nation.

This does not represent a sudden revelation in my life. Just before I became a public servant I undertook an enquiry for the Department of Immigration. It wanted to understand better the settlement needs of immigrants from non-English-speaking backgrounds. It was, dare I say, an exercise in social inclusion. I wrote the report with my friend and colleague, Loucas Nicolaou, now in FACSIA. Prompted by our consultations, we entitled our submission, *Why Don't They Ask Us? We're Not Dumb.*

On many occasions over the last 20 years I have reflected on the simple truth reflected in that title. Now I hope I can build the Centre for Social Impact to generate social entrepreneurship, to improve the managerial efficiency and political effectiveness of established not-for-profit organisations and to improve understanding of the role that they play.

And so, as I bid you a fond farewell, there is a sting in the end of my tale. You have not seen the last of me. I will continue, in my different role, to share an abiding commitment to public policy and a desire to promote the public interest. For that, I am glad.

8. Impressions, observations and lessons from a Canberra outsider[1]

Robert Cornall

Robert Cornall was born in Melbourne, went to school at Wesley College, and graduated in law from Melbourne University. He began his career in 1969 as a solicitor at Middletons Oswald Burt, becoming a partner there in 1972. From 1987 to 1995 he was Executive Director and Secretary of the Law Institute of Victoria. Then from 1995 to 2000 he was Managing Director of Victorian Legal Aid. This 19-year stint as a solicitor instilled in him a private sector mindset and has guided his approach to client service ever since. So when Robert Cornall began as Secretary of the Attorney-General's Department in 2000, he transformed the department and improved its performance by emphasising its outward or client focus – an approach he remained committed to until his retirement from the post eight years later.

My appointment as a secretary in the Australian Public Service was as much a surprise to me as it was to officers of the Attorney-General's Department. It came about in this way. The outgoing Secretary, Tony Blunn, rang me one day in November 1999 in my office at Victoria Legal Aid in Melbourne. He told me he was going to retire and he wondered if I was interested in being considered for his position. At that time, I had been the first managing director of VLA for four hectic years. It had been a hard and controversial task establishing that new organisation to overcome what both the Victorian and Australian governments assessed were the deficiencies of the former Legal Aid Commission. I had reached the stage where I felt I had completed that assignment but I hadn't started to think about looking for another job.

So I said, in a rather offhand fashion, that I might be. This was, I should say, a nonchalance brought on by the unexpectedness of the enquiry and a lack of any detailed understanding of the position's interest, importance and challenge.

Tony replied, in that case, it would be a good idea if we could meet as soon as possible to discuss the matter in more detail. He asked: 'How are you placed tomorrow?' I said I had some commitments in the afternoon so I couldn't go to Canberra but I would be available in the morning in Melbourne. Tony said he would be at my office at 11 o'clock. When I put down the phone, I thought: 'Bloody hell! He's serious.' After that meeting in Queen Street, I came to Canberra to meet with the Attorney-General Daryl Williams and, in rapid succession,

---

1   This speech was delivered in August 2008 at a function hosted by the Australian Public Service Commission.

to Sydney for an interview with Max Moore-Wilton. The upshot was that the Prime Minister announced my appointment on 8 December and I took up my position at Robert Garran offices a few weeks later on 24 January 2000.

First day

It's fair to say I was a bit on edge as I entered the front door on that first day. I was very conscious that I only knew about three of the several hundred people who worked there and none of the senior officers in the portfolio or the broader APS. I was also acutely aware that I had very little or no knowledge about many of the department's responsibilities, a limited background in public administration and no experience in dealing with a large number of portfolio agencies or negotiating the reefs and shoals of federal politics. However, I drew some comfort from the fact that I had gone through a similar experience twice before – at the Law Institute of Victoria and Legal Aid.

I adopted the same approach that got me through on those two occasions. That involved getting briefed and reading as much as I could as quickly as possible to learn how the department worked, consulting all relevant colleagues before making a decision and treating everyone with courtesy and respect. I made an effort to be friendly and open with all the staff, so I was surprised to receive some anonymous feedback towards the end of my first year that I had been perceived, at least in some quarters, to be a bit 'aloof'. I replied: 'Well, I am from Melbourne. We tend to be like that down there.'

I also found it interesting to observe how I was addressed on both formal and informal occasions. I made it clear I was perfectly happy to be called 'Rob' if people felt comfortable with that informality, but this was a bridge too far for some officers. To this day, some members of the Senior Executive Service who I have worked with for the whole eight and a half years have never called me anything but 'secretary', at least to my face. I might say this reservation didn't reach down to one young bloke who worked in the mail room. From day one, he called me 'mate'.

Early impressions

My early impressions of the department were that it was a good department faced with some difficulties. The major issue was that the Australian Government Solicitor had only just been established as a government business enterprise. Although that separation from the department had been coming for some years, its culmination in September 1999 brought home the stark reality that a large proportion of the department's principal function since 1 January 1901 — providing legal advice to government — had been transferred to a new agency within the portfolio.

The department was facing the challenge of redefining its position in, and contribution to, government after this significant administrative change. The impact this challenge was having on the department was reflected in a recent staff survey and research project which produced some interesting insights. The consultants reported that the department was inwardly focused and that senior management placed a commendably high value on quality of services but a noticeably lower emphasis on client satisfaction. I also found comments by outsiders were instructive. One person said the department was 'struggling for relevance'.

An agency head commented that the government was 'looking for someone to ground the department'. Another secretary said: 'The department's not a player'. I referred to these comments in a speech I made to SES officers in February 2000. I said: 'These perceptions — right or wrong — are interesting. They indicate dissatisfaction with the department's current level of performance. But I understood them to be more disappointed than directly critical. Generally I took them to mean they felt that the department has a key role to play in Australian government but it was failing to meet all of the challenges of, and opportunities in, that role'.

In confronting these problems, I was able to draw on two useful aspects of my prior experience as a partner for fifteen years in a commercial law firm in the Melbourne CBD. First, as a solicitor, you are always working in a team of at least two — that is, yourself and your client. Often the team got quite a bit larger and could include, say, other solicitors, an accountant, a barrister, a town planner, an engineer and so on, depending on the issue at hand. Working as part of a team — even across professional silos — was second nature for me. Secondly, while solicitors usually make a very valuable contribution, they are not always the principal actor or decision maker. So working to assist other agencies to achieve their objectives was also a big part of my professional mindset. But more importantly, I can now see that the department's ability to leave old tasks behind and take on new ones as the demands of government change is actually one of its great strengths. That capacity has contributed to it remaining today as one of only three out of the first seven departments of state (along with Treasury and Defence) that have served the Commonwealth under their original name and broad charter since federation in 1901.

APS — three early observations

When I recall my first impressions of the broader Australian Public Service, three now outdated points stand out. In 2000, the Portfolio Secretaries Group was a real men's club. Helen Williams was the only female in the room in her role as Public Service Commissioner.

The collegiality Peter Shergold later promoted wasn't the strongest feature of Max Moore Wilton's management style. And policy, agency and even divisional silos had not yet been overcome by the positive, if time consuming, forces of connected or joined up government.

Lessons learned before joining the APS

As I am one of the few secretaries who have come directly to their position from outside the Australian Public Service, I have occasionally reflected on the experiences and lessons learned in other places that helped me make that transition. I know these observations will not be anything new to secretaries and agency heads but I am putting them on the record for officers coming through the ranks of the APS in case they find them helpful. Six things stand out. The first is the value of money.

The value of money

Fifteen years as a private practitioner permanently etched in my mind the principle that every dollar spent is a dollar less net profit. Like a lot of law firms, we used to approach the 1 April due date for tax payments with a great deal of trepidation. It was usually preceded by urgent instructions to fee earners to render accounts for all completed work and anxious negotiations with our bankers about an increase in the firm's overdraft. These are experiences you don't forget. As a result, I have regularly asked my colleagues putting forward a new policy or spending proposal: 'Would you spend this if it was your money?'

Consultants

My second lesson from previous experience involved the use of consultants. My colleagues will tell you I have a great scepticism about the value – or lack of value – provided by many consultants. This scepticism is reflected in a change I introduced into the department's CEIs which requires every consultancy engagement costing more than $20,000 to be submitted to me for approval with a supporting business case.

However, I acknowledge that there are two sorts of consultants – those that add value and those that don't. Consultants that add value bring particular skills and expertise to bear on and solve, or at least contribute to the solution of, a management problem. I like those consultants. Then there are consultants that talk in the current management gobbledegook, provide template recommendations and contribute little or nothing. I don't like those consultants.

But it is not always the consultants' fault. Sometimes, engaging a consultant is a management cop-out. It can seem to be an appealing solution to flick pass a difficult and ill-conceived project to a consultant. This can give the temporary impression that some progress is being made and the unsatisfactory result can be blamed on the consultant. When I was engaged in the restructure of legal aid in Victoria, I was asked on one occasion: 'Who is helping you?' I said: 'We are doing it ourselves,' and was greeted with a look of considerable surprise that managers could manage their organisation without the assistance of outside consultants. However, it is possible.

Probity

My third lesson was about probity. As one of my colleagues at Victoria Legal Aid observed: 'People only have a go at you if you're making a difference.' This observation was made after we had both received a freedom of information request seeking details of all of our credit card expenses from the then Victorian opposition which used the FOI Act for the sort of information the federal opposition gets at Estimates. The point is this. If people want to stick a spoke in your wheel, they will use whatever chance they have, even though it may be totally unrelated to the cause of their irritation. The most obvious happy hunting ground is travel and personal expenses. In Victoria, I recall that concerns about expenses and the attendant media publicity brought about the demise of the state governor, the head of the tourism authority and the CEO of Museum Victoria.

Sound administrative process

The next point I was well aware of before I came to the department is the protection offered by sound administrative process. One of my more difficult tasks as secretary of the Law Institute was to prosecute solicitors for misconduct before the Solicitors Board. Some solicitors took a dim view of my decisions and they challenged me in court. One strongly contested case is reported in the 1995 Victorian Law Reports. The three judges in the Court of Appeal analysed every step I had taken in deciding to bring that prosecution in a 37 page decision. Any flaw in the process I had followed would have lost the case. Fortunately, the Court supported the referral to the Board and the High Court declined the solicitor's application for further leave to appeal. The case was finally heard by the Solicitors Board and the solicitor was found guilty of misconduct.

Media

The fifth useful experience was a background in dealing with the media. This started when I joined the Law Institute. We had an arrangement that the president, who held office for a year, represented the Institute in matters of legal policy and related areas. As executive director I would speak about administrative and educational issues and, as secretary, about disciplinary cases. This generally meant the president got the fun bits and I got left with questions like: 'What do you say to all the victims who have been defrauded by this $12 million defalcation?' Secretaries aren't often put on the spot in the media but my media training was very useful preparation for Estimates. It taught me the value of careful and thorough preparation. It taught me the value of short, accurate statements that clearly answer the question. I also learnt the need to avoid negative and uncommon words because you can't convey a positive message in negative language and uncommon words cause the listener to lose the thread of what you are saying.

Presentation

The final lesson I brought with me is about presentation. In my media training, I was taught that viewers form opinions about people appearing on television roughly like this: 50 or 60 per cent on how they look, 30 per cent or more on how they sound and about 10 per cent on what they say. So I have always tried to look, sound and act like a secretary. Some people may think that is paying attention to appearance over substance but I disagree. Leadership is more about persuasion and example than direction. Establishing a view or perception of yourself as a leader your staff are prepared to accept is, in my opinion, a precondition to success. As it isn't possible for leaders in large organisations to get to know all the staff personally, leaders have to pay close attention to the way people form impressions about them from a distance. The point was really brought home to me on one early morning flight back to Canberra from an interstate meeting. I was in seat 1C and I observed my fellow traveller in 1A.

I was – naturally – wearing a business suit but he was in jeans, T-shirt, open plaid shirt with the sleeves partly rolled up, Birkenstock sandals and socks decorated with cartoon character Yosemite Sam and the word 'cute'. I thought to myself: 'This guy could be a software multi-millionaire for all I know but one thing's for sure – dressed like that, he will never be secretary of a department of state.'

The role of government lawyers

Now I want to say something about how I see the role of government lawyers. I have always regarded good lawyers as legal problem-solvers – people who solve problems rather than create them. They take a close interest in a client's problem and accept personal responsibility to try to find an acceptable solution. I have to say I have not found this to be a universal view across the APS. One sometimes irritating aspect of my job is that, when attending a meeting, I have often been the only lawyer there.

On occasions, other participants (frequently led by Max) would look at me accusingly as if I was personally responsible for any perceived flaw in legislation, any court decision that went against the government or any legal advice, from whatever source, that the people present felt was unhelpful or impractical. To some extent, lawyers can provoke this attitude if we take too long to respond to clients or deliver turgid, verbose, impractical or unrealistic advice. To illustrate the point about the effectiveness of brevity and precision, I have sometimes relied on extracts from the *Opinions of the Attorneys-General of the Commonwealth of Australia* from 1901 to 1914 which was published by the department in 1981.

Those opinions provide great lessons in writing precise and useful advice. I will quote one of them to prove the point. The first Attorney-General, Alfred Deakin, was asked if the Commonwealth was liable to pay state stamp duty. On 20 January 1902, he dealt with the issue in these 55 words: 'I am of the opinion that stamp duty is not payable under State Acts, either by the Commonwealth or by individuals with whom the Commonwealth deals, in respect of any documents which are part of any transaction between the Commonwealth and any other party for the purpose of conducting the public business of the Commonwealth.' Of course, I have to allow that Alfred Deakin wasn't troubled by the need to take account of 105 years of High Court precedents. Nonetheless, we can certainly admire the simplicity and clarity of his advice.

Language

But while I have referred to legal examples, the objective of using simple and direct language is a challenge that can be put to everyone in the Australian Public Service. It may not be apparent to people who have lived in Canberra for all or a great part of their working life, but the nation's capital has a capacity for bureaucratic jargon that can be world class. I have identified two causes for this shortcoming. The main one seems to be the use of uncommon words that are not in everyday use and vague words that could have a number of meanings, leaving the listener to guess which one is intended. Words like 'drivers', 'methodologies', 'vulnerabilities', 'capacity-building', 'interdependencies', 'multi-faceted strategies', 'in this space', 'convergence' and 'industry best practice' really make my eyes glaze over. My pet hates include long sentences, passive verbs, dense paragraphs, bureaucratic words that have lost their meaning and generic language that gives no hint of the actual subject matter under consideration.

Another major cause is the apparently mandatory use of acronyms that end up sounding like a secret code only capable of being understood by a privileged inner circle. One of the most insidious characteristics of this 'bureaucratese' is that it's infectious. It would be interesting to count how many times in a week we hear 'at the end of the day', 'going forward', 'in this space', 'we have to have a conversation around that issue' and so on. This communication style doesn't work well outside Canberra.

I was at a ministerial council meeting in Victoria a couple of years ago where we heard a report from Bob Abbott, the Mayor of the Sunshine Coast Regional Council, about the response to Cyclone Larry. Bob came across as a very capable but down-to-earth Aussie bloke who you'd like to have on your side in a fight. He delivered his report in a very direct, conversational, easy to understand way. Then a Commonwealth officer made a report from the federal perspective in Canberra jargon. At the morning tea break, I commented to one of the ministers how impressive Bob's presentation was. The minister replied: 'Yes – not like that other bloke. He was talking bull dust.'

These bad habits translate into written work as well. One of my significant failures that I am prepared to own up to in public is that I have not been able to cure some of my colleagues from including definitions where no definition is required or, even worse, including definitions that aren't used at all in the letter, document or submission. I point out on occasions that ministers will know that ASIO refers to the Australian Security Intelligence Organisation and AFP refers to the Australian Federal Police but I have to acknowledge that, in some areas of the department, that is a minority view.

Policy pyramid

One of the most perplexing aspects of this dilemma is that these forms of expression run completely counter to the process of evolving good policy, which demands that the policy be simply and clearly expressed. I think of this process as a policy pyramid. At the base of the pyramid, policy officers do the research, explore the issues, run the arguments, test the counter-arguments, consult externally and develop a reasoned proposal. As the proposal advances to branch heads, first assistant secretaries and so on, the proposal is refined and the issues narrowed. Eventually, when it gets to the minister or to cabinet, the essence of the proposal has to be distilled into a few words or, at most, a couple of sentences. While it may seem counter-intuitive, this means the proposal has to get shorter and simpler as it goes higher up the ladder so that it is in its simplest, most basic form when it is considered by Cabinet.

Lessons learned in the APS

Now I would like to mention a few important lessons I have learnt during my time in the Australian Public Service.

Size and scope

The first lesson was to adjust to the size and scope of the Australian government. It was like moving from the under 15s to the seniors overnight. APS colleagues were spread out in offices all over Canberra, across Australia and in major centres around the world. This physical separation was important because it meant that I didn't have the close and regular contact I was used to in smaller organisations. The Victorian government, which had previously been so important in my career, was now just one of eight governments the Commonwealth dealt with when it had to. It took a significant mental adjustment to see myself as part of the small group of senior officers at the top of the now about 150,000 strong APS juggernaut. Once I had overcome that initial shock, it seemed to me the basic principles of management applied in much the same way as before – they just involved more people and more dollars. Commonsense and sound judgment were still the most valuable management attributes.

Information

This leads to the second lesson which was how to find out what I needed to know to do my job. It came as a surprise to me to see how much useful and important information is obtained from informal and indirect means, including the media. On reflection, this also is a product of the size and breadth of the Australian government. Ministers are away from Canberra for most of the year, so you can't rely just on face-to-face meetings, phone calls, emails or SMS messages to keep up with their thinking or policy directions.

The former Prime Minister, John Howard, expressed this obligation well when he said in 1997 that the task of public servants is to 'recognise the directions in which a government is moving and be capable of playing a major role in developing policy options.' So I developed a few strategies to try to keep up to date with what was happening across government. They include reading all submissions to our ministers and replies to ministerial correspondence, regularly checking my Capital Monitors electronic information service, skim reading the summaries of the daily DFAT cables and reading many of the reports and bulletins from other departments and agencies that come across a secretary's desk. I also accepted lots of invitations to attend speeches, launches, functions, receptions and dinners because they were often a valuable source of both formal and off-the-record information. I served as President of the ACT Division of the Institute of Public Administration for two and a half years. One downside was that one colleague observed I would go to the opening of an envelope.

Speed of decisions

The third lesson was to get used to the speed with which decisions have to be taken at the top level of government to get through the volume of business. This was exemplified on one occasion when I was attending a joint budget meeting of the National Security and Expenditure Review Committees. There was a proposal to shift a function – and all the associated personnel and resources – from one agency to another. I thought there were a couple of issues that merited discussion before a decision was taken. However, the PM said: 'This looks all right, doesn't it?' No minister objected and the matter was resolved in about 20 seconds. This example highlights two points. Firstly, the issue put to ministers for decision has to be simply stated (wherever possible) so they can just say yes or no. Secondly, the policy work that underpins the decision has to be fully developed so the steps needed to implement it are clearly laid out.

Value of good process

The next point is the value of good process. Obviously good process is essential to the Commonwealth's objectives in areas like merit-based selection and fair tendering. But it also has the benefit of protecting decision makers from any allegations of bias or unfair treatment. The important thing I learnt was that good process does not have to be slow or bureaucratic if the people in charge don't want it to be. So where the process is slow and clunky, senior officers should look at the way they are going about their business before they simply blame the applicable procedural rules.

International perspective

The final lesson I want to mention is learning to think nationally and internationally. One thing that really stands out when you come to the Commonwealth from a state service is the huge breadth of the national and international perspective confronted by the Australian Public Service.

Secretaries spoke of ministers and senior officials from other countries as their counterparts in a way I had previously spoken about officials in similar positions in other states. But where it really hits home is when you travel the world on the country's business and meet people most Australians would only ever expect to see on television. I know this international aspect has always been a large part of many departments' activities. But it greatly increased for the Attorney-General's Department as its national security responsibilities became so important after September 11.

So now I can look back on attending meetings with three US and two British Attorneys-General, two Home Secretaries, two Lord Chancellors, the Chief Justice of the United States, miscellaneous Law Lords, the President of Indonesia, the President of France (when he was the Minister for the Interior), the King of Cambodia, Senator John McCain, three heads of MI5, the head of the FBI, the head of the CIA, the Deputy US Secretary for Defence, two Secretaries for Homeland Security, the UN High Commissioner for Human Rights, one of the nine members of the Chinese Central Committee, high commissioners, ambassadors, senior officials from countries all over the world and so the list goes on.

Obviously a packed international itinerary is physically demanding, but two things have eased the burden. One is first class air travel and the other is the first class service provided by DFAT officers all over the world. What could be more welcoming in Beijing, Geneva, Washington, Jakarta, Ottawa, New York, Singapore or London than a smiling Aussie face at the top of the air bridge as soon as the plane door opens? This happy event is followed by facilitated clearance through immigration and customs, luggage being carried to a car waiting at the terminal entrance and assistance to go straight to your hotel room without passing reception. I once described travelling with a cabinet minister as being like travelling with minor royalty. But then I realised I had underestimated the service and I changed that to medium royalty. For many of you, that may all seem ho hum and old hat but I can tell you it was not an experience I ever expected when I was growing up in Moonee Ponds.

I think it's clear from what I have said so far that the Attorney-General's Department has grown and expanded over the last eight and a half years. This is illustrated by a few statistics.

On 30 June 2000, the department had 539 full time equivalent staff (excluding the Australian Protective Service and the Insolvency and Trustee Service Australia which operated as and were soon to become separate agencies). All of our staff were based in Canberra. In 2000- 01, the department had an appropriation of $99 million and administered revenue of $225 million. Today our total staff is around 1,550 officers. Our departmental appropriation for 2007-08 was $218 million and our total appropriation including administered funds was $1.152 billion. We have offices in Canberra, Sydney, Mount Macedon, Perth, Jervis Bay and Christmas and Norfolk Islands as well as officers in Indigenous Coordination Centres around the country.

The Department has grown in two ways. First, a number of our longstanding divisions have got bigger. For example, the Protective Security Coordination Centre and the security law, criminal law and international law areas have all grown in response to greater government demands over the last few years. Because our role is frequently as part of a cross-portfolio team, a lot of this growth and the activity that has generated it often isn't readily apparent. So I was interested to hear Michael L'Estrange observe, when he addressed our SES officers not long after he came back from London, how much more often DFAT and the Attorney-General's Department were now working together on projects like free trade agreements or international engagements like RAMSI and the Enhanced Cooperation Program in PNG. I could add to that list, as further examples, our work with Defence on the legal aspects of our deployments to Iraq and Afghanistan, our participation with more than half the public service in the Northern Territory Emergency Response, the development of the Commonwealth Corporations Act with Treasury, our conduct of whole-of-government counter-terrorism work including media awareness campaigns and our support for the National Counter Terrorism Committee.

The other way the department has grown is by acquiring new divisions or functions. They include the National Security Hotline, Emergency Management Australia, the AusCheck background checking service, film and literature classification, inter-country adoption, the Indigenous law and justice program, territories, establishing 65 family relationship centres and the development of a national personal property securities register. I have made the point to my colleagues more than once that getting a new task is an opportunity to do well but it doesn't come with a guarantee of success. The department is on trial each time that happens. Failure is a possibility. So each new task has to receive maximum care and attention. Despite that risk, the fact that we keep on getting more tasks suggests to me that we haven't done a bad job so far. In that sense, it has reinforced my view that the future of the department is bound up in its capacity to take on new tasks to keep its activities relevant to the needs of the government of the day. It also reminds me very much of private practice. Doing a job well often resulted in unsolicited referrals of more work.

A great privilege

So you won't be surprised to know that I regard it as a huge privilege to have had the chance to participate in, and contribute to, the government of Australia at this national level and, in doing so, to work with outstanding colleagues in the department and across the public service. After Daryl Williams retired from parliament, I wrote him a letter in which I said: 'I doubt many permanent public servants fully understand what an honour it is – and how exciting it is – to come to Canberra as a departmental secretary after holding other career positions elsewhere'. Daryl replied: 'The only reservation I had in recommending your appointment was whether you would be able to cope with a system with which you were not familiar. With the benefit of hindsight, I can now see that there was not only no cause for concern but in fact your coming from outside the department was a positive advantage. You could see more clearly than someone inside how the operations could be improved.'

Conclusion

However, in all my time in Canberra, I knew I was only here while I held this position. So my time in the nation's capital has been like a fabulous working holiday. But eight and a half year's is enough. It's time for both me and the department to move on. I do so with the best of memories and with thanks to all of you for your support and encouragement during my tenure as secretary.

9. An unlikely secretary — a boy from the outer agencies[1]

Mark Sullivan

Upon graduating from the University of Sydney with a degree in Economics, Mark Sullivan joined the Australian Taxation Office in 1971 as a cadet taxation officer. Over the next thirty-seven years he would enjoy a decorated career in both the private and public sectors, holding several prominent positions including head of corporate services at the Special Broadcasting Service (SBS; 1986-88); CEO of the Australian and Torres Strait Islander Commission (ATSIC; 1999-2001); Secretary of the Department of Family and Community Services (2002-04); Secretary of the Department of Veterans' Affairs (2004-08); and President of the Repatriation Commission. Mark Sullivan was appointed CEO of ACTEW, the ACT's government-owned water utility, in 2008.

My time as CEO of ATSIC was the best and worst job I had in my life, both at the same time. But it must also be said that the highs of that job far outweighed the lows. Like others who have become involved in Aboriginal and Torres Strait Islander affairs, it was an experience that was personally rewarding, knowledge-enhancing and friendship-building. To engage with and listen to the Dodsons, Pearsons, Yuis, Ross's, Perkins, Andersons, Scotts and the many community leaders across their lands was enriching.

It taught me the value of storytelling and the importance of wrapping a message or two within that. So I thought here I should recount a story of a career within the APS, a career a little different to many of my colleagues who lead the departments of state and agencies that make up the Australian Public Service.

My motivation to join the APS was simple. The notion of receiving a wage to continue my studies as an accountant full time and then be guaranteed a position as a tax assessor in the ATO was too good to resist. It's funny how many find it the opposite. So I joined as a cadet taxation officer in Sydney. I was a product of a determined recruitment strategy by the ATO. My career plan was to be a company tax assessor, a Clerk Class 6, not to be confused with an APS6. Even my provider of interim employment, Price Waterhouse, thought this a good idea, adding that a seat would always be available there if it didn't work out.

---

1   This speech was delivered in July 2008 at a formal function organised by the Australian Public Service Commission.

As happens in the APS and in particular the ATO, I met and fell in love with Bronwyn, a fellow tax assessor with a keen eye for detail. We married and left for the smell of the wood or oil fires of Canberra; a shift into the operational life of a big organisation, working in small project groups on both minor and major projects. We never really saw the top of the tree, the Commissioner. But we did see the Second Commissioner, Patrick Lanigan – brilliant, eccentric, mad, visionary – possibly all.

He changed Tax. A simple goal, collecting tax, not lodging returns or raising assessments, became his mantra. And he succeeded. Malcolm Fraser appreciated it. The ATO raised several hundred million more than the budget estimate – nothing these days, but enough then to see him promoted to Director-General, Social Security (later retitled Secretary). Lanigan did another thing. He had embarked on a large scale junior management development program with the ATO which he immediately imported to DSS. I had gone to DSS recruited by a branch head, who had been recruited by Lanigan. Again I was a beneficiary of a determined policy of skills development.

Lanigan departed, but DSS went on. I was leading project groups on larger and larger projects. I developed a reasonable reputation in DSS, which was difficult for an ex-Tax person. My career changed again in Brisbane when I met the then state Director of DSS in South Australia, Ron Brown.

Ron complimented me on my reputation, even described me as a bit of a hot shot – which I naturally concurred with – and then asked how many people I had ever managed. It was a dead giveaway when I asked if I could count myself. Possibly as many as four, I said. He made an offer I couldn't refuse – the management of DSS offices in South Australia, hundreds of staff and a personal commitment to develop me as a manager.

A growing number of people seemed willing to take an interest in me. Tony Ayers and Noel Tanzer in particular. I was prepared to take opportunities and the risk of moving cities at the same level to take on the challenging tasks.

I moved to SBS to a job destined to abolish itself. Nick Shehadie, on the recommendation of Ron Brown, had asked if I would like to work at SBS for a couple of years. His worry was the place ran as three organisations – Radio, Television and Corporate and the latter pulled all the strings. He wanted me to set about enlivening Radio and Television and significantly reducing the role of Corporate. It was different, it was fun and again I learned plenty.

At the end of this, I knew I couldn't go back to DSS so I resigned and joined a multinational, Wang, a name we all knew then. They were one of the world's hundred biggest corporations, as were Digital and Prime and now none of them exist. Microsoft and Apple were just start-ups. Wang taught me about a revenue-focused organisation. I learned that multinationals, particularly those a little fat and lazy, were as difficult a bureaucracy as any and came to reflect and appreciate the wonderful opportunities provided by the APS. This stage represented my half-time break and I could not wait for the second half.

That started in Immigration where I stayed for over a decade. I enjoyed every day of it in an organisation I considered one of the finest I had seen at the time. Three times I have worked in portfolios where a lack of politicisation generally through a reasonable level of bipartisanship helped drive a culture of achievement. Immigration was the first, ATSIC the second, and Department of Veterans' Affairs (DVA) the third. Introduce the political act, experience great divide in the approach of government and opposition and you see a fundamental shift in organisation culture and performance. Immigration has been to hell and back, ATSIC no longer exists, but fortunately DVA survives and prospers in a relatively harmonious political position.

In Immigration I learned to lead. While I still had the support and guidance of people like Helen Williams, it was now my turn to be looking out for and developing leaders of that agency and the APS of the future. As we come to appreciate the development we are granted, the onus shifts to us to develop the next generation of leaders. My personal development continued through participation in the inaugural Leading Australia's Future in Asia and the Pacific (LAFIA) development program. Exposing the APS leadership to Asia was a highlight.

Immigration was a chance to see the world and I saw it. Rarely the Peter Stuyvesant posts, but always interesting. I learned to eat for my country; to consume a couple of wonderfully sautéed cockroaches in China. If you are interested they eat like you would imagine, a squish and then chewy. Or the wonderful taste of snake blood and bile washed down by a thimble or two of Mao-tai. You would do it for fun but for work even better, and it was all great preparation for an RSL chicken and three veg sub-branch dinner.

It was also a chance to see what diplomacy was about. The strategy which led the Chinese government to accept the return of unauthorised boat arrivals in the 1990s involved many. Dennis Richardson led it, Chris Conybeare directed it, and I played a supporting role. To see the work of the then Ambassador, Ric Smith, the then Consul-General, Murray McLean and Immigration people in China taught me much about negotiation in a diverse cultural setting. Often the sweat trickled down your neck as you carefully explored the relationship between boat returns and Tiananmen Square incident students remaining in Australia. An exposure to the foreign relationship aspects of public service is a must. The broader involvement of the APS in bilateral and multi-lateral relationship is a very positive way of exposing many more to this aspect of the life of the APS.

Finally, Immigration introduced me to interaction with the media. Gerry Hand asked me to be the voice of Immigration – I responded as you would expect: 'Yes, Minister'. Boat arrivals, detention centres, high profile cases, HIV, Kosovo: you name it, I learned to talk about it. The late Paul Lyneham trained me. Confidence in dealing with the media is a developed skill providing an extra arrow in the bow, or bullet in the gun. When Peter Harvey arrived to do a boat arrival story at short notice, he told me that News had assured him I could provide both the questions and the answers – I took a bit of reflected pride in that. What surprised me even more was that 15 years later on a beach at Gallipoli he remembered. Like politics, the media and the APS are intertwined; the secret is to understand the division and where to draw the line.

In 1999 I was approached to consider the position of CEO of ATSIC. I immediately declined. Why? As I explained to the recruiter, I was a student of the sixties and seventies. I had a menu of demonstrations and causes. Vietnam, apartheid, canteen food, the full range. While I was being active on many issues I had never taken an interest in Indigenous affairs. I had no more than a couple of Aboriginal or Torres Strait Islander acquaintances and no Indigenous friends. And I felt the CEO should be Indigenous. End of the issue I thought. But with the persistence of the recruiter, the encouragement of Gerry Hand and the then Minister for Aboriginal and Torres Strait Islander Affairs, John Herron, twelve months later I was the CEO of ATSIC.

Pride in achievement is important for anyone. For me, ATSIC bought many proud moments, the highlights of which were:

- the building of Aboriginal and Torres Strait Islander talent within the organisation where at one point 80 per cent of the SES within ATSIC were indigenous, too many of them now lost to the Commonwealth;
- the point where ATSIC's relationship with the Australian government and the states and territories was at its best, despite major policy differences;
- a capacity to pursue the agenda of the board and work to the government on its agenda of 'practical reconciliation'; and
- the Indigenous contribution to the 2000 Olympics and centenary of federation and the proper pursuit of native title.

ATSIC's demise was unfortunate. It had been an experiment unique in the world. It gave Aboriginal and Torres Strait Islander peoples a voice within the framework of government. It offered a place to work within the Commonwealth for Indigenous young people as exciting as an ecologist would find the environment. And most importantly, on most fronts it delivered with the resources it had. Its housing and infrastructure programs and its management of native title were first-class.

The demise was also predictable and reasonable. The ATSIC Act set up a framework where policy clash between ATSIC and government was anticipated. As CEO the Act provided that the officer must obey lawful directions of the board; there's nothing unlawful about pursuing a treaty or an apology for the Stolen Generations. It was a government agency governed by the CAC Act and others. But the ATSIC Act gave the Minister the right to determine ATSIC's budget distribution. So a minister could say no money to be spent on treaty. The CEO and administration handled this delicate balance and from its inception they had managed this but the pressure was there. When you add the fact that the elected senior leadership carried too much of the weight of criminal and ethical suspicion, their behaviour at times gave their detractors heavy ammunition. ATSIC, the organisation, lost its capacity to operate the fine balance between its obligations to the board and to the government. Once that was lost it fell out with much of its board, the organisation was split, and it lost many of its Indigenous staff, particularly leaders. I greatly admired those who stayed on and understood those who did not.

It was a proud day when I sat in the gallery of the House of Representatives and heard the Prime Minister and the Opposition Leader say sorry to the Stolen Generations. The world didn't end, but this country made a huge stride.

The Northern Territory intervention is the subject of much debate today. My view, now that I can say it, is its boldness and scale should be applauded. For the first time, the scale of approach to the issues facing our Aboriginal and Torres Strait Islander communities has been recognised. A focus on primary health, particularly children, and housing is an excellent start. I remember being in Wadeye talking to one of the community leaders, a woman. She showed me her house and said her place was in the kitchen. She meant it literally. She slept there. She said it was a good strategic point to watch the house occupied by sixteen others. And we wonder why education suffers, sexual assault occurs and some seek comfort in drugs, legal and illicit.

We need to maintain the boldness. We need to get the support of Aboriginal community leaders. We need to remember the wonderful positives that come from embracing Aboriginal and Torres Strait Islander culture and practice and to recognise the enormous efforts being made by many communities themselves. We've made a good start on the government's bold targets, particularly around mortality; we need to finish the job.

Thinking again about APS development, the experience gained by the many executive level officers working within Aboriginal communities will be something that benefits them greatly and will bring a new dimension to policy advising on Aboriginal and Torres Strait Islander issues in the Commonwealth.

So finally, to my move to a secretary and seven years later a move out of the APS into the commercial, but regulated world of water and energy. Before I became a secretary, many said I would not make it. Not in a malicious way, but as keen students of form they advised that for a career public servant the lack of central agency experience was the death knell. I remember arguing with Max Moore-Wilton that as CEO of ATSIC I was part of the Prime Minister and Cabinet portfolio and had worked in a central agency. He abused and disabused me in a very short time. I liked Max, and I still do. I made the mistake of seeking feedback halfway through my term in ATSIC. He set about abusing me and blaming me for everything he could think of; many things far removed from the realm of ATSIC. My defence was swept away. I left somewhat dispirited and told Bronwyn that my career was over. Jane Halton was the first to tell me that I had been 'Maxed', that he had enjoyed it and felt I had given plenty. The next day I saw Max at a function and he embraced and thumped me. I thought there was still a chance for a boy from the outer agencies.

My memories of being Secretary of Families and Community Services (FaCS) and the Department of Veterans' Affairs are different. The breadth of FaCS was amazing and even broader now. We crossed segments of the community ranging from pre-natal through death. We administered huge appropriations. We were involved in every cross/whole-of- government issue. We worked with, struggled with, and usually got there, in our work with the Department of Education, Employment and Workplace Relations (DEWR) who never seemed to agree with our stakeholders' view of us being too hard and rigid. We somewhere between owned, directed, collaborated with or did as Centrelink wanted us to do – again I believe, reasonably effectively. My attachment to the staff of FaCS was strong. They had my admiration and support and they treated me well. They taught me what a non-blokey agency *was* like and what a non-blokey APS *could* be like.

DVA taught me about many new things. What a wonderful organisation. At one level the only piece of operational World War II infrastructure left while at another level coping with the pressures and impact of a regularly deployed defence force engaged in a diversity of operations. Most are surprised by its size and breadth of operations. Its data holdings are enormous and their potential assistance in understanding health and ageing in this country is yet to be fully understood. A longitudinal understanding of the health of up to one million World War II enlistees is there for the taking.

I understood the language of stakeholders. DVA taught me to live with real stakeholder engagement. From a grand organisation like the RSL to the veterans email forum – including the 'mad galahs' – makes you understand what they expect. Again, at DVA I found a strong and positive people culture. On average its members were four years older than the APS, or as I put it, 10,000 years more experienced. It was a large complex service delivery operation challenged with a changing business model – fewer and fewer veterans, more complexity, less resources. A challenge for anyone.

As I learned much about indigenous affairs, I also learned much about our military heritage and the ADF. The resurgent interest and pride in military history and commemoration is a good thing and continual challenge. Government rightly expects DVA to manage this aspect of its work. It may be to ensure the annual commemoration in Gallipoli meets the emotional and physical needs of those who attend. It may be that in the path to reconciliation with disaffected Vietnam veterans we commemorate battles like Long Tan, Coral and Balmoral. It may be that when some WWI diggers are unearthed in a rural community where they fought and died we solemnly re-inter them, or how we deal with the discovery of a mass grave at Pheasant Wood or the remains of the Cruiser Sydney. DVA delivers.

More importantly, when someone has to explain to a recent widow how the Australian government will compensate and care for her and her children, DVA does it with compassion and care.

Thirty-five years in the APS is a long time. Embarking on a new career I will carry and benefit from much of what I have learned here. The Australian Public Service has changed greatly over that time and will continue to change. We are part way through a change that has departments and agencies respond to issues through their ministers as part of the Australian government, not as an independent entity striving for the result that may suit it best. It is not long ago when we did not see the need to act cooperatively. Today we do and are learning how to do it. In my world welfare reform and indigenous affairs were examples of the new world starting to work. The COAG agenda has quickened the pace dramatically. This is one of the most positive changes I have seen.

Speed at one level is a curse. We have heard of the pressure of 24/7 news coverage and it is part of the picture. But the community demands more and more speed – a terrible case of child neglect needs a new national child protection response;the neglect of a response to climate change shocked into action by the drought means a decade of work is condensed into a year. Peoples' skills, energy and motivation are tested in such a heady environment. And we know the danger of speed – errors, inadequate research and analysis and possibly bad policy. We also know that the machinery of government service delivery often moves slowly. More than once have I been part of advice to government that says we can do the policy analysis this week, the legislation next week and we can implement it in two years. And I am not having a go at my friends in Centrelink. Speed is not a good or bad thing, it is just a fact of life. But seat belts, air bags and stability control are things to think about when speed is involved. For us the safety devices are work-life balance, physical health and emotional and mental health.

Ministers and their offices are a subject many have talked about. I have worked closely with over a dozen ministers and their offices and without exception I was able to establish a good relationship with them. Ministers have to be the risk takers, the policy promoter within government, the manager of the constituency, the MP and the participant within executive government. If they are well served by their department, they will be well informed in their role. If they are well served by their office, they will be across the portfolio. If they delegate the onus, it's with them to have trust and faith in their delegate. It is sometimes an enigma that the department will only trust its most experienced and knowledgeable to interact with its minister – as they have grown into that position of trust so too should the group of advisers around a minister. With few exceptions you cannot walk into any new world and be perfect immediately. Recognising that is sometimes a challenge.

While we have maintained a position of an employer of choice, it is now and will become a greater challenge to keep it going. The demand for labour, the ageing of our workforce and the efforts to improve our participation rates all mean a different approach to meeting our labour needs. While I feel job satisfaction is easy in the APS, it needs concerted efforts in recruitment, personal and professional development and the continual reinforcement of our position as an ethical, dynamic and diverse place of employment to succeed. The APS needs to view itself always as a whole; we narrow ourselves too much if we don't. And we need to recruit and develop with the service as a whole in our sights.

I believe the APS is strong, healthy, apolitical and robust. It is also challenged. It must do even more in succession planning. It must proactively scout for talent and through development and opportunity bring people to the fore at a younger and younger age. It must recognise that its policy development skills continually need re-honing and broadening but that at its core government services are delivered by large organisations meaning the APS's people skills must be world's best. It must test and retest whether the advantages of agency independence may have been maximised and whether the advantages of size, volume and consistency have a novel advantage while avoiding the disasters of such expeditions as whole-of-government IT outsourcing. Where the balance lies is the science of soothsayers.

For me the opportunity to serve has been a remarkable one. Many people have assisted me. The only one I will name is my wife, Bronwyn, who met me within a month or so of joining the Tax Office and who today stands by my side. I love her greatly and acknowledge the burden she has in me.

10. As if for a thousand years — the challenges ahead for the APS[1]

David Borthwick

David Borthwick graduated from Monash University with Honours in economics in 1972 and joined the Department of Treasury the following year. The son of Bill Borthwick, a former Liberal Deputy Premier of Victoria and the first Minister for Conservation/the Environment in Australia, David would go on to serve as Secretary to the federal equivalent of the department his father once headed. David left Treasury in 1974 to join the Industries Assistance Commission before returning to his old department in 1979, where he would stay for the next 19 years, aside from a posting as Australian Ambassador to the OECD (1991-93). Between 1993 and 2004 he held a number of deputy secretary positions, first in Treasury, then in the Department of Health and Aged Care, and finally in the Department of the Prime Minister and Cabinet. David Borthwick served as Deputy Secretary of the Department of Health and Aged Care between 1998 and 2001 and Deputy Secretary of the Department of the Prime Minister and Cabinet between 2001 and 2004. He became Secretary of the Department of the Environment, Water, Heritage and the Arts in 2004.

In April 1971, two years before I joined the Australian Public Service, the first meeting of Victoria's Land Conservation Council was held in the old Cabinet Room of Melbourne's Treasury Building. At that meeting, the Minister for Conservation gave a rousing speech and impressed upon the twelve new councillors their historic responsibility to make recommendations on the use of public lands 'as if for a thousand years'. The minister believed that the best conservation outcomes would be achieved if the councillors took a longer-term view.[2]

The minister was my father, the late Bill Borthwick. Today, I pinch myself that I am retiring from the Australian Public Service as Secretary of the Department for the Environment, Water, Heritage and the Arts when my father, as a member of the Victorian government, entered the ministry as Minister for Water Supply and went on to serve as Victoria's first Minister for Conservation. He founded the Victorian Environment Protection Authority and oversaw a vast expansion of the state's national parks system.

---

1   This speech was delivered in March 2009 at a function hosted by the Australian Public Service Commission.
2   Clode, D *As if for a thousand years: a History of Victoria's Land Conservation and Environment Conservation Councils,* Melbourne: Victorian Environmental Assessment Council, 2006.

I mention my father not because I intend to give you a blow-by-blow account of my family history or my career in the Australian Public Service, but because I think his was sage advice when he implored the Land Conservation Council to make decisions 'as if for a thousand years'. He firmly believed in taking a longer-term, national interest perspective.

For our nation to thrive in a rapidly changing and often confronting world, we need to be far-sighted in developing public policy, whether it be economic, environmental, social or foreign policy. The Australian Public Service has a critical role in helping governments to take such a longer-term view.

I would like to use this occasion to address some of the issues that I think are important for public policy and for Australia's national interest for the future. But firstly, and to provide some context for these thoughts, I would like to reflect on some of the forces shaping Australia and the Australian Public Service over my 36 years as a public servant.

Looking back

The Australian Public Service I joined in 1973 as a Treasury graduate was markedly different than that of today. Indeed, the nation was very different. In 1973, the Rolling Stones, Suzi Quatro, the Carpenters and Roberta Flack were topping the singles charts and people were tuning their televisions in to *Number 96*.

The number of people in Australia was less than 14 million and the population was much more concentrated in the south-eastern states[3] than it is today. Australians did not travel very frequently; the distance the average Australian travelled by air was more than four-fold lower than it is today.[4] Although telecommunications was a significant industry by the 1970s, many rural Australians were still without adequate phone lines. And it would be more than two decades before internet addresses became available to the general public[5] (and more than three decades before I fully figured out how to use mine). Australians were physically and technologically much less connected.

---

3   Source: Australian Bureau of Statistics (2008) Australian Historical Population Statistics (cat. no. 3105.0.65.001), viewed 30 November 2008.

4   A comparison of domestic air travel in Australia between 1972/3 and 2003/4. Average distance travelled in 1972/73 was calculated by dividing the total distance (kilometres) of passenger travel by air in 1972/73 by the Australian population in 1973. Average distance travelled in 2003/04 was calculated by dividing the total distance (kilometres) of passenger travel by air in 2003/04 by the Australian population in 2004. Source of air travel data: Bureau of Infrastructure, Transport and Regional Economics, 2008, Australian Transport Statistics Year Book 2007, BITRE, Canberra ACT. Source of population data: Australian Bureau of Statistics (2008) Australian Historical Population Statistics (cat. no. 3105.0.65.001), viewed 30 November 2008.

5   Source: Australian Bureau of Statistics (2001) A History of Communications in Australia (Feature Article) in Year Book Australia 2001.

The foundations of the Australian economy were also very different. Manufacturing was a much bigger component of the national economy, as was agriculture.[6] Since the 1970s, we have witnessed a boom in the services industry, particularly in the property, business, finance and insurance industries, and an increase in the relative contribution of mining to GDP.[7]

In the early 1970s, the Australian economy was wrapped in the cotton wool of tariffs, industry subsidies, tax concessions and ill-directed regulation. The effective rate of industry assistance for manufacturing was more than five-fold what it is today, and approximately double for agriculture.[8] To say that we had properly functioning labour and capital markets would be delusional. Government administration comprised more than five per cent of GDP, the highest contribution since federation, with the notable exceptions of the depression and possibly World War II.[9]

The Australian economy was a closed book. While we may have thought of ourselves as a substantial trading nation, we were not. The total value of goods and services imports, expressed as a percentage of GDP, was less than a third of today's value, and the total export value was just over half what it is today.[10] Thus Australians were not just less connected with each other; they were less connected with the world.

As a result of Australia's inward-looking approach, its rigid product and labour markets and undeveloped financial markets, the economy was in bad shape. Australia's GDP per capita, which had historically been well above the OECD average, was sliding towards a below-average report card.

---

6   Source: Australian Bureau of Statistics (2005) 100 years of change in Australian industry (Feature Article) in Year Book Australia 2005.

7   Source: Australian Bureau of Statistics (2005) 100 years of change in Australian industry (Feature Article) in Year Book Australia 2005.

8   Source: Productivity Commission

9   Contribution of the 'government administration and defence' industry to GDP was over 5% during the period 1972/3 to 1983/4. Between 1989/90 and 2000/01 it stayed in the narrow band of 4.1–4.5%. Government contribution peaked at 5.8% in 1930/01 around the start of the Depression (data is not available for World War II years, but it is expected that the contribution was higher still). Source: Australian Bureau of Statistics (2005) 100 years of change in Australian industry (Feature Article) in Year Book Australia 2005. The definition of 'government administration and defence' is based on the Australia and New Zealand Standard Industrial Classification (ANZSIC), 1993 version, and broadly equates to departmental spending for the general government sector.

10   Total value of goods and services imports was calculated by expressing 'Chain Volume Measures: Goods and Services Debits' as a percentage of GDP for financial years ending June 1973 and 2008. Total value of goods and services exports was calculated by expressing 'Chain Volume Measures: Goods and Services Credits' as a percentage of GDP for financial years ending June 1973 and 2008. Source of CVM: Goods and Services Credits/Debits data: Australian Bureau of Statistics (2008) Balance of Payments and International Investment Position, Australia (cat. no. 5302.0), viewed on 30 November 2008. Source of GDP data: Australian Bureau of Statistics (2008) Australian Economic Indicators (cat. no. 1350.0), viewed on 30 November 2008.

The Australian Public Service I joined in 1973 was in the throes of a debate between free trade and protectionism, or, as I saw it, a debate between economic common sense and the 'dark side'. This national battle of philosophies – of how to run the place – was reflected within the Australian Public Service. There was considerable ill will between departments, particularly Treasury, Trade and Industry officials, and personal, often heated, exchanges between departmental secretaries.

The Australian Public Service I joined – indeed Australia – was at a crossroads. Collegiality was minimal. Departmental officials believed that what was in their sector's interest was in the national interest. They fought hard to boost sectoral interests. Treasury was not immune either; although it was good at pointing out the failings of other departments, it too was guilty of overzealous regulation in its own patch.

But on this battleground, some powerful ideas emerged. Alf Rattigan was Chairman of the Tariff Board when I joined the service. He had been appointed back in the mid 1960s by the then Deputy Prime Minister, Sir John McEwen, because of his perceived protectionist leanings.

Sadly for Sir John, his appointed gamekeeper turned out to be a poacher. While Rattigan was initially cautious, he soon became a champion for economic reform. This period was a defining moment for Australia. The removal of the protectionist straitjacket in all its guises was led by Rattigan. Australia began to focus on issues of economic or resource efficiency, on stimulating productivity and lifting the nation's long-term growth potential.

Rattigan had a profound influence on the nation: he laid the foundations for Australia's future prosperity. He also had a profound influence on my career. I moved from the Treasury to the newly formed Industries Assistance Commission (the successor of the Tariff Board) in 1974. That period of the mid-1970s had a major impact on my approach to working in the Australian Public Service.

Rattigan shaped my views on the importance of pursuing the long-term national interest, rather than sectoral interests, and the importance of examining economy-wide implications of public policy choices. He impressed upon me the value of robust analysis, openness and public inquiry. Most importantly, he made me realise that public servants could exert a major influence on the course of the nation's fortunes. And so, all fired up from my early years in Treasury and the Industries Assistance Commission, I embarked eagerly on a public service career that has lasted 36 years.

What are the biggest changes I have witnessed over those 36 years? Firstly, I think the Australian Public Service has matured greatly. Today there is a much stronger focus on developing public policy that is genuinely in the national interest and, consequently, there is a much stronger focus on working together. Departments cooperate significantly more than they used to, and there is a greater sense of collegiality among the upper echelons of the service.

It is just as well that the Australian Public Service has matured – or perhaps it is not surprising – given that the issues governments are grappling with today are significantly more complex than they were in 1973. This is the second major change I have witnessed: an increase in the complexity of government business. Government business is more complex because Australia is more entrenched in the global economy and more exposed to the world in general. (The trade figures I referred to earlier are prime evidence of this, as are the massive financial flows in and out of Australia). In this world, governments must be on the front foot because competitive pressures are intense. And they must be ready to respond to global events, because, as we are currently reminded, the nation's fortunes can be buffeted by the rises and falls in other major economies.

Let me digress here and say a few words about the current international economic crisis. Economists are not very good at picking turning points, or the magnitude of events. They are, however, better at pointing out underlying pressures; at identifying the fundamentals. The growing major financial (and real) imbalances between the United States and China, to mention the most prominent example, have been apparent since the late 1990s. It was the main topic of debate in financial market meetings I attended during the latter part of the 1990s. These imbalances are truly massive: China's current account surplus peaked at around eleven per cent of GDP in 2007; the United States' current account deficit peaked at around 6.5 per cent of GDP. The vast flow of funds into the United States (that is the counterpart of their current account deficit) is reflective of persistent macro and micro economic policy failures in both countries.

The United States was not so much putting capital inflows into investments which could service the debt over time as into current public and private consumption, including housing. In essence, the capital inflows fuelled the boom that subsequently precipitated the collapse as the United States Federal Reserve belatedly sought to dampen domestic demand by tightening monetary policy.

The world is now wearing the consequences of speculative bubbles originating in the United States property market, inadequate financial market regulatory frameworks, and the collective loss of confidence affecting asset values, precipitating further contagion effects. Understandably, investors and consumers are confused. A return to more normal conditions is a long way off.

Inevitably, Australia has been swept up in such events; we cannot avoid the consequences of poor policy in other countries. But we can be prepared for them. Although we are being severely buffeted, we are in much better shape than most other countries because during the 1990s we reinforced the independence of the Reserve Bank, adopted longer-term monetary policy (aimed at keeping inflation in the two to three per cent range) and fiscal rules of thumb (achieving balance over the course of the economic cycle).

Of particular importance is the fact that in the 1990s we fundamentally changed the way we prudentially regulate the financial sector, forming the Australian Prudential Regulatory Authority covering essentially the entire sector. In this regard, Australia was well ahead of many other nations. Australia's prescience – or sound public policy – championed by the Treasury has stood us in good stead.

However, our situation stands in stark contrast to the financial regulatory shambles now exposed in so-called 'international financial centres'. One need only consider the ad-hoc and ill-conceived financial regulatory structure in the United States; look at the way administrations have run fiscal settings, particularly over the last ten years. Consequently, the United States now finds itself confronted with a disastrous budget deficit of around 12 per cent of GDP.

In short, good public policy – getting the underlying framework right – really does matter and in that regard, while we will undoubtedly have lessons to learn ourselves, we have been on the front foot and the Australian Public Service has been at the forefront of formulating good policy. Beyond the immediate economic issues, governments must be able to adapt quickly, because new ideas and technologies are developed and transmitted so readily. And they must be prepared and able to work with other nations because many problems – economic, social, and environmental – are truly global in nature.

Let me be clear. I am strongly of the view that Australia's greater engagement with the world, through trade and financial flows and our advances in communications, and the increased mobility of people and ideas, is a very good thing. However, as I have underscored by example of Australia's far-sighted fiscal and monetary policy management and financial market regulation, it does have consequences for the way Australia positions itself for those challenges. Let me elaborate further.

Challenges for government

Pursuing longer-term reforms

I started my address by emphasising the need to take a longer-term national rather than a sectoral perspective: 'as if for a thousand years'. One major challenge for government is pursuing a reform agenda in the face of extreme pressure from vocal single interest groups. Often the costs are upfront and obvious whereas the benefits, although much greater, are diffuse and long-term. Specific interest groups that stand to lose have become increasingly savvy at harnessing the power and reach of the media and the susceptibility of our politicians to push their particular cause. And, more than ever, governments are reactive to the intense pressure of the 24-hour news cycle. Sadly, responding to the shrill voices of sectoral interests too often gets in the way of long-term policy development in the national interest.

It is confronting this reality that I have found to be the most challenging and sometimes frustrating aspect of being a public policy adviser. The biggest tension between politicians and their public servant advisers resolves around this issue. The irony is, while we are much more enlightened now than we were in the 1970s regarding the importance of pursuing the national interest, it is always, unfortunately, a close-run thing.

Some might say: 'is there harm in making a few concessions here and there to sectoral interests?' But the fact remains that the accumulation of bad decisions or indecision will catch up with nations and is ultimately reflected in their standard of living. Of course, governments have to strike a balance. But exactly where that balance is struck needs to reflect the outcome of a fully informed assessment of where the national interest truly lies.

How can governments better ensure that the pursuit of longer-term reforms is not hijacked by the opportunistic demands of special pleaders? First, we need to undertake rigorous analysis of different policy choices drawing on economic, scientific and social considerations. Wherever possible, that should include cost: benefit analysis. Of course, not everything can be accurately weighed in dollar terms, but in all instances there needs to be a careful weighing of pros and cons so that quantitative *and* qualitative judgements can be made. We also need to remain realistic about what we can and cannot do: a nation cannot afford to fund every policy initiative which has a favourable cost: benefit ratio.

Secondly, we need to open up the debate over long-term policy choices. We need to better equip the public to understand the complexity of issues and the productive and contrary qualities of different options. Rattigan was a great believer in having transparent public policy processes. There needs to be more public releases of research papers, discussion papers and inquiries addressing policy issues of national importance. In this regard, some have criticised the plethora of reviews and inquiries currently being undertaken by the Commonwealth. While the proof of these reviews will be in the outcomes, this is a development that I welcome. It is certainly more effective than inaction or half-baked decisions that are taken on the run, often pandering to the squeakiest wheel.

Thirdly, the proper working of the cabinet system of government is imperative. I am concerned that we have slowly edged towards a de facto presidential style of government, without sufficient checks and balances. As an illustration, during my time in the Australian Public Service some of the most important decisions were made by the Prime Minister, sometimes with a small group of senior ministers. Cabinet was little more than a formality; a rubber stamp. Indeed, the Australian system is, in some respects, becoming more presidential in character but without the checks and balances that are on the President of the United States.

Governments usually start with good intentions but fall into bad habits. Ideas need to be debated and tested in a properly informed cabinet forum. I am not arguing that every idea needs to go to cabinet (in fact I think too many inconsequential items reach the Cabinet agenda), but it is critical that cabinet properly considers the issues of national importance.

Commonwealth-state relations

Another major challenge for the national government, which is a product of Australia's higher exposure to the world and the increased mobility of people and ideas, is a change in Commonwealth-state relations. Over time, our views on what issues should be handled at the national level have broadened and increasingly more responsibility has been acquired by the Commonwealth. The Commonwealth has gathered greater control via legislative means (High Court decisions, assertion of existing constitutional powers and occasionally, referral of state powers) and perhaps most significantly, via financial instruments such as specific purpose payments.

I believe this trend is unlikely to be reversed and the Commonwealth government will acquire more responsibility over time. Now this will not always be the Commonwealth's choosing, as Canberra will continue to be drawn into issues of state responsibility by the community, who view the Commonwealth as a de facto 'court of appeal'. Is this trend towards more centralised government a bad thing? Some would argue that it represents a departure from subsidiarity principle: that is, the Commonwealth is taking on responsibility for programs and services it is not best placed to deliver.

I do not believe this is the case, because these days physical proximity does not necessarily make a government better equipped to administer a program. The Commonwealth government is absolutely capable of developing strategies for managing complex projects at a local level, and delivering services across Australia which cater to the different needs of different communities.

Nevertheless, the acquisition of new responsibilities does bring with it new challenges. It puts the onus on the Commonwealth government and the Australian Public Service to do more of the longer-term, strategic analysis across a broader range of issues. This includes clarifying the boundaries in key areas of split Commonwealth-state responsibility such as health, education and transport to ensure the effective delivery of services.

The centralisation we are seeing on a national scale is also happening at an international scale. As I discussed previously, Australia is more entrenched in the global economy and will, increasingly, be shaped by global forces and events. We are most likely to thrive if we have a strong economy and a healthy society. This only reinforces the need for the Commonwealth government to be far-sighted in its approach to issues.

Issues for the Australian Public Service

I will now turn my attention to issues for the Australian Public Service. The Australian Public Service clearly has a critical role in helping governments to rise to challenges I have described. What then are the ingredients for a healthy Australian Public Service that can assist governments to pursue longer-term reforms across an increasingly broader range of responsibilities?

The first ingredient: finding the space for longer-term thinking

The quality of the Australian Public Service is the foundation of good government. It must have the capacity – the skilled workforce and the resources – to undertake the strategic thinking which underpins longer-term reforms. Institutions such as the Productivity Commission, which have a long-term orientation and some degree of independence from government, are vitally important. But they are not enough. The capacity for longer-term thinking needs to exist across the service, in each agency with policy responsibilities.

I think it is becoming increasingly difficult for the Australian Public Service to find room to do this. It has sometimes been said that the Australian Public Service is strong on policy but weaker on program implementation. Certainly officers with policy skills have tended to move up the ranks more rapidly. My concern is that the Australian Public Service is being tasked to do so much that the balance is tipping the other way. The immediate pressures of program and service delivery take priority over long-term policy development.

This is one of the great difficulties of being an agency head: we want to provide a longer-term perspective to government but our agencies are so flat out and stretched that we have scant capacity to invest in serious thinking. My concern is that the less we engage in thinking about longer-term policy issues, the less capable we become of engaging in it when it is required. I would hate to see the Australian Public Service become de-skilled to the point that it cannot participate in a meaningful way in setting out the nation's long-term agenda. Rattigan would have been dismayed.

The second ingredient: being business-like

I think the Australian Public Service needs to be more business-like in the way it develops, implements and evaluates policies and programs. All too often, we find ourselves landed with the daunting task of implementing a new initiative which has only been developed to the extent required to prepare the one page new policy proposal for the Expenditure Review Committee of cabinet.

Instead, we need to spend more time researching and assessing different policy options before picking a course of action. On this point, I refer back to my previous comments about the need for rigorous analysis to weigh up the merits of different policy choices; of taking the longer-term national perspective.

The Australian Public Service also needs to put more effort into rigorously reviewing and evaluating the success of different policies and programs, something we do not do nearly enough. We need to know which initiatives have not worked, or have not worked perfectly. That way, when governments need to make savings, they can target programs with a less favourable cost: benefit ratio. I do not think governments are serious enough about evaluating programs and closing them down when required; all too often, necessary savings are achieved by shaving funds at the margins across the board.

This presents a great dilemma for secretaries. Secretaries are responsible under the *Financial Management and Accountability Act 1997* for the financial oversight of their department. Yet under our system they do not really have the freedom to run their own shop. Ministers continually ask departments to do more but are rarely willing to cut things off. It is little wonder that departments are struggling to find the resources to invest in longer term strategy development: it is debilitating. One way around this may be to 'activity cost' everything we do, just like the leading edge of the private sector. In this world, if ministers want their departments to undertake a new activity then they should have to identify, at the same time, what they are not going to do. As things currently stand, the gradual accretion of new functions that have not been funded is debilitating to the capacity to focus on longer-term issues, yet it is an accepted part of today's APS.

The third ingredient: accountability

The Australian Public Service is by far Australia's biggest business and is arguably more complex than the businesses run by our private sector counterparts. But unlike our private sector counterparts, the Australian Public Service is not subject to market disciplines; it is a monopoly provider of services. The public has little choice but to deal with us. Consequently, it is incumbent on the Australian Public Service to apply high ethical and administrative standards, and to be accountable in general.

It is critical that we maintain 'accountability' institutions such as the Australian National Audit Office, the Ombudsman, the Administrative Appeals Tribunal and our accountability to parliament. Uncomfortable though it may be at times, we need to allow ourselves to be questioned and probed about the quality of service we are delivering on behalf of the Australian people, remembering that it is politicians who are ultimately accountable.

We need to be as open as possible about the way we do things, and we need to actively promote a pro-information disclosure environment (to the extent that it does not compromise the free exchange of ideas between the public service and ministers). Releasing more information into the public domain helps build trust in government and government processes and, most importantly, it encourages a more open debate on longer-term policy issues.

Concluding remarks

The Australian Public Service is a great asset to this nation and I have every confidence that it will rise to the challenges I have described. The quality of the service it provides and the standard of conduct is world class. So too is the capability and commitment of its people. Earlier, I spoke of the profound influence that one public servant, Alf Rattigan, had on turning around the fortunes of the nation. He is a fine example, but he is only one of many Australian Public Service 'heroes' who have made a difference, and who I have been privileged to witness at work over the past 36 years.

The Australian Public Service and the nation have fundamentally changed over the past 40 years; so too will they fundamentally change over the next 40. Reforms such as the Carbon Pollution Reduction Scheme, which today seem momentous, may well be viewed as minor adjustments 40 years hence. In 40 years time, we may reflect with nostalgia on the time when public servants congregated for work in the parliamentary triangle; where my generation saw the advent of the personal computer, the next generation may well witness the demise of the 'office and desk' and the creation of a more fluid, flexible and dispersed workforce.

I cannot predict how the Australian Public Service will change, short of predicting that the Commonwealth government will be doing more, but experience tells me it *will* change. I shall leave it to a future secretary to reflect on these changes in his or her valedictory address, 40 years from now.

Being in the Australian Public Service has been a rewarding experience. Many of my public sector values were instilled by my father and role models like Rattigan. While I will undoubtedly miss working in the Australian Public Service and the camaraderie that it has, the last couple of months away from it have confirmed that now was the right time to leave.

11. Reflections of an 'unabashed rationalist'[1]

Peter Boxall

Peter Boxall retired as a secretary following a one-year stint as head of the Department of Resources, Energy and Tourism in 2008. This followed six years as Secretary of the Department of Employment and Workplace Relations (2002–07) and five years as Secretary of the Department of Finance and Administration (1997–2002). An economist with a doctorate from the University of Chicago, Peter Boxall commenced his career with the Reserve Bank of Australia, then spent seven years at the International Monetary Fund in the US, followed by graduate studies at the University of Chicago and a graduate fellowship at the Brookings Institution. On returning to Australia in 1986, Boxall joined the Department of Treasury. He was senior economic advisor to the leader and deputy leader of the opposition in the late 1980s and early 1990s. He was next Secretary of the Department of Treasury and Finance in South Australia, then principal adviser to the then Treasurer Peter Costello, before returning to the APS in 1997. Peter Boxall is currently a commissioner with the Australian Securities and Investments Commission.

2006 interview with Paul Malone

The Secretary of the Department of Employment and Workplace Relations, Peter Boxall, says he really likes his job as head of DEWR. 'I had a background in labour economics, had an interest in it and I find the job intellectually stimulating'. He also has a reputation of being one of the 'economic rationalists' in the public service. 'I'm proud of it', he says when this is put to him. 'I like to think of myself as a classic liberal. I think that the market has so much to offer and that there are a few areas where the government might intervene, for political reasons or for other reasons usually to do with redistribution of income and issues like that. But I think the Australian based market economy has done very well, as have the other market economies'.

As a 'rational economic man', the pertinent question he says is: 'how does the person at the margin operate?' 'If you have an incentive structure, if you

---

1 This contribution is primarily based on an edited extract of an interview Peter Boxall gave in early 2006, while Secretary of the Department of Employment and Workplace Relations, to *Canberra Times* journalist Paul Malone as a series on the then 18 departmental secretaries. The second part of the chapter is based on an interview he had with John Wanna in February 2011, three years after he completed his term as Secretary of the Department of Resources, Energy and Tourism in 2008.

"

increase or decrease a price, then you will elicit a response from an individual or a firm at the margin. I believe that happens. I think it's very clear that happens. I think the data, the analysis and the evidence is unarguable'. The reaction does not have to be from everyone. 'There might be a bunch of people who might keep on doing things more or less indefinitely irrespective of what happens to the price. But the fact is that if you increase the price more people are likely to supply and less people are likely to demand it'. The other issue he says which is related, but which is not quite the same point, is the impact on business. 'People in the business sector have a bottom line and if you impose too many costs on them, they go out of business'.

He says he respects the political process which determines points of intervention. 'The people vote for the government and then the government needs to make a judgement about where it's going to intervene, to what extent it's going to redistribute, to what extent it's going to assist certain groups in the community. And that's the result of the political process and that's a call for the elected representatives. Our job as public servants is to advise on the public policy aspects, to point out the pros and cons of certain alternative policies and to be able to analyse them so that ministers have a full information set when they act — in particular to point out unintended consequences, both positive and negative. This is an issue which goes to equity and fairness. Equity and fairness is a value judgement. It's not something that economists or engineers or anybody else has a particular expertise in. Something that I think is fair, you might think is unfair. That's why it has to be a decision taken by politicians who are the elected representatives who have contact with their electorates.

'It's really our job to look at what is efficient, which is more measurable, and effective and ethical. And that's why in the *FMA Act* [Financial Management and Accountability Act under which Commonwealth departments operate] they have this section … which says that one of the duties of CEOs such as myself is the three Es, efficient, effective and ethical use of taxpayers' money. Fairness is an issue for the politicians'.

In 2006 Boxall's department had taken on additional responsibilities and grown to over 3000 staff in the five years he had been there. The immediate challenge for the department was the implementation of the government's policy agenda. The passage of the *WorkChoices* legislation was passed through parliament at the end of 2005. As a result the department gained a bigger role in compliance arrangements. There was also the *Welfare to Work* agenda to pursue and the successful tendering of the *Job Network* and other services to oversee. The department was also continuing implementation of reform to the *Community Development Employment Program* and increased Indigenous employment, where Boxall thought at the time that something was happening and things were moving in the right direction.

'My job is to keep on delivering those services and the way I do that is primarily through the selection of very good staff. I have a very good SES [Senior Executive Service]. I was lucky when I came to the department to inherit a good team of SES and I've tried to add to that. It's also to devise a compensation scheme which encourages people to give their best. But on top of that I need to keep my finger on the pulse, on the policy advice that's going to a minister. I need to intervene when I see something that's not quite going on track'. And the same with the service delivery. 'So it's very much a role of being in touch with my SES, being able to access all the ministerial briefs through the electronic network, being on top of issues of service delivery and being ready to intervene. The way I've operated, I've devolved the responsibility to my managers, who in turn devolve it to their managers and it cascades right down through the department'.

Boxall said in 2006 that his department had clear objectives because he and his executive had given a lot of thought to them. They aimed for three outcomes – employment, workplace relations and workplace participation. And, there was a one-to-one correspondence between each of his three deputies and the three outcomes the department sought to meet. He said the ministers of the elected government were their customers. 'We serve job-seekers and other clients of the department on behalf of ministers. It's very clear where the accountability is'.

He also said he applied a trusting, or some might say risky, process to handling ministerial briefs. Unlike many senior managers who cleared briefs before they left the department, Boxall's system allowed his executives to send briefs direct to the minister's office without his prior approval. The executives are expected to first discuss the issues with Boxall and then prepare the brief and send it to the minister. 'I read the brief electronically', he said. 'I read the summary and then if I need to, I read the whole brief. If I find there is something in there that is not quite right, I pull the brief and we re-do it'. By that stage the brief may have gone to the minister but Boxall said he usually got to it before the minister has had a chance to read it. This process, he said, avoids a bottleneck.

'If I had to clear everything in what is one of the biggest departments in Canberra and certainly has been the busiest in the last 12 months – we've had *Welfare to Work* and *Work Choices* plus the tender round for the *Job Network* – it would just be unmanageable'. But what if he's too busy and doesn't get to the brief? 'I'm now in my tenth year as a secretary at the Commonwealth level, five years in Finance and in my fifth year here and only once has a minister got to something that I wanted to pull, before I pulled it'. On average he was pulling a brief about once a month, perhaps rising to 1.5 a month because of increased volume of business. Boxall said managers accept that briefs get pulled. 'They're fine about it. They know how it works… I send them an email or I call them up and they pull it immediately. And then we just re-jig it or we might re-write it. Usually it's re-jigged'.

Unlike many other department heads, Boxall did not work twelve hour days. 'I get to work normally about 9 o'clock and I normally leave about six', he said. 'I try not to work on weekends. And I try not to work in the evenings, apart from official functions. Every now and then I have to do a little bit of email at night or on Sunday night just to clear the decks and make sure it hasn't backed up on me'. He said work/family balance was a big issue for him. In line with this he said he tried to be considerate of his staff. 'We don't normally call meetings before 9.30 in the morning and we try not to call meetings after about 4.30 in the afternoon,' he said. 'This is so people can come to work, not be rushed'.

As head of Finance, Boxall was responsible for the introduction of the system of accruals, outcomes and outputs that is now in place in the service. 'I think that this is a very important reform, a core budget reform with the outputs and outcomes and it has got the whole public service and for that matter parliament, focused more on the outcomes and outputs and what we're trying to achieve'. He said departments have had varying degrees of success in implementing accrual accounting. But what it has done is to get departments to focus on the true cost of service delivery, forcing them to take account of such things as depreciation. The outcomes and outputs were a major improvement because they focused on what the program actually achieved. Where ministers and departments had taken performance indicators seriously, they had been quite successful. 'It's not perfect but in my view it's much better than what was there in the past', he said.

But if the unemployment rate suddenly went up would he have seen that as his department's responsibility? 'Well one of the indicators is the state of the labour market and obviously there's more than us that contribute to that', he said. 'There's macro-economic policy in Treasury, and the Reserve Bank and others'. He said it is very difficult to disentangle to what extent his department's efforts might be at fault vis-a-vis other departments. 'We just have to try and do our best'.

About three quarters of DEWR's staff are on an Australian Workplace Agreement and they are eligible for a performance bonus. Boxall said if the unemployment rate went up and it was fairly clear that this was not due to mismanagement in the employment programs that would be taken into account in any assessment. But if there was major mismanagement of the employment programs by senior people in the department they would struggle to get a bonus, whether the unemployment rate went up or down.

Boxall was one of the department heads, which included Michael L'Estrange at Foreign Affairs and Trade, who have worked as an advisor in the politicians' offices. Having spent years in the public sector he took a job with Deputy Opposition Leader Andrew Peacock and helped prepare the opposition's 1990 economic action plan. Later, when the Coalition was elected to government he was chief of staff in Treasurer Peter Costello's office.

Few doubt the difficulties oppositions face in trying to draw up a comprehensive and defensible economic plan with the limited staff and financial resources available. Mistakes are costly and the best staff are required. Boxall said by the time he was employed by Peacock he was well aware of the issues confronting the opposition and was relatively experienced having worked at the Reserve Bank and the International Monetary Fund where, with colleagues, he had prepared macro-economic plans. 'You're at a disadvantage in a sense, but that's opposition', he said.

In Treasurer Peter Costello's office, Boxall worked on the Coalition government's first budget where major expenditure cuts were introduced. Subsequently, he went through six Expenditure Review Committees, possibly as many as anybody in Canberra, apart from the Treasurer. Asked if in making the expenditure cuts there was anything that caused him anguish he said: 'No. I don't recall actually. It was quite interesting that the public service didn't seem well prepared for it and a lot of it was driven by the new ministers'. However, they met resistance, he said, including from central agencies.

He agreed that he has wielded the knife for a fair bit of his career and, when asked if he preferred this to doling out money he said, 'I would not prefer to be doling out money because I have great respect for taxpayers money and I don't like supporting programs which I don't think are good value for the taxpayer'. But if he was given a social security type portfolio he said he would happily administer it 'because I'm a professional public servant and if the government decides that they should pay money to certain groups of people then I will pay it. But as a policy advisor it doesn't mean to say I would recommend that they do that'. As a classic liberal he thinks there is scope to continue to look at government expenditure to see whether programs are really necessary. This applies even when there is a significant surplus because then there can be lower taxes.

Boxall said when he was Secretary of Finance from 1997 to 2002 he was subjected to quite a focussed hostile campaign. While his stance had the backing of the government he believes he and some other secretaries were attacked as a way of attacking the government. But he will not say who precisely instigated the attacks. 'Did it make my life uncomfortable? Not terribly. It wasn't very pleasant'. When asked if he was more closely aligned with the views of Max Moore-Wilton, he replied: 'Look I don't really know because Max Moore-Wilton was head of PM&C and it's difficult when people are head of PM&C to work out what their real views are. That's not a criticism of him…you've got to be a collegiate player…[but] because I was Secretary of Finance I didn't have to be a collegiate player to the same extent'.

Today, do more secretaries share his views or does he think he is at one end of the spectrum? 'I think there are a spectrum of views of other secretaries. Not all other secretaries share my philosophical approach. Not all other secretaries have the same background as me. And so, in many respects, I am different'.

February 2011 interview with John Wanna

Interviewer: Has the role of secretary changed over time? If so, what are the big differences?

Boxall: I don't think it changed much in my twelve years as a departmental secretary. It changed slightly in my final year with the change of government and that's mainly because the current government has a more centralised approach or a less decentralised approach to the management of finances and public sector employment [than their predecessor]. I guess it was changing slightly in terms of the management of finances in my latter years, but otherwise I don't think it's changed that much.

Interviewer: You don't think the mix of policy and management and all the different stakeholders has changed much for them?

Boxall: I don't think it has changed much. I believe the role of secretary is principally a policy advisor and a public sector manager, and I thought that was very much how it was during my period. As for stakeholders, there is probably more management of stakeholders now – that's one change – though it was relatively subtle.

Interviewer: Many secretaries talk about the incredible pressure of modern communication management (Blackberries, email etc), which probably wasn't the case 20 years ago. Is this the case?

Boxall: I was overseas 20 years ago; I was first appointed as a secretary in January 1997. It's true that now we have Blackberries and emails and things like that, but in my view these forms of communication are incredibly powerful, as they allow the secretary to manage their department in a more efficient manner.

Interviewer: In terms of recruitment, do you think the pool from which secretaries are selected has been expanded sufficiently outside the APS?

Boxall: I don't think that is a real issue. It's difficult to appoint secretaries from outside Canberra unless they have substantive public sector experience because if you have someone who enters the public service as a graduate like I did, you become increasingly hard-wired to the public sector. On the other hand, a person who enters the private sector straight out of university and stays there

20 or 30 years becomes hard-wired to the private sector. This is apparent in the Australian Securities and Investments Commission, where you get people who have come in from the private sector and who, as a consequence, have developed skill sets or honed different skill sets. So it's often quite difficult — just as it would be quite difficult for someone who has been a secretary to move into the private sector at a CEO role.

Interviewer: There's been a push in recent decades to introduce more business practices into the public sector. What are your views on that?

Boxall: The idea of having a more decentralised approach to the management of finances, along with accrual budgeting and the appropriation of the price of the outputs — I thought were very important developments, but I think they have been wound back a bit in recent years. They were important because they forced secretaries to manage. Prior to that development, and prior to the public sector reforms under the Howard government (when Peter Reith was minister and the new *Public Service Act 1999* came about), secretaries had relatively less management discretion.

Interviewer: Do you think secretaries today are 'statesmen in disguise'?

Boxall: No I don't. And I think such a situation is dangerous because in our political system the elected government of the day has a policy platform and they are elected by the people to put those policies into place. To have a situation where you have a public service as some sort of 'constitutional bureaucracy' and the head of each department as a 'statesman in disguise' would hamper the elected government of the day from executing their mandate. Effectively, they would be hamstrung by non-elected bureaucrats with tenure, and I think that's a real danger.

Interviewer: Do secretaries still provide frank and fearless advice?

Boxall: I never felt that I could not give frank and fearless advice and what's more I did give it. I don't think it should be given in the public arena because then you are acting like a 'statesman in disguise'. I don't know whether all other secretaries did give it. I suspect some did and some didn't. I don't think it's a feature of the system. There are some people who are up to giving frank and fearless advice and there are others who prefer not to.

Interviewer: Often frank and fearless advice is required when you feel it necessary to discourage a government from going in a particular direction or pursuing a certain agenda — are they the most difficult situations that arise?

Boxall: There are those, and sometimes there is pressure to make appointments or not make appointments or you can have other issues concerning administration of public programs, but ultimately I don't think giving frank and fearless advice is very difficult. I don't think it's difficult at all.

Interviewer: When you were heading a department you had a fairly relaxed attitude to your senior people giving advice directly to the minister. Did this ever concern you?

Boxall: No, not at all, because they were giving advice to the minister within the parameters of what we had discussed in our department, and often I would discuss it with them before they went and did it. In my opinion this is better than having everything funnelled through the secretary, as I don't think that is a good or efficient way to run a department, especially if it is a large department. The trick is to create a framework and couple that with a selection of good people. I always had good people, so I always felt comfortable that the framework was there and the people were good. My people knew what our position was, what direction we were going in and the issues we covered, so I never thought that was compromised at all.

Interviewer: How active were your ministers in setting policy directions – John Fahey in Finance for instance? I'm trying to tease out the relationship between the secretary (and the department) and the minister (and the minister's office) in terms of who's taking the lead in terms of setting the agenda?

Boxall: I always thought that John Fahey was very interested in being Minister for Finance. He had quite a nose for detail and he would get into the detail in the Expenditure Review Committee and was heavily involved in about five of these events, and he was particularly interested in the assets sale side of the portfolio. He was active in promoting the government's policy to introduce accrual budgeting. That was a policy agenda item that John Howard took to the election in 1996. We [in Finance] very much set that agenda – but again it was filling in the agenda to implement government policy.

Interviewer: What was different when you headed up the Department of Employment and Workplace Relations?

Boxall: DEWR was a really great department. When I was there there was a lot happening on the employment side, the workplace relations side, and also in welfare reform and Indigenous employment. It was a bigger department. It had both a policy and a line agency role, and there was a lot going on. And it increased in influence considerably in the period that I was there, especially with the machinery of government changes. We were very much at the centre of the government's agenda. Also, the people in DEWR were very good. I inherited good people and I tried to maintain that. And I believe I successfully did do that.

Interviewer: You remained a secretary at the change of government [Howard to Rudd]. Was that a difficult time?

Boxall: At that time DEWR merged with Education to become the Department of Education, Employment and Workplace Relations [and given to the Deputy Prime Minister], and they gave me Resources, Energy and Tourism, a new department under Martin Ferguson. I was a secretary there for one year before I moved to ASIC. I was very fortunate to have Martin Ferguson as my minister under the Labor government, and that was quite good. But I did notice that there was a change in the approach to public sector management. Finance had started to become more active and central in the way the government were running their finances. That was already occurring but accelerated under the new government. Also there were changes being put in place with respect to public sector employment.

Interviewer: So did you see fairly big differences in the styles of the two governments, between Howard and Rudd?

Boxall: There were substantial differences between Rudd and Howard, and that's been written up in the press. But it's not so much Rudd and Howard as prime ministers; it's the regime. For example, there has been a change in the role of the Public Service Commissioner; a change of public sector employment responsibilities from DEWR – or DEEWR as it now is – to the Public Service Commissioner. Another change is the approach of Finance to budgeting, with more whole-of-government procurement and more whole-of-government processes which need to be gone through. And what that does in a sense is remove responsibility – or rather takes over responsibility for the management of some of these issues from the agencies and puts it with the central agency.

Interviewer: So you'd prefer the more decentralised approach where agencies could set their own employment terms and conditions, their own pay rates, source their own procurements?

Boxall: Yes, I would prefer that. I prefer appropriating the funds to the secretary and department to deliver the government's programs and I think that gets the better results. The point is we need to make sure the secretaries appointed are capable of carrying out such a role because it's a much different role compared with a highly centralised system where secretaries don't have the discretion to make some of these decisions, or they can only make those decisions within some very narrow parameters.

Interviewer: There's a lot of talk of returning to a single or unified APS. Do you think we will ever get back to a unified service? Do you think it's achievable?

Boxall: I think it is going to be very difficult to return to the single APS that existed a couple of decades ago. It's going to be difficult to do that, even if they wanted to.

12. Our custodial role for the quality of advisory relations at the centre of government[1]

Patricia Scott

Patricia Scott joined the APS in 1990. Her APS career included substantial periods in the Department of the Prime Minister and Cabinet and in line agencies including the Department of Industry, Tourism and Resources. She was subsequently appointed the inaugural Secretary of the Department of Human Services in 2004. She was appointed Secretary of the Department of Communications, Information Technology and the Arts in May 2007 before being appointed Secretary of the Department of Broadband, Communications and the Digital Economy in December of that year. In August 2009 she was appointed a Commissioner of the Productivity Commission.

I have had the privilege of serving five years as a secretary, four prime ministers and fourteen other ministers. For more than a decade, over the Keating and Howard governments, I was a frequent cabinet note-taker. Throughout this diverse experience I gained insights into the strengths of the Australian version of the Westminster system based on a rigorous, well informed cabinet process; and insights into the risks and problems created when good cabinet process is abandoned.

Also of vital importance to good governance are: clear lines of ministerial, ministerial adviser and public service accountability; respect for the respective strengths and roles of each; and recognition by ministers of the value of experienced, frank and fearless advice.

A rigorous cabinet process

I am a strong advocate for substantive cabinet consideration of all major policies on the basis of written submissions (not PowerPoint slides) and for rigorous coordination comments by all relevant departments. There are three key points to be noted here:

---

1   This paper was written by Patricia Scott in May 2011.

1. Written submissions formulated through genuine agency consultation allow a wider set of issues to be aired, key differences of view and risks to be considered and balanced recommendations to be formulated.

2. I consider it essential that the coordination comments provided by departments on cabinet submissions are not cleared by ministers or their ministerial advisers and that they be available to all cabinet ministers. This ensures that cabinet has the frank views of relevant departments.

3. Informed decision-making needs to be based on the consideration by ministers of the evidence and a variety of views, and not just the views of ministerial advisers and a limited few in central agencies.

No sensible individual would make a substantial financial decision on the basis of a PowerPoint presentation or a short paper. Why would it be fine then to have senior ministers or cabinet make decisions on that basis without substantive written analysis and alternative commentary available to them? Very infrequently there will need to be exemptions (national emergencies, global crises or unforseen urgencies), but over the last 20 years some of the worst decisions I have seen were done by dint of desperation, with insufficient written analysis, by a 'kitchen cabinet' or a select few ministers under intense secrecy (often without the benefit of implementation considerations or the valuable advice of agencies with program and stakeholder engagement experience).

Moreover, too often advice from line ministers and their departments has been undervalued by central agencies and such 'kitchen cabinets', resulting in a disempowerment of ministers and a subsequent detrimental impact on lines of accountability and implementation.

And while some good decisions have been made in such circumstances, one should only take such risks when forced to rather than making it the standard process. Policy making is at its weakest, and policies likely to be most compromised, when cabinet is merely a rubber stamp.

The role of public engagement

There should be the opportunity not only for well informed debate in the cabinet, but, on very significant reforms, also an opportunity for informed input from key stakeholders and the general public.

It might seem old-fashioned to develop proposals for public consultation (the old green paper) followed by further government consideration and then the release of the final policy detailed document (the white paper) but why not engage the general public, academia and stakeholders? As Gary Banks,

Chairman of the Productivity Commission recently noted, 'the experience has been that consultation is valuable not only to develop and get acceptance for broad reform options, but also to get the detail right in the option that is finally implemented.'[2]

My own experience in the Productivity Commission's study and public inquiry process is that there is much to be gained from transparent and robust engagement.

Good policy advice

Of course, good policy development starts a long way before cabinet. My singular piece of advice to young policy advisers and aspiring politicians is to take a few hours to learn and understand the basic economic framework regarding government policy. It doesn't matter if your policy expertise is not economics – all policy making involves making choices and opportunity costs. And the first place an economist wants to start is with the clear identification of the problem.

Unfortunately too many political advisers and public servants instead start with a solution before they have analysed the causes and the extent of the problem. In terms of basic economic principles, a few basic questions should always be asked:

- What is the problem, its extent and consequences? Who wins and who loses?
- Is the problem created by market failure?
- If so, which type of market failure as this would affect the remedy (externalities, public good characteristics, ill-defined property rights, barriers to entry or exit, insufficient information)?
- Is it an equity issue? What is the equity outcome being sought by the government?
- Will government intervention help or hinder a solution?
- Will the gains exceed the costs?
- Who needs to be consulted?

---

2 Banks, G. 2011, *Successful Reform: Past Lessons, Future Challenges* (Annual Forecasting Conference of the Australian Business Economists, 8 December 2010), Productivity Commission, Canberra (http://www.pc.gov. au/__data/assets/pdf_file/0018/104229/successful-reform.pdf).

And *if* the analysis suggests government intervention, what is the appropriate form of intervention (encouragement of private sector activity, direct government provision, regulation, tax, subsidy, funding to a non-government organisation, public private partnership, a fee for service, or a government ban)?

Furthermore, how should the intervention be implemented and by whom? Who needs to be involved in implementation? What is the sensible implementation timetable? What are the risks, and how can they be mitigated, and at what cost? What will be delivered and when?

And ultimately, will this intervention really address the problem? What will be the behavioural response of producers and/or consumers? What are the likely unintended consequences?

More generally, what is the opportunity cost of addressing this problem now relative to the other priorities of the government and how does it fit within a longer-term, strategic view of policy priorities?

Systematically addressing a problem this way may have a tinge of Bernard in *Yes Minister* asking too many awkward questions. But my concern is that not asking enough questions risks policy development descending to the desperation tactics of *The Thick of It*.

Relationship between ministerial advisers and the public service

There has been real progress in clarifying the role of ministerial advisers since the Code of Conduct for Ministerial Staff was introduced in 2008. To be effective, departments need to work closely with ministerial advisers and having clarity on their respective roles is vital. The Code states that: 'Ministerial staff do not have the power to direct APS employees in their own right and that APS employees are not subject to their direction,' and that 'executive decisions are the preserve of Ministers and public servants and not ministerial staff acting in their own right.'[3]

In his work on the postmodern presidency, Richard Rose suggests that advisers fall into four groups.[4]

---

3   Circular 2008/7 Code of Conduct for Ministerial Staff tabled in the Senate by the Special Minister of State, Senator Faulkner, 26 June 2008, Australian Public Service Commission.
4   Adapted from Richard Rose *The Postmodern President*, 1991 Chatham House p 171.

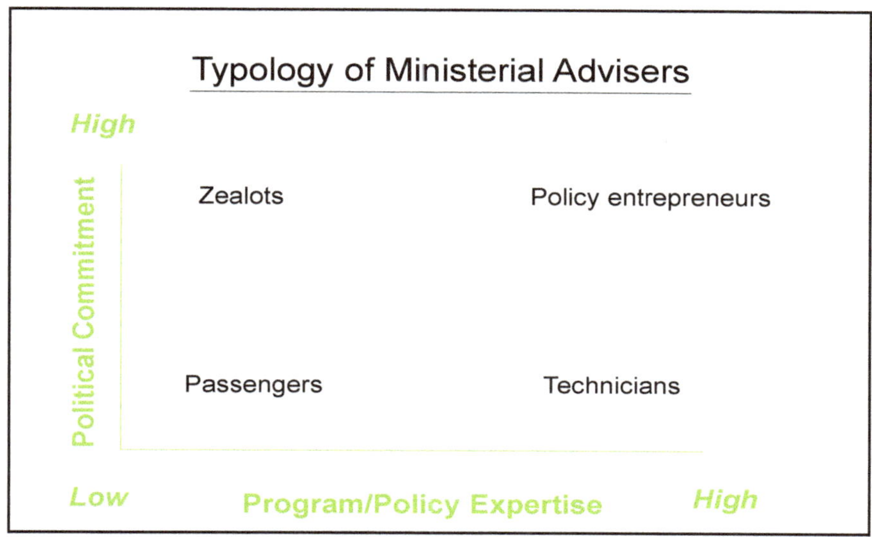

Figure 1: Typology of ministerial advisers

Clearly, having senior people in a minister's office who have both policy expertise and the confidence of the minister is preferable to the all-too-common experience of the adviser that is exclusively a political operative with little policy experience, overflowing confidence in their ability to discern policy on the basis of a quick Google search and an unrelenting focus on the short-term political imperatives (the zealots in the above typology).

There is much to be said for ensuring in ministerial offices a 'cross-fertilisation' of ideas and experiences between political operatives, senior departmental policy officers and people with diverse work and life experiences. The Hawke, Keating and Howard governments, for example, benefited from senior departmental officers playing key roles in senior ministerial offices (Dennis Richardson, Sandy Hollway, Rod Sims, Lynelle Briggs and Arthur Sinodinos just to name a few).

The Australian Public Service Commission should offer the government, the opposition and minor parties in parliament highly-regarded senior policy officers for advising roles, at times on a short-term secondment basis and of course subject to strict confidentiality arrangements. This would be seen as part of a rising career path rather than throwing your lot in with a particular party.

At present, while there is some recruitment of usually junior staff from the APS into ministers' and MP's offices, and talented junior officers are made available by departments as departmental liaison officers in ministers' offices, senior advising positions are most likely to be held by political apparatchiks. A greater mix would lead to better policies and a better appreciation of the challenges of implementation. How can the opposition and then new governments avoid over-promising and under-delivering if they don't have advisers with sufficient policy and implementation experience?

Not only would the placement of more senior public servants in ministerial offices assist informed policy decision-making, it would also aid the Australian Public Service in terms of interaction and insight. For a year or so I worked as a ministerial adviser in the Assistant Treasurer's office under the Keating government focusing on competition policy reform. Looking back now, that office's policy staff was largely drawn from Treasury, the Department of the Prime Minister and Cabinet and the Australian Taxation Office. Without exception those public service advisers rose to very senior ranks, have served governments of both persuasions faithfully and were better advisers because of the different perspectives gained on policy issues and exposure to the stress and strains of political life.

Ensuring continued strengths

The Australian Public Service has a long and proud history of providing strong and confidential advice. Within their confidential circles, sensible ministers and governments encourage a diversity of views. I have great respect for those ministers who welcomed confidential debate and valued criticisms of policy proposals and existing programs and were prepared to engage on alternative options.

It is easy to create a veneer of greater openness by reforming Freedom of Information laws but then have a minister insist that the most sensitive material is never provided in writing or have political advisers inappropriately seek to reprimand departmental officers for committing views to paper that would be 'unhelpful' if they were made public. At the same time, self-censorship by public servants in advising is a dangerous trap that is easy to fall into.

I am delighted that I took the decision to work in the Australian Public Service. It has remarkable strengths – these are most easily on display to the public in the efficient and remarkably reliable payment system of Centrelink (imagine the uproar if Medicare and Centrelink were unable to process funds safely, as some banks have encountered recently). My experience in policy and especially in establishing the federal Department of Human Services, and in working with large and small delivery agencies, is that there is tremendous talent and dedication within the service. For example, I saw during the recovery efforts after Cyclone Larry the tireless dedication and real innovation of the APS in serving the Australian public.

I am delighted to have the opportunity to work in and with so many departments and agencies, and consider the APS is an important underpinning for Australia's wellbeing.

But times change and new arrangements bring different risks. In light of the increasingly substantial funds now dispersed through contracts both by officials and Commonwealth entities, I consider that it would be prudent for anti-corruption arrangements like NSW's Independent Commission Against Corruption to be established in relation to the handling of Commonwealth expenditure.

Governments are as partial to fads and fashions as teenagers. A strong and vibrant Australia needs government adherence to good cabinet processes. It also needs a strong, vibrant and impartial Australian Public Service that is always prepared to question, analyse and, where necessary, offer sometimes unwelcome but confidential advice and to implement programs as if their family's and other taxpayers' funds and services are at stake (which they are!).

13. A road less travelled — reflecting on three professional pillars of support[1]

Michael L'Estrange

In 1981, Michael L'Estrange joined the Department of Prime Minister and Cabinet, having studied at Oxford University from 1976 to 1979. From 1989 to 1994 he worked for several leaders of the opposition in a range of policy advisory positions. In 1995, he was appointed the inaugural Executive Director of the Menzies Research Centre in Canberra. In 1996 he was appointed Secretary to Cabinet and Head of the Cabinet Policy Unit, a position he held until becoming Australia's High Commissioner to the United Kingdom in 2000. He served as Secretary of the Department of Foreign Affairs and Trade from 2005-2009, and was appointed Director of the ANU National Security College upon his retirement from the Australian Public Service.

This perspective on my years as Secretary of the Department of Foreign Affairs and Trade from 2005 to 2009 is more a brief personal reflection than any attempt at a thorough-going assessment of the professional relationships and decision-making processes that shaped the carrying out of my responsibilities in that period.

It is inherent in the positions departmental secretaries hold that many personal confidences are entered into with the expectation that they will be respected in both the short and longer term. Departmental secretaries are involved in many frank and sensitive exchanges of view, often leading to significant policy or administrative outcomes. The context in which those exchanges took place, and the relationships of trust that underpinned them, also need to be respected over time. In this context, I believe that senior public servants have an ongoing and particular responsibility. It is not a responsibility that prevents or should inhibit them, if they so wish, from systemic analyses of public administration and how it can be improved. It is, however, a responsibility that demands respect for the professional relationships of trust and confidence in which they were involved.

In my view, this ongoing responsibility of senior officials is of a different order to that applying to elected decision-makers and representatives. Those who are elected to public office campaign on a commitment to pursue particular policy

---

priorities; they work to implement them; and they are judged at the polls on their actions. Some choose, and are fully entitled, to provide their perspectives on deliberations that led to particular policy outcomes when they were in office. Senior officials have different entitlements and constraints in this respect because of the different roles and accountability that they have.

In this brief retrospective, therefore, the insights that I give into the role of being a departmental secretary do not lie in revealing confidences or the internal deliberations that led to particular outcomes. Nor do they lie in re-fighting old policy battles, or exhuming the bones of administrative actions long ago. They lie more in focusing on the broad challenges I encountered as secretary, the pillars of support I valued most in meeting those challenges, and the inherent strengths of the department I had the honour to lead. This focus also embraces some reflection on a number of important administrative matters which encompass the Australian Public Service generally, and the contours of which have changed significantly over recent years.

It was Robert Frost who wrote:

> 'Two roads diverged in a wood, and I –
> I took the one less traveled by,
> And that has made all the difference.'

I came to the position of Secretary of DFAT in January 2005 by a 'road less traveled'. That was not a deliberate choice with any particular destination in mind. It was a product of chance, circumstance and opportunity. Its route, staging posts and end point were anything but pre-determined. Unlike most secretaries of DFAT, I was not a career departmental officer. I brought to the position of secretary a different kind of background. It was one associated with the work of DFAT officers and with the issues on which they were focused. It was not one with as deep an immersion in the ways and structures of the department as most of my predecessors had experienced over a much longer period of time, but it was a background that reflected a different range of institutional perspectives on Australian foreign policy and its processes.

The background I brought to DFAT included broad experience on foreign policy, defence and national security issues as an officer of the Australian Public Service (in the Department of the Prime Minister and Cabinet), as a Policy Adviser in the Office of the Leader of the Opposition, as Secretary to the Cabinet (1996-2000) and as High Commissioner to the United Kingdom (2000-2005). This was a background that reflected a range of different involvements with foreign policy issues and relevant institutional architecture at official, parliamentary and executive levels. It also included the practical challenges of leading one of

Australia's largest diplomatic missions overseas (in the United Kingdom) during a period of significant international crisis generated, in particular, by the global reach of terrorist networks.

In the future, 'the road less traveled' of the kind that I followed may be a less uncommon route to positions of departmental leadership than what it has been in the past. That may well be the case because the next and subsequent generations of leaders in the Australian Public Service, together with their colleagues in the non-government sector, are likely to be more diverse in the breadth of their individual experiences, more determinedly mobile in their employment preferences, and skilled in a more adaptable way.

The skills needed to be an effective DFAT Secretary (or indeed an effective secretary in any other department) are not exclusively cultivated in DFAT, or in the APS more generally. The skills necessary include a genuine belief in, and practical commitment to upholding, the values of the APS. They require subject matter knowledge, judgment, policy vision, attention to administrative detail, decisiveness and integrity. Those skills also need to combine an institutional empathy with an embrace of change that will make the institution a more productive one. In particular, a DFAT Secretary needs to understand the department's distinctive evolution and to identify with the day-to-day challenges that its officers (and their families) face, particularly those relating to the diverse and demanding operating environments in which those officers are required to carry out their responsibilities. A DFAT Secretary needs to know the difference between traditions that give enduring institutional strength and those that entrench outdated thinking and inefficient practices. And he or she also needs to stand up for the department's interests and its record without rationalising its inadequacies and shortcomings in particular instances.

These skills and attributes of leading a department such as DFAT can certainly be developed within DFAT's own career structure. But that is neither necessarily nor always the case. Those skills and attributes *can* be developed and honed outside DFAT, and applied effectively within it. Although others will make their own judgments, my own experience at DFAT was that I never felt my background inhibited my capacity to carry out the responsibilities of the position. I felt welcomed in DFAT from my first day as Secretary, not least because of my involvement on foreign policy issues over a lengthy period, because of the working relationships I had developed with many DFAT senior officers, and because of the particular departmental connections I developed in my four-and-a-half years as High Commissioner in London. I also enjoyed a strong sense of support from, and professional camaraderie with, fellow secretaries in the APS and with senior officers of other agencies and departments. I certainly never felt any sense of being put – even implicitly – in a different category to others who had risen to positions of APS seniority in different ways and through different backgrounds.

A DFAT Secretary's role is one which brings him or her into constant contact and interaction with departmental officers (in Canberra and at overseas posts), with officers of the APS more generally, with ministers in the Australian government, officials from other countries as well as leaders in business and non-government organisations. Yet for all this interaction with others, there are responsibilities that a departmental secretary alone needs to assume. They include being ultimately accountable for overall organisational effectiveness and efficiency. At DFAT, that responsibility and accountability entailed final judgment calls on policy advice and implementation, on administrative arrangements and on decisions relating to career development of departmental officers. These responsibilities are some of the inevitable consequences of organisational leadership but they are no less demanding, consuming and sometimes lonely because of that.

For a Secretary of DFAT, these leadership responsibilities have some added complexities. In organisational terms, DFAT is relatively small in scale but it is complex in administrative and financial terms – operating, as it does, in many parts of the world, being subject to the laws of countries in which Australian diplomatic posts operate, employing a significant number of locally engaged staff in those countries, and being responsible for the Australia-based DFAT staff and their families who are deployed overseas.

In addition to its administrative and financial complexity, DFAT has policy responsibilities that engage diverse and critically important aspects of Australia's international interests and that include the provision of a range of services to the Australian community. Those services include the issuing of passports, the availability of consular assistance to Australians in difficulty overseas, and the responsibility for up-to-date advice to Australians travelling to particular countries.

Meeting these policy and management responsibilities provides ample scope for sleepless nights. But they also offer an extraordinary opportunity for service in the national interest as well as for personal and professional challenges of a uniquely demanding kind.

It is critically important that secretaries bring to the fulfilment of their responsibilities an understanding of departmental work cultures, policy challenges and management issues as well as an awareness of important APS-wide issues generally. But that understanding and awareness can be acquired in more ways than one. The true bedrock quality that a secretary needs to bring to his or her responsibilities is not an exclusively departmental or APS-focused career background but far more a deep, abiding and practical commitment to the values and purposes of the APS itself, and to the principles of public service more generally. Those principles include an apolitical responsiveness to the priorities and decisions of the elected government of the day.

In this context, as in most things, it is a balanced approach which is needed – and such an approach has clearly been adopted over time. To have a majority of 'external' appointments to senior APS positions of leadership would be as unrealistic and inappropriate as an internal APS 'closed shop'. The challenges that face public administration and public policy generally in Australia demand as broad a talent pool to draw on as possible, and that reality will only become reinforced over the period ahead.

In addressing the policy and administrative challenges I faced as Secretary of DFAT, there were three professional pillars of support that made a critical and positive difference.

The first lay in the Foreign and Trade ministers for whom I worked – Alexander Downer, Mark Vaile and Warren Truss (2005-2007) and Stephen Smith and Simon Crean (2007-2009). I valued the different but very productive professional interactions I had with each minister. I found them all, each in their different ways, constructively demanding of the department in terms of standards, policy rigour and administrative effectiveness. Though each operated in his own particular framework of policy priorities, I found all of them encouraging of new departmental thinking on foreign or trade policy issues that reached out well beyond those priorities. Obviously, not all of that new thinking progressed to the next stage of the policy development process but all of it received due ministerial consideration. The fact is that, like other policy advice, foreign and trade policy advice is highly contestable within government and beyond it. A secretary is wise to recognise that fact, to encourage departmental openness to and development of new thinking (lest such thinking become the preserve of others), and to have considered views on those elements of new thinking judged to be unwise or impractical as policy alternatives.

Where there were uncertainties or areas of imprecision, I felt I could raise such matters openly and frankly with portfolio ministers with a well-founded confidence of having them addressed directly, and clarified for the purposes of policy implementation by the department. From my perspective as Secretary of DFAT, the professional relationships that I enjoyed with each of the ministers for whom I worked were indispensable assets in the carrying out of my responsibilities. I valued that support greatly, knowing that such productive professional relationships are critical for the effective management of complex organisations.

In my role as DFAT Secretary, I found a second critical pillar of professional support in the quality and commitment of DFAT officers themselves. As a young officer in the Department of the Prime Minister and Cabinet in the early 1980s, I recall being very impressed (perhaps overly so) by a comment made by the department's then Secretary and one of Australia's truly great public servants, Sir Geoffrey Yeend, about prevailing stereotypes of his department, particularly 'its alleged struggle for supremacy in the economic or welfare or foreign policy field or somewhere else'. Sir Geoffrey wrote that officers in the department responded to such depictions with 'a tired smile'.

I often felt the same kind of response to stereotypes of DFAT over recent years. That is not to say that all criticisms of DFAT were based on misunderstandings. DFAT always had lessons to learn from particular experiences as well as from its own mistakes. It needed to remain committed to continuous improvement as an organisation, and not to defensive rationalisation of shortcomings where they existed.

One of the real challenges of leading an organisation like DFAT is to weigh carefully the criticisms made by others but also to distinguish those that identify genuine inadequacies from those that rely more on assumption and caricature than substance. In my view, for example, those who argued that DFAT had been forced to become consumed with process at the expense of substance, or that it was disproportionately focused on functional tasks to the neglect of immediate and longer term policy creativity, significantly misrepresented the department's activities. Such criticisms simply do not reflect the reality of the output that DFAT produces on a day-to-day basis: whether it be in terms of policy advice and policy-relevant reporting from posts to portfolio ministers, or responses to topical issues, or potential policy initiatives, or input to ministerial speeches, or briefings for important meetings, or draft cabinet submissions, or comments on other cabinet business brought forward by other ministers.

The functional workload for DFAT is significant and important. Meeting those responsibilities did not require the department to abandon or seriously degrade its other policy-related roles. The fact is that the stereotype of a DFAT narrowly focused on limited functional activities does not reflect in a realistic way the full range of what DFAT actually does. This is particularly the case in relation to DFAT's reporting to its ministers on the implications of the forces of change affecting Australia's international interests, particularly the changing power relativities among states, the challenges and opportunities of economic globalisation, the constraints of sovereign decision-making, the limits of multilateralism, the changing dynamics of bilateral, regional and global diplomacy, but also many other issues. To claim that DFAT's functional responsibilities had somehow become a substitute for these wider policy-related responsibilities would be both inaccurate and ill-informed.

Some of the stereotypes to which I refer had their roots less in the reality of what DFAT officers actually did and more in the perceived implications of DFAT's relative decline in budgetary resourcing – relative both to some other Commonwealth agencies and to benchmark countries internationally. The claim that, with additional resources, DFAT could do more in more parts of the world was plainly true. The real issue, however, lay more in how such additional resourcing could be accommodated within the Commonwealth's overall fiscal framework, and how it would add net value to achieving progress on the government's foreign and trade policy priorities. What was plainly not true, in my view, was the claim that, with prevailing levels of financial resourcing, DFAT could not effectively carry out its responsibilities. Prioritising certainly became more important. Pressures on particular departmental areas did need to be carefully managed. The limits of departmental capacities did need to be explained, including at times to ministers. But the claim that existing resource allocation prevented DFAT from carrying out its responsibilities effectively was not, in my view, a sustainable one on the evidence of what the department was actually producing for the government (not all of which was publicly accessible).

I have never subscribed to the view that Australia has experienced a lost 'golden age' of public service. Public administration faces many very different challenges to a generation ago. It is addressing them in often very different, and certainly less hierarchical, ways. But in my view it is doing so no less effectively.

Similarly, I do not subscribe to the view that DFAT has witnessed the demise of its own 'golden age'. Perspectives on the past can become very selective, idealising it beyond the facts and sometimes beyond recognition. Diplomacy in the past served Australia's national interests with high professionalism and great effectiveness. But it operated in a very different environment to current realities – different in terms of public accountability as well as contestability within and outside government. The Australian diplomacy of the past operated in a context in which foreign policy and domestic policy were more starkly demarcated than they are today, and in which foreign policy was far more compartmentalised within government advisory and decision-making structures. The interests of Australian foreign policy were generally more precisely identified and more narrowly pursued. Community expectations of Australian diplomacy were, in general, judged by less precise, demanding and informed standards than they are today. The involvement of non-government organisations was less apparent. Media coverage was less intense and questioning. The Australian Public Service generally, and Australian diplomacy in particular, operated in more labour-intensive ways. They also operated in a world in which international news coverage was narrower and in which access to international communications was far less easily accessible for most Australians.

These and other factors make comparisons between the character and operations of Australian diplomacy in different eras complex, and sometimes misleading. In relation to skills, for example, modern Australian diplomats are, in my view, certainly no less impressive than they were in the past; their commitment is no less resolute; and their effectiveness is no less significant.

There have been claims made over recent years that DFAT officers, and the APS generally, are more compliant with ministerial perspectives than they were in the past, and less prepared to present contrary views. I've always thought such claims to be hollow. Certainly in my time as DFAT Secretary, I did not encounter a reluctance to convey views candidly to ministers. I cannot make personal comparisons with departmental practice from 20 or 30 years ago because I do not have personal experience of such practices. But on the basis of the accounts of others and my own knowledge of contemporary practices, I do not believe that a massive backsliding from fearless policy advice to a culture of compliance is, in any way, an accurate description of DFAT's evolution.

The calibre, attributes and high professionalism of DFAT officers – whether in Canberra, around Australia or at posts overseas – are vital assets in advancing Australia's national interests. They embodied a capacity that I constantly valued and relied on, and without which I could not have begun to fulfil my responsibilities as Secretary.

A third vital pillar of professional support in the carrying out of my responsibilities as DFAT Secretary was the practical sense of belonging to a wider APS network. This was a great source of advice, comparison and professional support. I derived real benefit not only from 'bilateral' interaction with senior officers in other departments but from the 'multilateral' discussions at leadership levels that also took place on the challenges that the APS faced – short and long term – and how the future of the APS needed to adapt in order to respond to those challenges.

This kind of interaction with senior APS officers covered a wide spectrum of issues. It provided a useful point of reference in benchmarking DFAT's performance and planning. It generated real insights into important aspects of public policy development and the quality of public administration. It facilitated much valued networks of wise counsel, sound advice and insights from long experience. This was the important broader context of co-operative and collaborative APS leadership in which the focus on some familiar particular issues needs to be set.

For almost two decades, contract employment for secretaries has been a focus of debate, not least among secretaries themselves and those aspiring to such leadership positions. During my period as DFAT Secretary, my sense was that the intensity of this debate was diminishing, that the prospects of a return to 'permanence' for secretaries were (quite accurately) seen as negligible, and that it was the terms of contract employment, and not the issue of its appropriateness, that focused attention.

Performance pay for secretaries, and for the wider APS, was also a point of contention for some. I respected and understood their views, but differed in important respects from them. Performance pay, in my view, has never fulfilled the best hopes of its champions or the worst fears of its detractors. It is not some brooding presence that shapes professional responses on a daily basis. I strongly believe that secretaries make calls on the basis of their knowledge, judgment and integrity, and not the prospects for their performance pay. Their departmental role is reviewed in a performance pay framework but that framework does not shape the decisions that secretaries make on a day-to-day basis, nor the ministerial advice they give. That was certainly my personal experience in my time as DFAT Secretary, and how I saw others approach their responsibilities. By the time in their careers when individuals become Secretaries, they are prepared to back their own professional instincts, experience and values as they are applied to contemporary challenges. And they are also prepared to accept the consequences of their actions taken in that context. I share Peter Shergold's view that the provision of frank and sometimes unwelcome advice by secretaries to ministers is a question of character, not of contract.

The issue of performance pay in the Australian Public Service more broadly (which goes back over 20 years) is a complex one. There are many variations in its application across departments and agencies, and there is ongoing debate about its consequences for organisational coherence and effectiveness. There are many ways other than performance pay to provide APS officers with career advancement, or teams within departments and agencies working on particular issues with special recognition. In my view, these mechanisms and incentives other than performance pay are going to have increasing attraction in the period ahead.

The progression from 'turf wars' and sectional bureaucratic interests to greater collegiality focused on whole-of-government priorities has been the defining characteristic of change in the Australian Public Service over recent times. DFAT has been deeply involved in that process, as other agencies and departments have developed their own international priorities, linkages and presence, and as many of the old barriers between domestic and foreign policy have broken down. In this evolution, a next phase for DFAT (and for a range of other departments and agencies) is the development of a national security community, and the new linkages, interaction, coordination and collaborative leadership that it will encourage. This development will entail significant institutional change. Knowing the calibre of DFAT as an organisation as well as the attributes and adaptability of its officers, I have no doubt that it will meet those challenges and opportunities to the advantage of Australia's national interests.

14. There's a telegram for you — fashioning Australia's unique model of public administration[1]

Ken Matthews

After graduating from the University of Sydney (BEc) in 1974, Ken Matthews embarked on his career in public service with the Department of Defence in 1975. There he stayed for eight years before transferring to the Department of Industry, Technology and Commerce in 1983, where he was responsible for advice on manufacturing industry policy and technology policy. He next joined the Department of Primary Industries before in 1997 heading the Wik Task Force in the Department of the Prime Minister and Cabinet, providing advice to the Prime Minister on Native Title. The next year Matthews was appointed Secretary of the Department of Agriculture, Fisheries and Forestry, and in 1999, Secretary of the Department of Transport and Regional Services, a position he held until 2004. From 2005 until his retirement in 2010, Ken Matthews served as the Chair, Chief Executive Officer, and one of the seven government-appointed commissioners of the National Water Commission.

In January 1975 my wife Margaret and I stepped off a plane after backpacking around Europe in the months since we finished university the year before. We were handed two telegrams (they still had telegrams then). The first offered Margaret a job as a teacher in Hoxton Park in the western suburbs of Sydney. The second offered me a job with the Department of Defence in the Australian Public Service in Canberra.

Frankly, I could not remember having applied for a job with the Department of Defence. Indeed I had spent the last few years at university 'railing against the machine' and protesting against what *Rolling Stone* magazine called the 'military-industrial complex'. To this day I suspect there had been a mix-up in the Defence recruitment mail room. My fit with Defence was, on the face of it, so poor that one of my startled friends asked which side I would be fighting for.

Margaret and I discussed our telegrams for all of fifteen minutes before we decided to give Canberra and the Australian Public Service a go – at least for a while. There was about that much science to it. The rest is history.

---

1   This speech was delivered in October 2010 at a formal function hosted by the Australian Public Service Commission.

So it was we went to Canberra and I went – sceptically – to work at the Department of Defence. But I was quickly struck and swept up by an ethos I just had not been expecting but which I found enormously stimulating. Defence turned out to be an organisation with a set of public service values and ethics handed down through generations of fine public servants. Here was an organisation whose vision was truly national. Here was an organisation that had to make hard calls, an organisation that managed billions of dollars, millions of assets and tens of thousands of people. Here were issues that were in a very real sense about the destiny of our nation. Here for the first time in my life I encountered an organisation which insisted on intellectual, analytical and systematic rigour. And here was an organisation which was actively searching out the best and the brightest new young staff. They also took me.

What followed for the next 36 years was the privilege of being involved in six portfolios – Defence; Industry, Science and Technology; Primary Industries, including agriculture; Prime Minister's (for Indigenous issues and some years later, back again for water); Transport and Regional Services; and Environment (for water again).

I have served the governments of seven prime ministers, and have been lucky enough to form powerful working relationships, and sometimes firm friendships, with ministers on both sides without any of them ever knowing my own political leanings. Indeed, throughout my career in public service I have kept this a closely-guarded secret, something which I believe has benefitted my relationships with ministers. I have also been fortunate enough to serve, at secretary or statutory chair level, six portfolio ministers and countless junior ministers and parliamentary secretaries. Plus of course, many more at levels before I became CEO.

I have been privileged to have been involved in some of the great public policy issues of Australia's last 36 years – tariff reform, reform of the car industry, the collapse of the former Soviet Union, development from a zero base of the biotechnology industry, mining impacts on the environment including mining at Coronation Hill, ecologically sustainable development, September 11 and counter-terrorism, native title and Indigenous disadvantage, how best to deliver our multi-billion dollar infrastructure program, the second Sydney airport, reform of our agricultural industries, science and technology policy, national energy policy, natural disasters preparedness, water policy, regional development and regional disadvantage, and trade policy – among many others.

Claiming to have been involved in trade policy is a slight exaggeration. I include it only because once when I was in China I was more or less pushed into a room by the Australian Embassy to informally spruik to a key Chinese vice Minister for Trade what was then a breathtakingly bold idea of a Chinese bilateral trade agreement with Australia. I suspect a visiting Transport Secretary was seen as sufficiently senior – but at the same time sufficiently remote from DFAT – to fly the kite without causing diplomatic embarrassment if the Chinese turned us down. To our delight the vice minister showed immediate interest, and although the wheels have since turned slowly, this trillion dollar idea is coming to pass and all Australians will one day benefit in a big way.

But my main point about this long list of terrifically interesting public policy issues is that I have indeed been fortunate, probably privileged. I have sometimes said to new recruits to the Australian Public Service that had they joined instead for example a medium sized manufacturing firm in Sydney, the most strategic decision they could hope to take – if they worked their way right up the greasy pole over many years – would be to decide whether to establish the new factory in Wollongong or Geelong. But by joining the APS, new recruits are almost immediately exposed to public policy choices which are worth billions of dollars and which influence the daily lives of millions of Australians. First year recruits will often see 'their' issues on the evening television news; public policy and the APS can be big picture, stimulating stuff. Stuff that matters.

I have been fortunate enough to lead and manage as CEO, organisations as large as 3000 and as intimate as 50. As I have moved through them, I have had the opportunity to experience the full spectrum of public administration work: intelligence and research, policy development, administration, regulation, program management, people management, organisational leadership, intergovernmental negotiations, assessment, audit and evaluation, and even a modest public advocacy role in the work the National Water Commission does to press the case for water reform.

Regional Australia

But rich though that diet was, partly because of my background as a boy from the bush I never lost my personal interest in policy issues as they impact on rural, regional and remote Australia and the people who live there. It is no secret I grew up on a farm. I still know a Jersey cow from a Guernsey, I can still ride a horse and I attended a regional high school. I could even probably still milk a cow – if paid enough. I learned to debate in a rural youth club, I have seen country towns rise and fall, commodity cycles turn and turn again, and droughts come and go. When I married Margaret I inherited a lifetime of free advice from her extended family about what needs to be done by the government for regional Australia. And with the benefit of that advice stiffening my back after many a long weekend, I have continually been dispatched back to Canberra with renewed insight and resolve.

Thus having worked on issues in agriculture, mining, environment, natural resources management, water, regional services, and regional infrastructure, regional Australia has been something of a unifying theme for my career. In fact as I stand here tonight and the drought is breaking, commodity prices and the terms of trade are at historic highs, both major parties are committed to dealing with our shameful Indigenous disadvantage (usually regional and remote Indigenous disadvantage), and we have a new government brimming with commitment to regional Australians, it is clear that I can with a clear conscience pack up, retire and say to myself, 'Job done. I can go now'.

I wish that were really so. A serious message I wish to discuss here is that regional Australia is a much bigger policy and delivery challenge for the Australian Public Service than most public servants so far realise. We joke that Sydney differs from Melbourne, but compared to metropolitan Australia, our regions have so much more variation and usually, so much less resilience. When a job is lost or an industry folds in a regional community, the options are much more limited than in the cities and the human and community consequences greater.

The challenge for public administrators is therefore more than simply to introduce one parallel 'regional' policy to complement our traditional metropolitan-oriented policies. Many of our policies and programs will have to be comprehensively regionalised and localised – to multiple regions and localities. How well equipped is the APS to understand multiple regional perspectives when we have grown up with a much more homogeneous metropolitan world view? How will the public service gain an accurate understanding of the needs, aspirations and opportunities of the many different regions of Australia? In my view it would be weak to rely only on parliamentarians and ministers to tell us what we should know. They may have their ears to the ground, but we will need our own channels too, into, and out of, Australia's regions. We do not have them today.

I also ask myself whether we will be able to adjust our usual analytical tools to accommodate regional policy requirements. I ask that because one of the policy achievements of which I am proudest is the progress we made during my time in the Department of Transport when we introduced a national transport infrastructure planning process – then known as AusLink but since carried forward under other labels. I am proud of it because it introduced some well overdue simple principles to infrastructure decisions – principles such as an insistence on cost-benefit analyses before transport investment decisions, mandatory comparison of alternatives before decisions, and the development of longer-term strategies before decisions about individual infrastructure projects.

These principles have not always been observed by governments since, but they were, and are, good principles. Yes, we still have a way to go, but our AusLink white paper – which was an initiative of the APS – began the inexorable movement away from decades of using infrastructure as shameless election bait and towards strategically planned, benefit/costed investments in the economy and society.

But how well these same principles work for regional Australia may be another question. For example in most cases, a dollar spent on a metropolitan ring road carrying tens of thousands of cars a day will be found to be a dollar better spent than on a lonely country road. In the future, the APS will need more sophisticated project selection methodologies to capture the non-monetary, community and externality values of the rural road. There is more to this than just political judgment by ministers.

What else might the APS expect in our 'new paradigm' of priority for regional Australia? Like metropolitan Australians, regional Australians over the next decade will be looking for more accessible agencies – on the screen, on the phone and in the home. Like metropolitan Australians they will increasingly expect more timely services and correspondence. Time frames for email are obviously different from 200 years of snail mail and the public service cannot afford to be the last national institution to be responding in snail mail time frames. Like metropolitan Australians, regional Australians will expect more personalised and tailored public services. They will want to know by name their contact officers in the APS and will be impatient with agencies' constant re-organisations and staff changes. They will also be impatient with apparently artificial functional separations between different agencies, and for that matter, different levels of government. Governments will have to organise themselves to be more unified externally and to 'keep the spaghetti behind the counter'.

However, unlike metropolitan Australians, regional Australians will more than ever be expecting government services to be localised and spatially delivered. They will want their services to be tuned to their particular communities and their regions. On the one hand they will expect to be able to participate in decisions about their regions. On the other they will sometimes startle the city-based Australian Public Service by exhibiting consultation fatigue (because so often in smaller communities it is the same people who must front all the consultation processes). They will be looking for governance arrangements that maximise decision making and accountability in the local area – where they are comfortable – not back in Canberra where we are comfortable.

The APS will also need to be ready for a certain amount of pent-up frustration in regional communities. I detect parallels between the situation today and in the years leading up to the emergence of the One Nation Party in the 1990s. I was at that time working for a National Party minister. The rising tide of anger in regional Australia had not yet been recognised by the commentariat outside regional Australia but every time I dealt with regional people or opened regional newspapers (and you must do both every day in the Department of Agriculture!) the language was stronger, the temperature higher and the alienation more evident. I became increasingly alarmed but could not persuade others that there was a real issue emerging.

In the end, I clipped fifty angry headlines from regional and local newspapers. I took the clippings and sat with my minister for an hour and talked him through them. Later that week he launched a political response to what was essentially a rural revolt – just in time to meet One Nation head-on. To his great credit, and this would have been hard for a National Party minister, the minister publicly acknowledged his senior bureaucrat's early policy warning when we moved to different portfolios years later.

Other public administration suggestions

Beyond regional issues, there are some other public administrative suggestions I can now luxuriate in inflicting on the public on the eve of my retirement. I shall articulate them as questions I suspect many public servants have already asked themselves in the honest hours of the night.

Firstly, is it inevitable that the APS must forever be in a state of structural and staffing change? Must there perpetually be a new face every time a client or stakeholder rings? We know it drives our stakeholders mad. We know it introduces management risk. We know it adds confusion, costs and time. We know it makes the service look inexperienced and shallow. We know these things, but we seem to accept restructurings and personnel changes as unavoidable features of the public service. We grumble to each other that just when our staff get good at their job they are promoted to start at the bottom of the curve all over again. But we keep doing it to ourselves. We know – as APS insiders ourselves – that this churn has high hidden costs. There are things that can be done: promotions in place; abolition of duty statements and functional statements; mandatory cost-benefit testing of restructurings; and so on. I wonder whether as a professional service we cannot do better than we are.

Secondly, do our recruitment and promotion processes always justify the investment? How often do these complex, time-consuming and resource-hungry selection processes actually lead to a different outcome? They can, but how often is the process more to boiler plate against objections by documenting mechanical process, rather than focusing on results – that is, the selection of the best person for the job? When we know the right answer from the outset, why do we not more often put our own name on the line and make ourselves accountable for the merits of our staff selections rather than the detail of the processes we followed?

Thirdly, and here is one to provoke my colleagues from Treasury and Finance, why do we continue to encourage governments to load so much into the annual budget process? Yes, it enables tradeoffs, and yes it facilitates macroeconomic management and parliamentary process. But it seems to me to have a high cost in terms of foregone political and policy opportunities. Policy initiatives well worth a front page spread in their own right find themselves on page six of a very congested budget supplement and sinking without trace by the following week. Worthy, but not critical spending measures can be seriously delayed because they are forced into a 'one shot a year' budget cycle. I suspect impact could be enhanced, quality improved, government timeliness and responsiveness restored, and pre-budget chaos reduced if clusters of related policies were to be routinely developed and announced at different scheduled times through the year.

Fourthly, have we developed internal probity and fraud control processes out of proportion to the objective need? Internal APS-specific probity and fraud processes are costly, constraining, time-consuming and frustrating for all involved. I wonder whether we should not be placing more reliance on generally available legal processes to deal with the very small number of crooks. Our processes are too often designed as though crime, corruption and unethical behaviour were endemic to the APS. They are not. Indeed, for me one of the inspiring features of the APS has always been the deeply embedded ethics, values and principles of the organisation's culture. In a way, so extraordinary was Godwin Grech that he was the exception that proved the rule. The most powerful way to avoid a repeat of this unfortunate chapter will never be internal processes. Rather, it will always be cultural clarity about just what is acceptable and expected around here – messages sent by an organisation's leaders.

And finally on this long list of self indulgent free advice, I wish to propose a more strategic question: are we becoming a 'docile and unassertive' service. Like a frog in boiling water, have we been imperceptibly persuaded to think of the APS not as the great national institution it is in its own right, but simplistically and solely as the instrument of the government of the day? Of course, we are the instrument of the government of the day, a fact I have spent many hours explaining to my staff over the years. Individual public servants cannot all independently pursue our own personal notions of the public interest. That is why Australians elect their representatives. Public servants propose; ministers dispose.

But I acknowledge that while the APS is the instrument of the government, it is also much more than this. In my view we need to find a better point of balance between accountability to ministers and responsibility more broadly. For example we do have a responsibility to keep pointing out uncomfortable truths even after the government has made its call. We do sometimes know facts and have access to analyses not easily available to the public or its elected representatives. We do have the history.

It follows that we have a responsibility to argue forthrightly when politics is compromising good outcomes. I bet most public servants can think of instances where the decisions of the properly elected government were clearly and objectively not in the national interest. If we are serious as professional servants of the public it is a cop-out just to shrug and snigger knowingly and say that the elected government decides what is in the national interest. Yes, the public service is an instrument of the government of the day, but it is not mindless. Backing up and speaking up can be uncomfortable but we have a responsibility to keep doing it.

Have we become docile and unassertive in the way we put – or more accurately, fail to put – our biggest-picture national strategic views to incoming ministers? Are we (at least our line departments) waiting too long for political parties' policy announcements and then weighting them too heavily in their incoming ministers' briefs? By all means we should shape the colour and texture of our advice to the goals, directions and style of the government of the day. But it is too easy to merely build a line department's portfolio policy agenda only to the blueprint of an election platform often produced in a rush by political parties with much less depth than the APS – and much more constrained by the sensitivities of a political campaign. We can do more and better than that.

Have we become docile and unassertive in giving up when our advice once given is rejected? There was once a saying that advice given three times is courageous. There are several ways of running genuinely good ideas back into the system after a knock-back. Talented, creative, process-smart public servants can and should do that. Have we become docile and unassertive in our dealings with ministerial staffers? Despite the newish guidelines for ministerial staffers I still see many middle-ranking public servants bending unthinkingly to 'the office' mistaking these meretricious cameo-players for the minister. They are not.

Have we become docile and unassertive in Senate Estimates hearings? There is nothing wrong with being assertive in an Estimates Committee hearing; you are not a victim, nor on trial. In a sense an Estimates hearing is nothing more than one set of public officials questioning another. A public servant must be accurate and honest of course but there is nothing wrong with showing a bit of spine when required. Indeed my own view is that one reason the most senior APS people should be present at Estimates hearings is to provide air cover if a more junior colleague begins to struggle under fire.

Have we become docile and unassertive in media and academic debate? When we hear inaccuracies or downright lies on current affairs radio over breakfast should we not be getting the facts out there? I also think we have a responsibility to be more active on the conference circuit, including alongside academics. Yes, we need to be mindful of the public profiles of our ministers, and yes we need to avoid partisan issues, but there is a lot our great APS institution can say that can be constructive and will advance the public debate. We do have a choice: we can sit back and complain about the standard of public policy debate or we can do something ourselves to improve it. To clarify what is legitimate in public comment perhaps we need a 'new deal' with our ministerial executive, parliamentary committees and accountability bodies such as the Australian National Audit Office.

Further, our top executives have a special role in the public debate. For example, although it has been contentious, I applaud my colleague Ken Henry's persistence in his regular public economic and reform contributions. These are respected, needed and heeded. Given the caning he has sometimes received, Ken might have given up long ago. But to his great credit, he has not.

Have we become docile and unassertive in speaking up for the APS itself? This obviously does not apply to Terry Moran, who spoke up for the APS after the (admittedly awful) insulation affair. But the prevailing wisdom in the media and the parliament is that the Commonwealth as a whole (the APS) cannot manage programs. Yes, the program management failures have been substantial and damaging to our professional reputation. But it is a shallow, intellectually indefensible conclusion to say that the feds should therefore be out of program management in all portfolios and for the indefinite future. An assertive APS would be saying so; for my part, that is exactly what I am saying here today.

On a more positive note for the APS, let me switch, in a schadenfreude kind of way to a story about the very popular institution of the Senates Estimates Committee. On one occasion, immediately following the collapse of Ansett Airlines, I was called as the sole witness to a Senate inquiry on the last day before parliament recessed – for an election I think. The opposition, the media and indeed most of the nation was outraged that Ansett had collapsed and were baying for blood. It was known that I had been up to my neck in the last weeks of work to manage the collapse. (Our departmental view was that it was a painful event but that the tide could not and should not have been resisted.) The smell of blood was in the air and I was dreading the hearings. Despite my hours of swotting overnight I knew that only misery could come from the day.

When I arrived my heart sank even further to see approximately twenty journalists including several TV cameras milling around excitedly to see and record the bloodletting. For once the senators seriously outnumbered the (single) public servant. It was clear that whatever I said would be national news and worse, would likely be taken up in Question Time later that day.

Well, I am pleased to report that despite some punishing questions, I was so painstakingly precise and detailed in my answers; so pedantically accurate, boring, dull, lengthy and comprehensively non-telegenic that I had the inward satisfaction of watching the disappointed media steadily drift away over the next hour, well before the questions got anywhere near anything dangerous. When the inquiry had finished, my minister's chief of staff, probably having roused himself from a deep Ken Matthews-induced sleep, rang to congratulate me. I have always considered it my modest little triumph of the dead bat over the fast bowlers.

'Ausminster' — Australia's Westminster system

Consider now how the Australian Public Service interacts with the nation's parliamentary system. The Australian system of government is often referred to as the 'Westminster system.' The APS is not a pure Westminster system; nor is it, as is sometimes claimed, a 'Washminster' hybrid. It is already uniquely Australian — I sometimes refer to it as the 'Ausminster' system. The uniquely Australian features of Australian government administration which have evolved over time derive from many sources. These include the differences in the Australian Constitution from other countries' foundation documents. Legal case law has evolved in characteristically Australian directions. Parliamentary processes have evolved to meet uniquely Australian political and administrative needs. Uniquely Australian public administration institutions and processes have evolved. There is certainly a uniquely Australian 'culture' in the APS.

In my view we should be very proud of our uniquely Australian model of public administration. For me the fact that it has evolved far from its Westminster origins is thoroughly positive. It captures the dual ideas of the APS as a great, continuing national institution — but one which at the same time is responsive and ready to change — that is, a willingness to continue to adapt to Australian circumstances and national needs. Here in Canberra we should never forget that there is no special community respect for the centuries-old Westminster model. The Australian community wants a model that works for them in their current circumstances. We should be applauding not apologising for the progressive departures over the years from old models originating in old countries, and assertively affirming the resulting strengths of the younger, tailored Australian model of public administration.

And that model will and should continue to change. The case for necessary further public administration reform can be built around the uniquely Australian policy challenges ahead. The strength of Ausminster is its fluidity and capacity to continue to adapt to Australia's own

future. We have moved sufficiently close to our own Ausminster model I think it is time to stop using the Westminster misnomer.

The Australian Public Service

Clearly, I am a fan of the APS. However it is no secret that at least outside Canberra, not everyone is. Public servants seem to spend too much of their time apologising. It was partly for those reasons that when I was the president of the Institute of Public Administration in the ACT over the period including 2001 we decided to make a concerted effort to improve the self image, and the public image, of the Australian Public Service. The year 2001 was of course the centenary of federation and therefore the centenary of the Australian Public Service. At the Institute of Public Administration Australia we decided to go for broke and organise an unapologetic celebration. After all, no-one else was likely to organise one for us.

To celebrate this occasion, we held what was then the largest ever dinner in the Great Hall of Parliament House. We saluted past and present public servants, including representative middle and junior level public servants invited along for the night. The [then] Governor General [Sir William Deane] himself immortalised the public servants of 2001 in a centenary plaque which you can find outside the administrative building. There were many other agency-specific events organised. For example, Defence built a monument to intelligence officers past and present – an anonymous group of public servants never before publicly acknowledged. We even startled the tourist visitors to Canberra by having APS centenary flags flying along Commonwealth Avenue for the week as though we were a visiting football team. It was a fun week but with a serious message. We were acknowledging 100 years of public service by the Australian Public Service. And not before time.

Canberra

I wanted to say a word or two about Canberra. Though many of our public servants are not Canberra-based, Canberra is clearly the home of the APS. Canberra gets bad press. It is said to be out of touch, theoretical, unrealistic and elitist. Visitors, we are told, get lost in Canberra in many senses. They say that Canberra goes in circles; is a waste of a perfectly good sheep station; the best thing about Canberra is that there are good roads out of it; it is only three hours from Sydney and two hours from the coast; and so on. But Canberra to me is a critical part of the aforementioned unique Ausminster model. Canberra's business is government. No dinner party happens without a spirited exchange about public policy. Ideas move in and around the city much more easily than they would if our national capital were a five million person diversified urban giant.

Australia may be a big continent, but it is a small nation governed from a small city. For that reason it is much more governable than for example the United States or Europe. From my own experience, when I have issues that need to be resolved – I almost always know the people involved – either in Canberra or in the state governments. Consequently, I can pick up the phone and if not resolve the issue then and there, at least have the opportunity to do so. But managing issues in that way is much less feasible in the US or Europe and would certainly be much less so without our Canberra. Government business works when the business of government is the business of the whole town.

Having said that, Canberra has come a long way even in the time Margaret and I have been here. Canberrans support – almost insist on – fantastic art, cultural and recreational opportunities, Australia's best educational standards, world class science and brain-based enterprises, flagship national institutions such as The Australian National University, the national collections and a burgeoning services sector based on consultancies (which are often themselves spawned from people and ideas from the national government). Canberra is a stimulating top-end intellectual environment. Canberra and the APS feed off each other and long may it continue.

The National Water Commission

My most recent appointment has been as Chair and CEO of the National Water Commission. I approached then Prime Minister Howard requesting that appointment after two successive appointments as portfolio secretary. I well remember David Borthwick, then Deputy Secretary of the Department of the Prime Minister and Cabinet, being incredulous that a secretary would do such a thing – ask to move to a non-secretary role. He did not understand at all. I equally well remember David confiding in me years later that he was about to pull the plug on his own appointment as Secretary of the Department of the Environment, Water, Heritage and the Arts. I reminded him of our earlier conversation; he understood well by then.

My six years with the National Water Commission have been among my most rewarding of all my years in the APS. The Commission is a unique creature in public administration. It is an independent statutory body formed for the express purpose of criticising the federal and state governments that created it. It exists to blow the whistle if the water reforms to which all Australian governments have committed are not delivered. Unusually, it has a public and media advocacy role – a role I have exercised with discretion and, I hope, judgment.

The Commission is at once a critic, as well as a player on the water reform stage. It provides not only policy advice, but also manages programs, initiates action and facilitates cooperation among water reform players. It comprises commissioners nominated by the states and others nominated by the Commonwealth. In a conspicuous breach of good governance principles, it produces a public report card on the achievements of the very minister to whom it reports. ('Talks a lot in and out of school. Could do better'.) It is definitely a bold experiment in the design of public institutions.

I am enormously proud of what the Commission has done. But I am more proud of how it has done it. The Commission has been scrupulously principled from the outset. It has criticised, yes, but always with careful attention to the evidence. It has been decent in its dealings with officials from the states and territories but has always told it like it is. It has worked hard and systematically on its stakeholder relationships. To this day it enjoys warm support from dark green environmental groups, red-necked industry groups, uber-rational science groups and soft, people-focussed community groups. It prides itself on its integrity.

Around the Commission table itself some of the commissioners have quite literally forgotten whether they were originally nominated by the states or the Commonwealth. They act, as required by their Act, in the best interests of the Commission, not their antecedents.

The National Water Commission is in some senses a mirror of my APS career. The APS values and ethos that so attracted me all those years ago when I followed my telegram to Defence permeate the Commission. It works on a vital national issue and is prepared to tell truths when they need to be told. The work of Commission staff has a hard edge: they insist on logic, rationality and evidence. But there is also a softer team culture of decency, affection for each other and respect, including respect for the many different water stakeholders. The commissioners, who run the place, are unfailingly decent in their dealings with the staff, who do the running. That sort of culture attracts able people. It attracts people who take ethics, values and decent behaviour seriously.

It has been a privilege to serve alongside such principled people for thirty-six years. It says something about the APS culture that so many public servants have attended this valedictory lecture despite the fact I am sure they have many more important tasks to address. But somehow, given the Australian Public Service collegiate culture we share and which we will pass on, I am not surprised.

15. The opportunities, challenges and policy responses for the Australian economy[1]

Ken Henry

Perhaps the highest-profile Australian public servant of his generation, Ken Henry was appointed Treasury Secretary in 2001 after a diverse career which had included teaching economics at the University of Canterbury (New Zealand), advising former Labor Treasurer Paul Keating and serving as Minister (Economic and Financial Affairs) in the Australian delegation to the OECD in Paris. During a decorated career in Treasury, Henry was closely involved in tax policy advice to the Hawke/ Keating governments in the 1980s/early 1990s and the Howard government's GST in the late 1990s. In 2008 he headed Australia's Future Tax System Review Panel, charged with examining all aspects of the Australian tax system with a view to reform. He retired from the Treasury after 10 years as Secretary in early 2011. He remains an adviser to the Prime Minister.

In 1930 the legendary Tasmanian economist Lyndhurst Falkiner Giblin (1872-1951) wrote a series of articles in *The Melbourne Herald* called *Letters to John Smith*. These letters attracted widespread attention, becoming influential in developing a broad understanding of the challenges facing Australia during the Great Depression. In a series of ten letters, Giblin explained, in simple language, the economic issues facing Australia at the start of the Depression and described a pathway by which the country could find its way back to prosperity.

In Giblin's honour I will attempt in this valedictory to outline some of the challenges facing the Australian economy today and make some remarks on our pathway to future prosperity. At a time of extraordinary upheaval for Australian society, when the fears of mass unemployment, inflation and economic instability gripped the world, Giblin's ability to explain economic issues clearly and simply proved to be of immense value.

Today we are again going through a period of unusual upheaval in the global economy: a historic transition in economic power from West to East that, having been in progress for a couple of decades, then accelerated abruptly in 2007-08 with the onset of what we call a global financial crisis; a crisis that, more

---

1 Dr Henry chose to make this lecture his valedictory address upon his retirement in March 2011 in lieu of an APSC-hosted event. This is an edited version of that speech, the 2011 Giblin Lecture, presented at the University of Tasmania.

accurately, would have been labelled a 'Western financial crisis'. That crisis hasn't played out fully as yet; many globally significant financial institutions remain weak and heavily reliant on government support arrangements. And questions are now being asked about the sustainability in several Western countries, not only of those government financed support arrangements, but of government finance itself.

So I'd like to take this opportunity to take a look at the nature of the economic transformation occurring in Australia in Giblin's time, and consider the relevance of the lessons learned then for us today, in another period of economic transformation.

A perspective on Giblin's Australia

It is impossible to do justice, in this short chapter, to the mammoth topic of Australia's economic evolution during Giblin's lifetime. What follows is a rough sketch.

Economic advancement – the rise of manufacturing

The three decades prior to the Great Depression that hit Australia from 1929 set the scene for Australia's economic development through the rest of the 20th century. Despite the interruption, forced adjustments and price instability caused by the Great War, Australia experienced steady population growth; the uptake of new technologies in areas such as automotive engineering and heavy industry; and increasing openness to foreign investment.

Buoyed by those currents, the manufacturing sector was destined to become one of the most significant performers in the Australian economy in the 20th century. It had been one of the major beneficiaries of the dismantling of interstate tariffs at federation. Employment in manufacturing expanded rapidly – almost doubling in the first decade of federation, rising from around 190,000 to 361,000 people by 1910-11 – accounting for more than 20 per cent of total employment. The dominant categories of manufacturing during this time included the processing of clothing and textiles, metal, wood, food and drink, and agricultural products.

In the two decades that followed, however (that is the 'teens' and the 1920s), manufacturing only broadly held its share of total employment, despite a number of factors that might have been expected to assist it. These factors included:

- the industrial requirements of war;
- isolation from foreign competition afforded by the war;

- heavy tariffs being imposed to nurture and protect an emerging diversity of domestic manufactures;
- improvements in technology and economic infrastructure; and
- the establishment of large automotive plants to meet a burgeoning demand for motor vehicles.

While statistics about production for the early periods of Australia's history should be read with caution, estimates of manufacturing's share of domestic output in those decades would suggest a broadly similar story to that told by the employment numbers. While manufacturing as a share of GDP doubled between 1866 (six years before Giblin was born) and 1910, it only broadly held its share over the period between 1925 and 1930. What was going on?

Economic advancement – moving to 'newer' more advanced manufacturing activities

Drilling down into manufacturing industry detail yields some useful insights. What was happening within the manufacturing sector was part of a longer-term trend – a 20th century gradual 'changing of the guard' if you like.

While manufacturing's share of output and employment did not substantially increase much in the second and third decades of the 20th century, the composition of the sector changed dramatically. Broadly, more advanced manufacturing activities developed at the expense of the more traditional, lower-value industries.

Processing industries that were relatively intensive in manual labour experienced a long-term relative decline. One reason for this was that wage costs facing producers in Australia were very high relative to its trading partners. During the mid-1920s, coincident with a surge in the terms of trade from trough to peak of more than 130 per cent, Australian wages were 50 to 100 per cent higher than those paid to workers in comparable activities in the United Kingdom.[2] Low skills manufacturing was simply uncompetitive; or, to put it in more technical language, the real exchange rate was too high to accommodate continued expansion of these sorts of manufactures. This may have been an early example of a large terms-of-trade induced real appreciation affecting the structure of the Australian economy.

On the other hand, more advanced, emerging industries like motor vehicles, metals, engineering, drugs and chemicals were expanding. Chart 1 shows employment in selected manufacturing sub-industries as a proportion of total

---

2   Griffin J (ed.), *Essays in Economic History of Australia*, p250, Jacaranda Wiley Ltd, 1967.

employment in manufacturing between 1908 and 1929. Since the second half of the first decade, employment in more traditional activities — the processing of agricultural and pastoral products, clothing and textiles and wood products — recorded a trend decline. In fact, even during the Roaring Twenties, a number of these industries were actually shedding labour, especially those associated with rural exports.

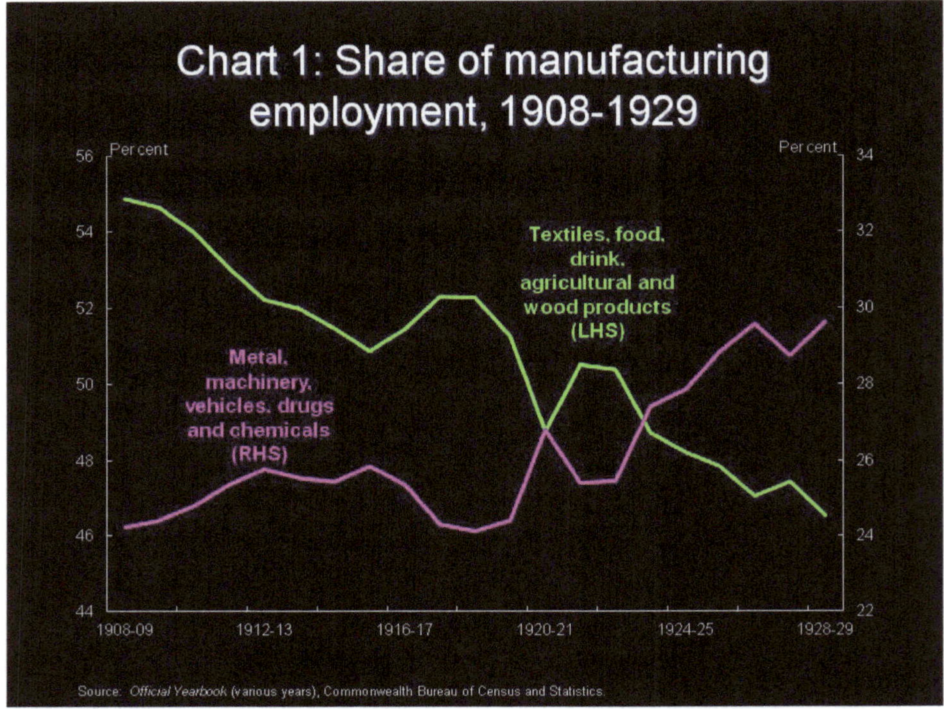

Chart 1: Share of manufacturing employment, 1908-1929

The purple line, on the other hand, represents the 'newer', higher value industries which took off post war — like motor vehicles, machinery assembly, drugs and chemicals. While the Great Depression hit these more advanced activities hard,[3] they were the ones that led the recovery and the surge in manufacturing's relative importance in the thirty years following. Consider the following chart on industry GDP shares over time.

---

3   For example, industrial metal and machinery shed more than a quarter of its employees in 2 years (*Yearbook*, various years).

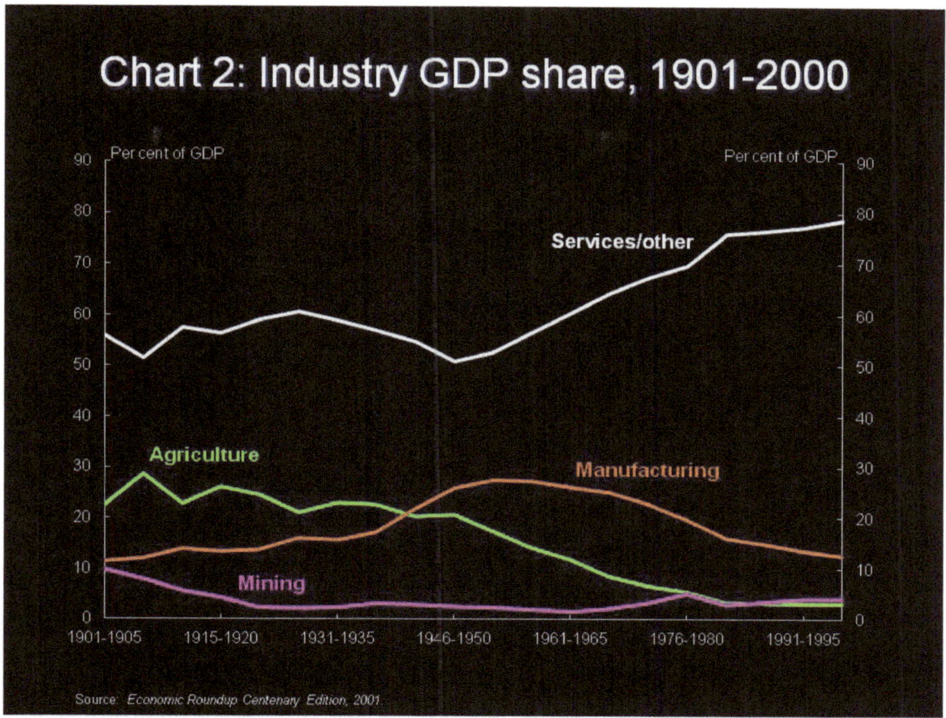

Chart 2: Industry GDP share, 1901-2000

Boosted by the heavy production requirements of World War II, the 1940s saw manufacturing overtake the traditionally dominant agriculture sector. In the 1950s and 60s[4] manufacturing remained buoyant, while services provided the engines of growth (with economic growth in these two decades some way above the 20th century average).[5] In contrast, primary industries declined gradually as a share of GDP. Incidentally, this shift had been keenly anticipated by Giblin and Brigden in the 1930s. Through productivity gains and deregulation rather than protection, it was thought that the relative expansion of the secondary industries would absorb more people, lift employment and drive the recovery.[6]

From Giblin's Australia to the present day

It turns out that the 'changing of the guard' observed in Giblin's time is just one among a large number of historical examples of large-scale structural change in the Australian economy. Structurally, this is an economy that has never sat still.

---

4   Sinclair WA, *The Process of Economic Development in Australia*, pp211-262, Cheshire Publishing Ltd, 1976.

5   Commonwealth of Australia, *Economic Roundup Centenary Edition*, 2001.

6   *Giblin's Platoon* pp113-114.

Economic advancement – embracing the trend towards knowledge industries

Just as the more advanced parts of the manufacturing sector overtook primary and lower value industries towards the end of Giblin's life, the second half of the 20th century saw a rise (relative to manufacturing) in the higher productivity, higher value, knowledge based goods and services. This experience is common to the economic development of virtually all advanced economies over the past half century. The shift towards higher value, including knowledge-based, services has been driven largely by changing tastes and preferences arising from higher incomes, technological change and demographic change. But the pattern of comparative advantage was also shifting in the second half of the 20th century, as rapidly industrialising Asian nations emerged as labour-abundant competitors. And the trend toward services persisted, despite the impost of heavy protectionist measures in advanced economies.

There were two key features of Australian protectionism. One was a naïve desire to promote exports, depress imports and shield economies from external fluctuations. This was an argument primarily mercantilist in nature: a protective wall comprised of tariffs, import controls and other regulatory features was considered necessary in order to grow an Australian manufacturing industry and protect the economy from swings in commodity markets.[7]

The second feature of Australian protectionism arose from a far more considered exposition of trade theory. The Brigden enquiry, 'The Australian Tariff: An Economic Enquiry', was prepared by Brigden, Copland, Dyason, Giblin and Wickens at the request of Prime Minister Bruce. It reported its findings in 1929. The report alluded to many of the insights of trade theory that were popularised subsequently by the Hecksher-Ohlin-Samuelson trade model and, in particular, it foreshadowed the key results of the celebrated Stolper-Samuelson theorem.

The report had three key conclusions: tariffs have costs that can outweigh the benefits; real wages are not necessarily higher under free trade; and the available evidence doesn't allow a more precise statement on either of these two effects. Today we understand that the imposition of a tariff can increase the real (producer) wage if the import-competing sector of the economy is relatively labour-intensive. This is the standard Stolper-Samuelson result established in 1941. One can imagine the power of the theorem in the early 1950s with movements in the terms of trade advantaging capital-intensive exports, and a concern that slower real wages growth would undermine the pursuit of rising living standards.

---

7   Volatility in global capital markets was also a concern of economists and the broader public.

In fact, protectionist measures proved unsuccessful in holding back the tide of economic development. It seems likely that they simply shifted the pain of adjustment to those workers and businesses not shielded from foreign competition and hurt consumers generally. Today, the services sector — capturing many of the new knowledge-based activities, including information and communications, professional, health, finance and scientific services as well as more traditional services like retail, hospitality and tourism — has risen to almost 80 per cent of total Australian output and employment. Manufacturing, which peaked mid-century, has since declined over time as a share of GDP to a level similar to that at federation.

This trend is typical of the advanced economies against which we usually compare ourselves. Chart 3 compares employment shares by industry for the United States, the United Kingdom and Japan against education per person employed.

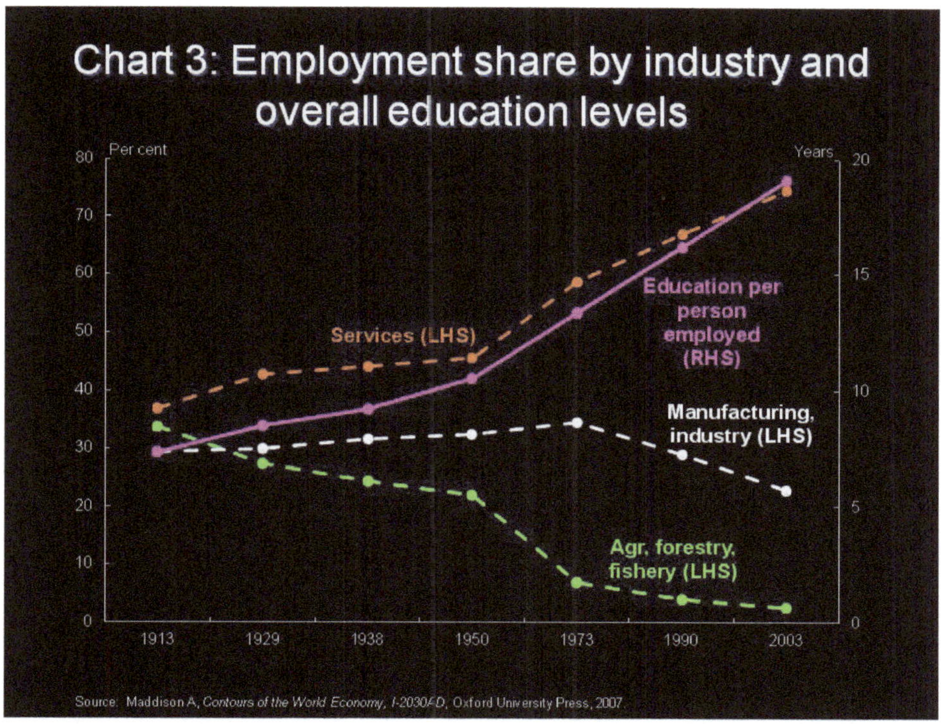

Chart 3: Employment share by industry and overall education levels in the USA, UK and Japan

As those employed in services tend to have a higher incidence of post-school qualifications than other sectors, it is not surprising that the services industries have expanded with improvements in education levels.[8]

In these countries, primary and manufacturing industries, on the other hand, have declined in relative importance in the latter half of the century — following a similar trend to that seen in Australia. At the risk of gross over-generalisation, it seems fair to say that trends in industrial structure tend to be of long duration and fairly immune to policy intervention — with the probable exception of those policies that affect rates of factor accumulation, including policies affecting education and training, immigration and levels of capital investment.

While our industrial structure has shown a marked trend decline in manufacturing and agriculture post-WW2, with flat mining output, trends in export shares have been very different. In the 1950s commodities made up more than 85 per cent of goods exports. Textile fibres — which is predominantly wool — alone represented nearly 50 per cent of goods exports.

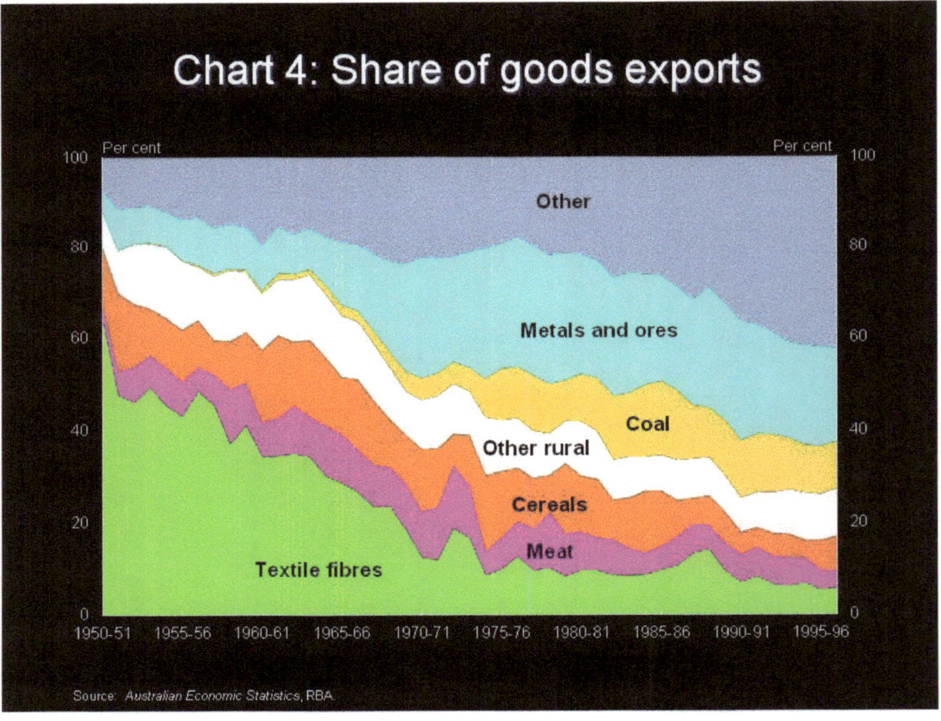

Chart 4: Share of goods exports

---

8   For the services sector in Australia, 62 per cent of those employed in services between the age of 15 and 74 have some form of post school qualification in 2010. On the other hand, 54 per cent of those employed in manufacturing, agriculture and mining have post school qualifications (ABS cat no 6227.0).

Of course, the large share of resources in Australian exports in the second half of the 20th century reflected our natural endowments. But it was an export performance tied also to the post-war reconstruction and rapid industrialisation of Japan. The Japanese post-war industrial expansion contributed to strong terms of trade in Australia, and these were taken to extraordinarily high levels in 1951 with the Korean War surge in demand for woollen military uniforms. Asian growth is once again having a pronounced impact on our terms of trade — a matter to which I will return in a moment.

The Australia in which Giblin lived embraced the emerging technologies and industries of his day — the world of motor vehicles, chemicals, pharmaceuticals, engineering and metal industries. Today, there is a case for embracing the emerging technologies and industrial opportunities of the 21st century. Technology improvements, particularly in information and communications, will continue to transform the way we do business and the way we live. And they will transform the structure of the national economy — just as the manufacturing sector transformed the economy in the first half of the 20th century.

Technological advancement has also opened up new sets of opportunity. It will continue to bring new and innovative goods and services into the marketplace, giving Australian consumers expanded opportunities and more choice. For producers too there is the promise of expanded opportunity, with new technologies offering opportunities to secure productivity gains through innovation and adaptation.

Those opportunities can be expanded with policies that support flexible education systems; protect financial systems; and reform to taxation systems to facilitate more rapid rates of physical capital renewal and accumulation and a more productive allocation of the capital stock.

Such policy prescriptions would have force in all advanced economies, in which the strongest growth sectors are likely, increasingly, to be knowledge-based industries. But there are features of the Australian economy that distinguish it from most other advanced economies, in which the factors of production are, themselves, largely produced — whether it be manufactured capital equipment or skilled labour 'produced' from unskilled labour in the education sector. Our factor endowments include substantial natural resources. And that peculiarity sets us apart in important ways. Most significantly, it means that we view the re-emergence of the Asian giants quite differently.

The re-emergence of Asia

The mining boom

The re-emergence of China and India has created a rapidly growing demand for energy and mineral commodities. Global supply of these commodities has expanded rapidly, with some of these doubling in the past decade. Even so, it has not been able to keep pace with demand, and prices have skyrocketed.

In addition, growth in the manufacturing sectors of China has led to an increased global supply of low cost manufactures. With increases in the prices of the commodities we export and falling prices of manufactures that we import, Australia's terms of trade have improved significantly. Improved terms of trade increase real national income. Specifically, the purchasing power of exports increases.

The Governor of the Reserve Bank put it quite nicely recently — five years ago, a shipload of iron ore was worth about the same as about 2,200 flat screen television sets. Today it is worth about 22,000 flat-screen TV sets — partly due to TV prices falling but more due to the price of iron ore rising by a factor of six.[9]

Australia, as a net exporter of resource commodities and a net importer of manufactured goods, is in a prime position to benefit from China's development. At some point, growth in the global extraction of commodities like coal and iron ore should start to outweigh continued strong growth in global demand, driving down prices. But nobody knows when, or by how much.

My view is that a reasonable case can be made for considering that the terms of trade will remain significantly higher, on average, over the coming decade or two than they were before the start of the mining boom. The boom has contributed to a strong exchange rate and has drawn labour and capital into the mining and related construction sectors. Both of these effects have placed significant pressure on other sectors of the economy, especially other trade-exposed sectors like tourism and manufacturing.

Over the past decade, jobs in mining and construction have almost doubled, from around 750,000 to around 1.3 million. Employment growth in mining has grown by 8.6 per cent a year for the past five years, compared with 2.4 per cent across the non-mining economy. Even so, most of the growth in employment has been in construction rather than mining per se. Over the same period, manufacturing has lost roughly 50,000 jobs, down to around one million people employed; its share of the workforce dropping from 12 to 9 per cent.

---

9   Stevens G, *Address to the Committee for Economic Development of Australia*, Melbourne, 29 November 2010.

The mining boom seems to have accelerated a long-term adjustment away from manufacturing. But it would be a serious mistake to forecast the death of Australian manufacturing. That industry has a track record of remarkable resilience and adaptability – just as agriculture adapted to industrialisation and changes in global markets in the 20th century. As Australia's tariff barriers came down in the 1980s and early 1990s, our manufacturing sector successfully shifted its focus away from products in direct competition with low cost producers, to higher value-add manufactures.

More recently, manufactures for the domestic resources and construction sectors have grown strongly. A substantial decline in output for industries like textiles, clothing, wood and paper products has, to some extent, been offset by a shift into manufactures related to mining and construction. This trend might be expected to continue for some time.

A burgeoning Asian middle class

The mining boom is the most remarkable consequence for Australia of the rapid growth of China and India. Many commentators, in Australia and elsewhere, have expressed concern about our economy appearing to be so heavily dependent upon continued Chinese demand for our natural resources. What happens when Chinese growth slows down or, even worse, collapses as Japanese growth did at the end of the 1980s, they ask? What happens when global extraction of mineral resources catches up with Chinese demand and commodity prices collapse? And what if, when these things happen, we find that we have 'hollowed out' our manufacturing sector and have nothing to fall back on?

These are understandable, if somewhat bleak concerns. But I would suggest that they are exaggerated. Indeed, there is instead a strong case for optimism. At the end of the 1980s, Japan was our largest trading partner. After 20 years of poor macroeconomic performance, characterised by several recessions, Japan remains our second most important export destination – only very slightly less important than China, despite that country's stellar economic performance. For the Australian economy, Japan remains a very big market, even when it is growing slowly. A weakly growing Chinese economy would present an even larger market than Japan.

A second observation is that, given the very long term trends in industrial structure that we have already observed in the past half century – with services growing strongly as a proportion of total employment and manufacturing employment falling from about one third of the labour force to less than 10 per cent today – it is a bit odd to be referring to this as a China-induced 'hollowing out' of manufacturing.

A third observation concerns the consequences for industrial structures of real incomes growth associated with economic development. Today, we see China as a manufacturing powerhouse, reliant upon raw materials that we happen to have in abundance. But as the Chinese economy develops, its industrial structure will also change. It won't become a smaller producer in manufactures in absolute terms. Indeed, Chinese manufacturing output will probably grow at least as fast as the Australian economy grows for as long as any of us can project. But other sectors of the Chinese economy will grow even faster, in time. As with all other stories of economic development, real income growth and the emergence of a large middle class will generate a demand for an almost endless variety of goods and services. What sorts of goods and services? Who knows? It could be premium tourism, it could be fine wine, financial services or it could be some other good or service not yet invented. At other times in our history we have witnessed some of the opportunities that income growth in emerging markets presents for Australian exporters.

Consider tourism services, for example, and the strong Japanese demand that drove its development. With increased demand for tourism services from emerging markets, there is considerable potential to attract a greater share of increasingly wealthy travellers to Australia for business tourism, holiday packages and to visit family and friends.

According to the United Nations World Tourism Organisation, the number of international tourist arrivals globally reached 935 million in 2010. That's an increase of 58 million, or seven per cent, from 2009. Emerging economies continue to drive global outbound tourism expenditure growth – for example, 17 per cent for China in 2010 – outstripping growth in traditional markets like Japan, the United States, Germany and the United Kingdom.[10] Australian tourism stands to benefit from these global developments.

We have also already seen a greater appetite for particular goods produced by Australian exporters. For example, while Australia's largest wine export markets continue to be the United States and the United Kingdom – and while there is currently pressure on this industry from the high exchange rate – wine exports to China have grown strongly, increasing from 1.9 per cent of total wine exports in 2007-08 to 6.1 per cent in 2009-10.

A sensible way forward

None of us knows with certainty for how long this mining boom will last. Nor do we know precisely what will be the shape of the global demand for

---

10   *UNWTO World Tourism Barometer*, United Nations World Tourism Organisation, January 2011.

Australian goods and services when it ceases. So it should be no surprise that economists have difficulty describing in any detail the industrial structure that will maximise economic opportunity for Australians in the world of the future. One thing we can be certain of, however, is that it will not be the industrial structure we have today, nor any drawn from our history. In the world of the future there will be no benefit to be drawn from turning back the clock.

Don't turn back the clock

Today's economy has responded much better to the mining boom than it did during any previous terms of trade spike. Three settings in particular have contributed to our flexibility and our ability to respond to the boom. First, a flexible exchange rate has done a better job of curbing demand and price pressures.

Secondly, while Giblin addressed the problem of inflexible wages,[11] including in his *Letters to John Smith*, three-quarters of a century later a significantly more flexible labour market has helped facilitate a reallocation of labour among sectors of the economy while avoiding economically damaging aggregate wage adjustments.

Thirdly, the sectoral reallocation of labour has been made easier by more open and flexible product markets nurtured by the dismantling of trade protection, deregulation of utilities and other components of the economic infrastructure, and the development of a sophisticated domestic competition policy. It is important that there be no temptation to wind back the clock on the reforms that have helped get us where we are today.

Just as importantly, we should not allow ourselves to think that all the necessary reforms have been done. Giblin's Platoon understood the risks of complacency in their day. They were not carried away by Roaring Twenties euphoria. And with good reason. The Australia of the 1920s was overregulated and underproductive. As Brigden had said on a number of occasions:

'The conditions of high tariffs, heavy borrowing overseas and high standards of living are not conducive to enterprise or efficiency...People of all classes seemed to expect the Government not only spend for them but to think for them.'[12]

---

11   See for example his *Letters to John Smith* and the so called 'First Manifesto' (*Giblin's Platoon* p112).
12   *Giblin's Platoon* p110

In fact, Australia had not roared at all in the twenties. Rather, the 1920s were one of four decades in the 20th century to have had average annual GDP growth below that of the century average – along with the teens (which experienced the Great War), the thirties (which had the Depression) and the seventies.[13]

Reforms to facilitate a more flexible economy – an ongoing task

Today, I sign off after a decade as Treasury Secretary. Yet rather than use this contribution as an opportunity to be reflective about my career, I have instead chosen to look ahead to the economic landscape upon which future Treasury secretaries will be developing policy advice for Australian governments. With those successors and future governments in mind, there is one reflection I will leave with you.

It is a reflection on political economy – of just the sort that preoccupied Giblin in his day. The hardest part of this job has not been figuring out what the 'right answer' to a policy problem actually was. I hope you won't dismiss as arrogance a reflection that, for a Treasury equipped with robust analytical frameworks, good evidence and capable of exercising sensible judgment, even very complex policy questions have, for the most part, proved tractable.

Thinking about present and future challenges, the 'right answers' for Australia today include: maintaining fiscal policy settings that lift national saving, including private saving, over time; pursuing further micro-economic reform, including tax reform, encouraging competition and improvements in education and health policies to expand the nation's supply capacity by lifting participation and productivity and to promote economic flexibility; and constructing policy settings relevant to population that support an expansion of the nation's supply capacity, but in a socially and environmentally sustainable way.

On numerous other occasions I have detailed the reforms, in the areas of participation, productivity and population that could be pursued to lift supply capacity. I don't intend reprising those here. I do want to say, however, that most of them would do more than boost aggregate supply potential. Many would make a direct contribution to tackling the extreme capability deprivation suffered by many Australians, especially Indigenous Australians, and would also deal with the considerable forces that continue to threaten environmental sustainability on this vast land mass of extraordinary biodiversity.

Like Giblin, I think we do know what needs to be done. What we don't understand so well is how to get it done. Right through the 1980s Australian

---

13   Commonwealth of Australia, *Economic Roundup Centenary Edition*, 2001.

policy makers, haunted by another deep recession attributable to policy failure over many decades, found themselves on a burning platform. With high inflation and high unemployment, and another negative terms of trade shock that threatened a further hit to living standards, the imperative for action was broadly understood and accepted. I'm not saying it was easy. It wasn't. And accounts of that period that would have you believe that it was not politically contentious – and I've seen more and more of these accounts popping up in recent years – are simply wrong. But the circumstances were so confronting that action was inevitable.

Today we find ourselves having avoided a recession that paralysed the rest of the developed world. We have low inflation, low unemployment, and a terms of trade boom that has, to date, boosted average living standards. How does one, today, communicate the imperative for action? That is the question. And the answer? Well, that is for you to figure out. To borrow from the man we honour today, Lyndhurst Giblin, in a letter to the prominent English novelist E. M. Forster: 'For God's sake, don't feel that [this] demands [my] answer. It is enough to have got it off my chest.'

16. The boss in the yellow suit — leading service delivery reform[1]

Lynelle Briggs

Over an APS career spanning three decades, Lynelle Briggs worked for the Department of Social Security, the Department of the Prime Minister and Cabinet, the Treasury; the Department of Health and Aged Care, and the Department of Transport and Regional Services. From November 2004 she fulfilled the role of Australian Public Service Commissioner, a position to which she was re-appointed in 2007. During this time, she was Board member and President of the Commonwealth Association of Public Administration and Management. In August 2007 Lynelle Briggs became the Chief Executive Officer of Medicare Australia, retiring from this post in July 2011.

Leadership is about setting a vision, devising a strategy to deliver on it, and putting in place mechanisms to motivate people to get you there. But transformational leadership is much more than that — it is closer to the concept of heroic leadership.[2] It requires passion, belief and trust if it is to be successful. That means leaders need to motivate both the hearts and minds of those travelling with them and convince the fellow travellers that they can be relied upon to deliver what might actually be beneficial to everyone involved.

Service delivery reform is one of those transformations. It has been both an enormous task and an enormous opportunity — and one that I wouldn't have missed for quids. In this valedictory address I will recount the story of service delivery reform and the associated leadership issues, and will do so as the first step in a long road to embed and grow the reforms that Kathryn Campbell[3] will now lead.

Service delivery reform involved bringing together three great Australian public service institutions — Centrelink,[4] Medicare Australia[5] and the Department of Human Services[6] — to create a new way of delivering health care, income support and child support services to the Australian community. That new way is all about:

---

1   This speech was delivered in July 2011 at a major function at ANU University House hosted by the Australian Public Service Commission.

2   The concept of heroic leadership is derived from Max Weber's 1947 model of transaction and transformation leadership authority, where the characteristics of the ideal types are set out.

3   Katherine Campbell is the first Secretary of the new Department of Human Services, formed on 1 July 2011, incorporating the former Centrelink and Medicare Australia agencies.

4   Centrelink was the social security delivery agency.

5   Medicare Australia was the Medicare and other health payment agency and, at the time of the announcement, was the 4th most popular brand for quality in Australia.

6   The Department of Human Services was made up largely of two other delivery agencies—Child Support and the Commonwealth Rehabilitation Service.

- merging our services so that they are refocussed to deliver better results for people;

- ensuring our staff have the necessary information and tools to assist Australians gain access to a range of community or other services that might meet their needs;

- Australians feeling that they are able to work with us to devise new services that better meet their needs, share in the design of those services and advise us on the best method of delivery of the services to them; and

- transforming our operations electronically and procedurally to provide the basis for all of this to happen.

Few people appreciate the cost and energy involved in such a massive change. To start to appreciate the leadership dimension involved, consider that there are around 40,000 people,[7] about 5000 middle managers and 220 senior executives in the human services portfolio. We have large physical networks with some 550 offices and many outreach services across Australia, virtual networks such as call centres and online servicing options, and extraordinary ICT capabilities, all of which must be combined. We deliver about 170 different programmes and services. We are in contact with 99 per cent of the Australian population during the course of a year. We are truly the face of the Australian government in the community.

In mid-2009 when I joined Medicare Australia, the portfolio was being propelled to change by national developments and by our staff working on the front line who could see the opportunities to do things differently and to deliver better results.

As a country we had become wealthier and we had been able to deliver all the basics of a quality national health and welfare system, but our people expected more from us. Today, Australians expect quality services from the government, reliable advice from expert service staff, and convenient online access. They expect to be treated like individuals with particular needs, rather than to be treated like everyone else and told to take it or leave it, or to go somewhere else to get something that they might need. They expect to be treated with respect and courtesy and they expect to be able to trust the public sector to support them when they need it.

These developments were apparent to our staff living across the country. They knew that simply providing income support or Medicare payments and getting through queues in offices or handling calls quickly wasn't enough to deliver truly great service. They told us time and again that our services needed to

---

7   This is about $\frac{1}{4}$ of the Australian Public Service, so is a large exercise.

be more inclusive, more respectful, more convenient, and more joined up with other parts of government and other service providers, and that serving people more holistically was obviously beneficial and long overdue.

Ideas about citizen-centred services and new ways of relating to communities had begun to take hold. We had done a lot of work with policy departments to bring them on board with the need for change. The problem remained that there was no clear vision to make the reform a reality and without that vision there could be no transformation.

We needed a vision that would be important symbolically to both our staff and to the Australian community for service delivery reform to have any traction at all. It had to be clear, simple and aspirational, and set a higher service standard for the reforms. And, it had to have really passionate, genuine leadership commitment to promote the vision and drive the changes necessary to make it a reality.

The starting point, as with all great ideas, was very simple. Five good people developed the vision in a couple of hours one afternoon in my office by simply talking about what we understood the Australian community wanted from us: convenience, correct information, sound advice, less bureaucracy, great service, helpful staff, efficient service, delivering results, joined up services, and getting paid on time, all morphed together into the catchphrase 'easy, high quality and works for you'.

Our minister took this further and decided that 'easy, high quality and works for you' should not become another dry policy statement; it should be the basis for our entire approach to service delivery reform. And so the vision was born and we had our rallying cry for transformative change.

To deliver on this bold reform promise, Finn Pratt, Carolyn Hogg and myself[8] knew that we needed a plan for integration and a set of initiatives that would deliver better services to Australians. Given the size of what was involved and the absence of any significant new investment from the government, this was an enormous undertaking and required several months of discussion, ideas development, intensive negotiation, priority setting, careful costing, and dialogue with Australians, our staff and the policy departments. The numbers of people involved and the levels of project planning undertaken were staggering – it stretched us all. Consequently, the three of us met once a week for several hours to keep it going and push it along – taking some pretty challenging decisions as we went.

---

8   The three of us led the Department of Human Services, Centrelink and Medicare Australia respectively at the time.

The process involved all of us opening up our minds to new opportunities, being prepared to drop existing practices, and refocus on the best way forward.[9] The balance between investing in foundation systems changes and value added services was a tough call,[10] particularly because the closer we engaged with our policy departments the more the opportunities to deliver genuine service improvements became apparent. We knew, however, that we had to fund the foundations first.

At the forefront of our thinking was the need to progressively take the portfolio to another place where we could truly put people at the centre of everything we do. Design and delivery of services would be 'outside in', with Australians telling us what they want and need – as opposed to the more traditional internally driven 'tell you' model – and with the service offer being based around people's life events and needs and local issues, and not the requirements of the support programs involved.

To start to appreciate the leadership dimension involved in this transformation, let me share some simple examples of what a transformed service might look like. Starting at the straightforward end, we anticipate that in a few years most Australians will be able to do their business with us online or over the phone, or we'll do it for them behind the scenes – meaning that they won't need to go to an office for a service. At other times in people's lives when things aren't going as well, we will be there to help them. We see the department increasingly becoming the 'go to' body for Australians to seek help and support when they need it.

Imagine a situation where a woman's husband dies. Rather than just adjust the widow's pension or Medicare card, we'll identify her individual and complete needs. That might mean identifying grief or financial counselling. We might also connect her with some local support networks and let her know what community care options are available or what steps are involved in her being assessed for care. This sort of reassurance is what we are about.

After a marriage breaks down, we can help take some of the stress away by connecting up the information and services that will support both parents and their children. We can do this at the first point of contact, so that they can plan

---

9   A special tribute should be given to our deputy secretaries and deputy chief executive officers who drove much of this work and established genuine collaborative partnerships across our agencies and with policy departments during this time. They did a great job.

10   It was a tough judgement call that was governed as much by money as desire because we knew that, unless we provided the systems and procedural changes necessary to free our staff up to do more value added work, staff would be propelled to continue to do transactions work and we would not have the money to fund that better quality work.

their next steps with greater knowledge and confidence and, if it's necessary, we can provide more intensive support. This sort of early intervention is what we are about.

When a family realises that they have a disabled child, their immediate priorities are usually about getting help for their child. The parents may or may not know where to turn first, and this is where we can help. The department won't deliver all of the programs that parents may be eligible for, but we will certainly know who does and be able to link the parents to them at the local level, particularly as the child moves through school. While the parents are focusing on the needs of their child, we can help make sure that their needs are met too – such as through co-ordinated and streamlined access to income support or ancillary payments, Medicare rebates, referrals to respite services or other programs to increase their well-being. If we think and act to address the needs of the entire family, we can help protect them from the financial and personal pressures that can so easily impact on their relationships and health. This sort of preventive and caring service is what we are about.

These examples show what an 'outside in' approach can mean for people – and the rewards they can bring for staff – and how collaborative schemes involving government working together with people, service professionals and the third sector can improve public service delivery in ways that rigid program structures fail to do. By integrating the sources of information we have around life events or local services and providing things like 'warm' transfers to other services for those with multiple, complex problems, we can improve overall wellbeing.

We are also building a new way of designing services called 'co-design' where all parties have a say in the shape of the service and a role in its implementation. Already, co-design principles are being embedded in our operations and it's been wonderful to see the enthusiasm with which our staff have embraced them to devise better services.

Not only have we found that the more we engage with Australians the more we can do to help them, but also that delivering services in ways that suit them can also save money because it minimises rework and maximises prevention.

For me co-design is all about power – a transfer of power from provider to user. This is one of the touch points for truly transformational leadership. A shift in power is often not willingly given or comfortably managed. Transferring power involves a shift in obligations and responsibilities, something that has to be negotiated between us and the person receiving the service. To manage that shift properly, we need to understand the people we assist – seeing the world and the situations they are in as they see them.

We need to further embed the co-design concept and its associated processes into the mainstream way we do business. To do so in an informed way, we need to redevelop our standard user satisfaction surveys, adopt approaches such as ethnographic research, map how our customers really interact with us around life events, and start to invite them in to be part of our design teams. We will need to expand the opportunities for community engagement in all aspects of our business. We have to accept that we don't know best – or even know at all – so we should go out and actively seek ideas and input. Most importantly, we need to take time to make sure we are asking the right questions.

Our leadership focus needs to be not on the *how* of service delivery but rather the *why* – knowing the outcome being sought. For too long our key performance indicators have really been about management information – how long did the phone call take or how long was the wait time at the counter – rather than whether the interaction met its purpose – did the person get a job, did the homeless kid get referred to a service that could actually help her, and was the elderly carer connected to support services?

I don't want to give anyone the impression that our everyday transactional services aren't important. They are the core business of the human services portfolio, and getting the mainstream right is a crucial element in freeing up resources to focus on the more difficult, more complex services the government wants us to deliver. More than that, if a pension doesn't get paid or a Medicare benefit wasn't provided, we would be severely denting trust in our capacity to deliver transformative outcomes. I can say that despite the level of reform activity, there has never been a risk of that occurring, ever.

That doesn't mean we get everything right. Carolyn Hogg[11] says that 'a complaint is an opportunity to improve our service'. Our service leaders need to see that opportunity, and embrace it.

Service delivery reform sees us trialling a range of activities, and a focus on a 'can do' culture that will see us move from a rules based hierarchical approach to one that is more devolved and discretion based. If complaints are opportunities to improve services, so too mistakes can tell us where we need to direct attention, and what works and what might not. Obviously no one sets out to get things wrong, but nor will we change behaviour by doing all the same things and punishing attempts to do things differently.

---

11   Carolyn Hogg PSM is the former Chief Executive Officer of Centrelink and was a close friend, colleague and confidante throughout the reform. I can remember several occasions where we shared a glass of red wine and sorted out our differences about the way forward. She was a truly great public servant and, without her, this reform may never have happened.

Just as a shift in power is a necessary external component of service delivery reform, a shift in control is equally as necessary internally to bring this 'can do' focus to the fore. Control is anathema to the creativity and innovation we need from our people to get true transformation. They obviously need to work within the law and the parameters set by the government, but they also need the room to create real, local solutions. *Amazon* is a good analogy – a large global delivery system within which niche marketing not only exists, but piggy backs the system enabling it to flourish.

It should be readily apparent by now that service delivery reform is not simply a structural change, and that the challenge for leadership in what is occurring is revolutionary, not evolutionary. But there is more to the story.

There is fear involved in transformational change, and the worst aspects of leadership can occur when fear is about. The lowest points in my career have been when I saw people's fears and prejudices brought out and deliberately and cynically exploited for political ends. It is easier to manipulate fear than it is to harness passion, heart and good spirit, but any outcome achieved that way isn't worth having. Modern leadership takes people to a better place. Modern leaders work with and within the cultural fabric of an organisation to bring out what is best in their people.

The fears we are dealing with are both internal and external. When we first talked about combining Centrelink and Medicare offices, I heard it said more than once that 'my wife says she will never go into a Centrelink office'. There are also fears about the extent to which our new single department will share personal information.

Internally the fears are about the effect the integration will have on staff and working arrangements. None of these are unusual in large scale change – fears of a takeover by one agency over the others, fear of job losses and job changes, fear of being powerless while change is happening, fear that staff will be expected to be experts in everything, and generally just being afraid of the unknown.

Our approach in addressing these fears has been to acknowledge that they are real, and then to stop and think about the best way forward. The way to avoid claims of a takeover is by valuing the approaches of the smaller agencies too. You deal with customer comfort concerns by treating all of our customers with respect and courtesy and by setting a standard for your offices, call and online services that any Australian would be proud of – tatty is simply not good enough. You deal with staff fears, by active and sustained engagement with them about the change and what is to come, and by delivering on the promise of the future. At the core of our staff engagement program is a suite of change management initiatives; regular, effective and sustained communications; quality learning and development; and talent management.

In all these things, the way Carolyn Hogg, Finn Pratt and I worked together was fundamentally important. We were in a fairly unique situation and not one I had encountered before in my professional career. We had three separate organisations, each with either a secretary or CEO in charge, and over which neither of the other two could exercise control. There were three leaders and three separate legislated responsibilities.

From the start we decided to forego the bureaucratic formalities of MOUs[12] and legalistic operating arrangements. Instead, we simply trusted each other. We respected each other and the different perspectives we brought to the table. We spoke up when things needed to be said and we had robust discussions with the aim of achieving an agreed way forward. Sometimes it took a little longer than we might have liked, but that was a natural consequence of wanting to find a right and proper outcome that took us all forward together, not one that suited any particular organisational interests. More often than not we agreed because we had the same vision of what was possible.

It also showed that we were prepared to play the way we expected others to play. We talk a lot about modelling behaviour as leaders, and we talk a very good game. What leaders must focus on, especially to get significant change, is walking far more than talking. Studies have shown that people will do what they see a leader do; even when that leader tells them behaving that way is unacceptable.

We knew we needed to be united and supportive of each other. Everyone's eyes were on us, and our confidence, commitment, united focus on the vision, and energy were fundamental to the transformation.

We waited out the old 'consent and evade' culture in parts of our organisations — where people smile consent, fail to commit and do nothing. We knew that if we let one part of the show let us down, we would all fail. We just kept at it until either they came around or we found a better way by working with them to achieve the same goal.

We confronted quite a few sacred cows, and significant vested interests. For instance, our new operating model is structured around 16 geographic service zones. Given that Centrelink is by far the biggest integrating agency, we could have moved everyone else into one of their 15 existing areas, and minimised the level of disruption. But, we knew that would have fed the takeover fear, with the associated risk that people in Centrelink would have thought they had simply gotten bigger, as opposed to having become something else. It would have also missed the opportunity to transform key roles and the service focus across our service delivery network.

---

12   Memorandums of understanding are the typical way that agencies agree operating arrangements between them to ensure that their needs are understood and met.

So we moved the boundaries, refocussed the region offices, abolished the area manager role, and then put new service leaders in charge of making it work. It was made clear to our service leaders across the country that they were responsible and accountable for customer service and stakeholder engagement in their zone – they were no longer primarily just administrators of services, but the key people tasked to ensure that the services met the expectations of Australians.

As we move forward, jobs will change, structures will continue to change and people will continue to be affected. Leadership in those circumstances cannot be immune from that change. You won't get transformational change by insulating yourself from the effect of the change around you, by expecting others to bear the consequences but not you. To lead transformational change, you must be prepared to change yourself.

From day one, Carolyn Hogg and I knew we were doing ourselves out of a job. We could have sat back and waited for the legislation to bring that about, taken care of business as usual, and then let the new secretary take charge on 1 July this year. To do that would have not only wasted 18 months but been an abject failure of leadership.

So without the niceties of being a single agency, we merged our human resources and other enabling functions. We had people working in each other's agencies, performing functions in one but formally reporting for accountability purposes to someone in another. With enormous goodwill from our staff, we forgot our structures and worked around our agency boundaries. We put in place what were effectively cross agency committees so that our people could get to know each other and learn about each other's programs and ideas. We restructured and merged our agencies in advance of the legislation to align the business units to be closer to what we knew we wanted.

And, it worked brilliantly. We have devised new and world-leading people and leadership practices; we have crafted a new ICT strategic plan and redesigned our ICT around the new business; we have merged governance arrangements; and we have delivered 10 per cent savings – all done before we were a single department.

We were supported by enormous goodwill on the part of our employees to whom we owe a debt of gratitude. They got on board with the vision, which meant we had 40,000 people pushing it forward, and they made and will continue to make their own sacrifices as we go along.

It has been great to see office managers lining up to be co-located and provide merged services, and it's been terrific to see how staff and customers appreciate the combined services as we provide them. Without that goodwill, we might not have been able to deliver a new set of service commitments or liaise so effectively with community groups, and I commend them for that. Our staff are the heart and soul of the new organisation and we couldn't ask for a better bunch.

Regular and massive senior staff meetings and dialogues with all players from APS 5 upwards have been incredibly important to keep everything on track. Our senior leaders have participated admirably in these forums and visited all of our offices to spread the word about service delivery reform and to learn about each other's business. Their tireless efforts at communicating the vision and direction to our staff have not gone unnoticed.

I have to say that not everything has been quite so enabling. There were processes and outright bureaucracy put in our way that reflected a very traditional public service approach. At times, planning to assure others has seemed like an end in itself. We endured a barrage of consultancy assistance, strategic implementation plans, gateway reviews, first and second pass business cases, P3M3, project offices, design authorities and so on − and, for all the investment to manage the risk, I'm not sure that it has been either necessary or worth it. We have behaved professionally at all times and nothing has gone wrong. It might be better if the funds devoted to these tasks were reallocated to actual service delivery improvements.

While we have pushed on in advance of integration, becoming a single department of state will be a significant impetus.[13] It will give policy clout to service delivery. More fundamentally, service delivery is now being recognised as a valid policy stream in itself.

It is fair to say that in the beginning the policy departments were somewhat sceptical about service delivery reform. Through an enormous amount of energy and by meeting what was asked for by those policy departments, we have turned that scepticism around so that they are now among our strongest supporters. This is evidenced by us now being invited to the policy table, which means we will be able to ensure that the strategic value of service delivery information informs and guides policy development. That is not something that I think we have had before in the way that is now possible.

Integration will also be significant from a cultural perspective. We are reporting back to staff what they have told us in co-design sessions and surveys about what they want in our culture, and we are using that as a lever for change. We also appreciate that if you want to change culture, you change work and that changes behaviours, which invariably changes attitudes and...cultures.

---

13   Not least of all because we will no longer have to do things like run multiple sets of accounts and prepare multiple annual reports.

We have a strong starting point – great systems, strong core values, a firm commitment to customer service, and the desire to get things right and to deliver on time. We also have remarkable symmetry between our senior leaders' values and what they aspire to, which makes it easier to deal with what's not so good about our culture. We intend to build on that by giving less direction from the centre and providing more opportunity to innovate and respond personally at the coal face.

We have made a commitment to our senior executive service that we will 'value you as a person, respect your leadership contribution, develop your leadership capability, support your leadership aspirations, give you the room to lead, and encourage your innovation.' That is the approach that we want all of our senior leaders to adopt with their staff as well, so that everyone has more room to move and more chance to improve the lot of Australians. The fact that the senior executive service has, in turn, committed[14] to the vision of 'easy, high quality and works for you' and to 'engage and empower the public we serve', will drive cultural change.

What we don't have, though, is a new name – we wanted one and we had one. In terms of melding a new single departmental identity, the leadership challenge to unite our staff would likely have been much easier if we had jettisoned the old names altogether, and been known by a new moniker, just as Centrelink was when it was first created. But, integration is not about what is better for us, and the people seeking our services will likely be more comfortable with the fact that the trusted and well known brand they are familiar with is not disappearing overnight.

To help remind our leaders of that, our new leadership strategy contains the following aspirational statement: 'People in Australia experience our leadership every time they engage with us. We want them to feel the difference our leadership makes to that experience.'

This statement neatly encapsulates what it is we want from leadership. All public service leaders should be looking to make a difference for the public, and to make that their leadership aim. If we think of leadership as being about our own career development, or the basis of our next promotion, or another term for managing staff, or a means to an end other than a public outcome, we fail both ourselves and our institution.

---

14   The SES has committed to serve the minister; drive better service outcomes through easy, high quality and works for you; engage and empower the public I serve; strive for innovation; inspire the people I lead; model the APS values; and work well with others.

When we refer to feeling the difference leadership makes we are acknowledging that leadership is about more than what might be called bricks and mortar — implementing a set of projects, reorganising our structures and funding change. Leadership is emotional, and to do it well takes inspiration, courage and passion. That passion will ignite the efforts of those whom we lead; just as surely as its absence will see those efforts flicker, but little more.

This encapsulates the heroic leadership concept I raised at the outset: passion, emotion, personal commitment, character, personal attributes, and empathy are all too dryly described as emotional intelligence. If you appreciate that these are all elements of great leadership, then you will see what I have believed throughout my public service career that we should all aspire to as leaders.

Some of these emotional attributes have been called the soft side of leadership, although it is by far a harder set of attributes to bring to bear than those more traditionally learned technical ones. This is to mistakenly denigrate the core of great leadership. It is also why women make great leaders.

We are blessed in the Australian Public Service to have more than half our employees female, and to have strong women in senior positions. Not enough yet, but it is improving all the time. Maintaining that momentum requires those strong women to be seen and to refuse to be 'blokes'.

When I joined the public service, less than one percent of our leaders were women; when I was promoted to the senior executive service, only two per cent were female. We were still an oddity and it was hard to be given a voice. I have been in senior executive positions for just on 21 years.

I got a lecture early in my career about how to dress as a senior woman — long sleeves, high collars and no trousers. I made a pact with myself to steadfastly ignore that lecture, and have deliberately tried throughout those 21 years to at all times be a woman.

The so called 'feminine touch' is really about caring for people, tending to their needs and nurturing their aspirations. By being feminine, and by being feminine as a leader, we are saying these things matter. And when they matter, it both enables and empowers the blokes to be feminine as well.

I can't imagine a better bedrock on which to reform service delivery. So I say to all of you, don't just be another boss in a grey suit. Get out your yellow suit or tie, and all that it encompasses. Be strong, be seen, and be bold. People in Australia are depending upon it.

17. The challenges for the public service in protecting Australia's democracy in the future[1]

Terry Moran

As the outgoing Secretary of the Department of the Prime Minister and Cabinet, Terry Moran is the most influential Australian public servant to leave office since former Treasury Secretary Ken Henry. Moran's public service career began in 1973 as a Commonwealth Public Service Board Administrative Trainee; he would spend half his career at the federal level. Before commencing his role as Secretary of the Department of the Prime Minister and Cabinet in 2008, Moran had held several influential posts in public service, including Chief Executive of the Victorian State Training Board, Chief Executive of the Australian National Training Authority and Director-General of Education in Queensland. In 2008-09, Terry Moran worked closely with departmental colleagues, the Prime Minister and senior ministers on the formation of the Economic Stimulus Plan.

Democracy has at its heart a simple goal – government by the people. Power and authority rest with citizens, not with a narrow elite. The people's interests are sovereign. The idea is simple, but the practice of democracy has grown and changed over the centuries. Australia's system of parliamentary democracy has its roots in the 'Glorious Revolution' in Britain of 1688. Democracy looked different in those days. For one thing, the elections themselves were much more arduous and time-consuming. Orders to conduct the election were issued and carried to every town in the realm by men on horseback. They were pinned up in prominent places for all to see. After a suitable interval, ballot papers were distributed in a similar way, and only then did voting occur. Another big difference was that only one in ten of the population had the right to vote. And their choice was no private matter; the electorate was confined to a small knot of voters who generally obeyed implicitly the orders of their landlord. It took months to tally the vote and announce the result.

In 1901, when Australia went to the polls for the first time as a nation, the telegraph and the railway line had transformed not just elections, but many other aspects of life. Trains carried ballot papers promptly across the country, while telegrams provided running updates on election results. Yet even with these technological advances the process was still a drawn-out affair. In Sydney

---

1   This is an edited version of the John Paterson Oration, delivered by Terry Moran at the Australia and New Zealand School of Government Annual Conference, Sydney, 28 July 2001.

on election night crowds thronged outside the offices of *The Sydney Morning Herald*, where a tally board had been erected to display the results. The Prime Minister, Sir Edmund Barton, had been appointed three months earlier, pending the first election. He set up residence in a hotel directly across the road from the *Herald* to monitor the tally board. Even with these facilities, it was more than a week before the outcome was known with confidence.

That first Commonwealth election was conducted under state electoral laws – as the Parliament had not yet convened to make any laws of its own. By the time of the next election, in 1903, the vote had been extended to all adult British subjects resident in Australia for six months – although there were exceptions, notably for Indigenous Australians, Asians and Africans; defects that were not fully rectified until 1962.[2]

Today, the franchise has been extended to all adult Australian citizens, and we have come to expect to vote during the day and know the result before we go to sleep. Today the process of counting votes and transmitting the tally has been vastly accelerated by improvements in communication. Last year's delayed outcome occurred in spite of technology; of course the delay wasn't because of any problem in counting votes and transmitting the result, but because of the political negotiations required to form a government. It may be reassuring that the human dimension of politics at times can trump technological advance, but of course the two forces are bound inextricably together. Democratisation and industrialisation have been among the most crucial forces for change in the modern world. The technological advances brought by the industrial revolution have changed democracy in significant ways. And the advent of democracy was a key driver of the industrial revolution.

Democracy came first, and contributed to industrialisation. The Glorious Revolution weakened the power of the monarchy, helping create an affluent middle class. The middle class had influence and interests separate from those of the monarchy and the aristocracy; its rise led to the greater empowerment of individuals. Industrialisation and democracy together brought improvements in education and drove the growth of the public service.

These changes continue to affect the nature and conduct of democracy. We should embrace, not fear, such change, while making sure we remain faithful to the overarching goal of democracy – government by the people.

---

2   This was separate from the 1967 referendum that gave the Commonwealth the power to make laws relating to Aborigines.

Australia's democracy

Australia's democracy is one of the oldest and best in the world. We have our own versions of the institutions and practices that make a democracy. Our liberal democracy is based on democratic institutions of governance, a liberal conception of the rights of individuals and a market-based economy. The institutions of our liberal democracy divide power between levels of government – federal, state and local – and among three branches of government – the legislature, the executive and the judiciary. By convention there are informal divisions within the executive branch. On the one hand, there are its leaders – the prime minister and his or her ministers – and on the other the departments of states and various agencies that provide ongoing support to them.

The formal institutions of our democracy have not changed greatly since 1901. But the practice of government has. There have been changes in the balance of power between the legislature and the executive; changes in the balance of power between ministers and the prime minister; and changes in the balance of power within the policy and administrative arms of the executive – that is, between the cabinet and the public service. The current minority government arrangements have also prompted changes, with modified parliamentary procedures and a greater role for private members' business.

The biggest change has been in the broader environment that shapes the way our democracy functions – an environment shaped by interest groups, the media and by society as a whole. A key aspect of this changing broader environment has been in the ways we communicate within society. It's not trivial that the conduct of elections, and news about politics, are transmitted instantly these days by fibre optic cable or satellite – not on horseback, as in the 17th century, nor by telegraph, as in 1901.

The executive and the legislature

Over our history, power has been shifting from the legislature to the executive. This has occurred because of changes in practice, rather than in the structure of government. The argument is sometimes made that this shift has diminished the 'separation of powers'; but this overlooks the historical origins of our system. The close links between the executive and legislature in Australia originated before federation. The American emphasis on the separation of the executive and the legislature is tempered in Australia by the principle of responsible cabinet government, derived from Britain, where it evolved in the mid-19th century. The cabinet comes from the legislature, but its function is to rule the nation. As Walter Bagehot wrote in 1867, cabinet is 'a hyphen which joins, a buckle which fastens, the legislative part of the state to the executive part of the state. In its origin it belongs to the one, in its functions it belongs to the other.[3] Where the Australian system more closely resembles the American is in the separation of the judiciary from the legislature and the executive.

One driver of the shift in power to the executive was the increasing dominance of political parties, which imposed tight discipline on their parliamentary members. This occurred very early. The period without party dominance was an aberration, a quirk of the period before the political alignments of the first parliaments had a chance to settle. As early as the 1903 election, parliament was dominated by three political groups. By 1910 these had coalesced into a two-party structure. The composition of the party groupings has changed since then, but the structure has persisted. This structure underpins an avowedly combative and adversarial approach to politics in Australia.

The dominance of the political parties allows party leaders to exercise considerable control, reducing the discretion of individual members.[4] Australia has one of the strongest cultures of party discipline of any Westminster system. This has provided much greater stability for governments. Bagehot described the lower house of the British parliament as being 'in a state of perpetual potential choice'.[5] It would be more difficult to support that notion now. Today in Australia, and in Britain, governments tend to be more stable than in the world Bagehot was writing about.

Another trend that many consider troublesome is that over the past century, the executive branch has increasingly dominated the legislature. As the volume of legislation put before the parliament has increased, the time and resources available to consider legislation has declined. Together with the strength of party discipline, this has led to greater deference to the executive. As a result, the role of the parliament as a forum of contestability and accountability has been reduced. It is true that the current minority government stands against this trend. But minority government is the exception in our system, not the rule.

Other factors have contributed to the strengthening of the executive. The growth in the size and scope of government administration empowers the executive. It is ministers who control the administration, not the Parliament. There's a chicken-and-egg question here. Did the growing size of government make the executive stronger, or did a stronger executive exploit its position to increase the size and

---

3   Bagehot, The English Constitution, 1867, p 15.
4   Summers, Woodward and Parkin, eds, *Government, politics and power in Australia* (3rd ed, 1990), at p 14ff.
5   Bagehot, The English Constitution, at p 176.

role of government? Suffice to say it was a bit of both. The executive had become stronger because of greater party discipline, but there were also external factors that increased the size and scope of government.

Two world wars greatly increased the role of government. And after World War II government expanded further with the growth of the state-sponsored social welfare system. As in other countries, industrialisation led to – and relied on – growth in services such as education, health and transport.

The growing weight of legislative business has also played a part in the growing power of the executive. The legislation is drafted by the executive, and there is so much of it that the parliament has less opportunity to give it detailed scrutiny.[6]

These changes are important, but we still have a strong and effective system of formal and informal checks and balances that includes the states, the Senate and the public service.

Accountability within the executive

The public service barely rates a mention in the Australian constitution. Its role as the administrative arm of the executive took root in Britain after the Northcote-Trevelyan Report of 1853, which led to the development of an apolitical, professional civil service. By the time of federation in Australia the independent role of the public service was taken for granted.

The role of both arms of the executive has continued to evolve, along with the relationship between them. There are well established checks and balances between the cabinet – traditionally regarded as the policy arm of the executive – and the public service – the administrative arm.

The predominant institutions of the executive arm are departments of state. Their role is: to provide impartial professional advice, including strategic advice; to administer programs; and to offer caution to ministers in the face of risky decisions.

Within the administrative arm there are other agencies with varying degrees of independence and different accountability mechanisms. For example, the Reserve Bank and the Australian Competition and Consumer Commission have high degrees of independence. Their activities are conducted on an entirely professional basis, without being subject to the pressure that inevitably arises in

---

6   John Summers, Dennis Woodward, Andrew Parkin, eds *Government, politics and power in Australia*, 4th ed.

departments under the direct authority of a minister. This relationship between Cabinet and the Public Service is one of the checks and balances in our system of government with origins in conventions which predate federation.

But a new element has emerged that has muddied the water – the rise since the 1970s of a new sort of public sector employee: the ministerial adviser. The support that leaders of the executive branch receive from advisers varies from country to country, and is the subject of robust debate. In the French system, ministers are supported by a *cabinet*, comprising a majority of highly capable public servants and a minority of political officers. The *cabinet* system influenced a proposal by the Labour Party in Britain in the late 1960s that ministers be supported by a political staff of up to four people.[7] The proposal was not immediately taken up, but the Conservative Party experimented with the idea in the 1970s, and nowadays ministers are supported by special advisers, a practice which continues to stimulate political and academic debate.

In Australia, the reformist tendencies of the Whitlam government led to a significant reshaping of ministerial offices. The new arrangements were influenced by the British experiments with partisan advisers.[8] 'Ministerial officers' have increased in number. There were 209 of them by the end of 1974.[9] Their ranks have swelled further since then, with a growing proportion of political appointees compared with advisers whose backgrounds are in the public service. In recent years, though, their numbers have been cut and their remuneration capped.

The growing number and role of advisers raises some questions for the functioning of our democracy, as the role of this cadre of officers of the Commonwealth is poorly defined. In a sense, they are an extension of the persona of the minister. They are portrayed by many as a source of contestable advice on public policy.

But the mechanisms for holding advisers accountable are murky. Unlike other public sector employees, they are not called before parliamentary committees, nor are they subject to some of the other bodies that oversee public servants. Nonetheless, the government now operates under a formal code of conduct for ministerial staff that is exacting in its guidance.

The real issue here is actually best viewed through the prism of ministerial responsibility. The doctrine of ministerial responsibility has contributed to the rise of advisers and lies at the heart of uncertainty about their role. Tradition has it that ministers are answerable for all actions taken by the departments

---

7   RFI Smith, in Royal Commission on Australian Government Administration, Appendixes to Report, vol 1 at 293.
8   Ibid, at 293.
9   Ibid, at 298.

under their control.[10] But the size and scale of modern government makes this impossible. Do we really think ministers can be responsible for every significant transaction and all manner of decisions in every part of a complex public service? And it is hardly more plausible that even with a bevy of advisers they could overcome this problem. In seeking to track so many matters through advisers it is possible that ministers find themselves accepting a very broad view of ministerial responsibility, a view at odds with the reach of all the other mechanisms established by the parliament to hold the administration accountable. We must strive for the right balance in the exercise of executive power, and clarify ministerial responsibility.

The arena of democracy has changed

The greatest source of change in our democracy has been the immense changes in society at large. British sociologist Anthony Giddens has described some of the dilemmas in public policy that reflect — and are driving — these big social changes.[11] I want to focus on four of the dilemmas he identified — and I will add a fifth factor. The four dilemmas identified by Giddens are globalisation, the new individualism, the changing nature of government[12] and ecological issues. These four issues are driving changes in society that demand flexible and creative responses from government.

Globalisation not only means increasing economic integration, it also refers to the transformation of time and space in our lives thanks to revolutions in communications and transport. The second dilemma, 'new individualism', is linked to the retreat of tradition and custom, partly a response to globalisation. The first two dilemmas have led to a third dilemma, a change in the role of the nation-state and of national government which requires governments to find ways to reconcile the divergent claims of special-interest groups and of an increasingly diverse community. Engaging citizens in policy and service delivery is one way that government is addressing this. The fourth dilemma, responding to ecological issues, requires policies that focus on the idea of sustainable development.

These four dilemmas are forcing changes in our traditional approaches to government. The fifth dilemma that I would add to Giddens' four dilemmas arises from the changing nature of communications media.

---

10   Singleton, Atkins, Jinks, Warhurst, *Australian Political Institutions*, 7th ed. at p 171.
11   Anthony Giddens, *The Third Way*, 1998, at pp 27ff.
12   Giddens calls this the dilemma of 'political agency'.

Democratic discourse has changed

In some respects, the changes in the media are deeply troubling; yet they also hold hope for improvement. Competition within the *mass* media is becoming more intense. Technological changes, the growth of the internet and the advent of social media are diversifying sources of information, changing the commercial drivers of the mass media, and weakening the implicit subsidy for strong journalism that advertising sometimes provides.

Not so long ago the changes in mass media would have been the end of the story. But today the change goes beyond the mass media: new technologies are dispersing our channels of communication much more widely, making it much easier for individuals to communicate through the new social media of the internet such as Facebook, Twitter and YouTube. All these changes occur and are influenced by broader changes in society and the economy. And many of them are connected.

The advent of social media is changing political debate, both by increasing the channels of communication and giving politicians and the public avenues for sidestepping the traditional media and the filtering it applies. Some of this is noisy and ugly, but other features of this change are encouraging. The new media will continue to evolve, strengthened by the National Broadband Network, and will create further new channels of debate. My hope is that a new generation of trusted institutions will provide the means for a new breed of online analysis and commentary, driven by serious contributors to the policy debate who can bypass the mass media and go directly to the sources of information and to their audiences.

As for the traditional media, you could call me a health nut, but I am depressed by the increasing saturation of traditional news media with high energy, low nutrition debates. One reason for this poor news diet is that commercial pressures are increasing the populist tone of newspapers, the traditional outlet for informed political debate. In the electronic media, the increasing number and diversity of media outlets intensifies the pressure.

Newspapers are declining in importance. The proportion of people buying daily newspapers has been steadily falling for decades, eroding their profits. So for many proprietors, maintaining a newspaper is almost a philanthropic activity, and many newspapers rely increasingly on fringe advertising and cross subsidies from other activities to survive.

News used to come in 24-hour cycles shaped by daily newspapers. Nowadays the need to feed electronic media has increased the tempo of the news cycle. Journalists and politicians all work harder and faster to keep feeding the beast.

This is driving populism, and displacing reporting of difficult, longer term issues. It contributes to the decline of trust in the traditional media that was reported recently in an *Essential Research* poll. The professionalisation of politics – often inspired by developments in the US – adds to these pressures. Political operatives are becoming more skilled in techniques for appealing quickly to wide and varied audiences – but often at the cost of more considered debate.

A few weeks ago a writer in *The Economist* argued that the changing character of the media was undermining the legitimacy of government – as an aside, it's interesting that this article was published not in the printed magazine, but in one of the paper's blogs. The writer argued that a key feature of a healthy democracy is that citizens communicate problems to government so that government can respond. In his view,

'The constant crisis-atmosphere contrarianism of the current media and internet environment overwhelms the signal-to-noise ratio…and preoccupies government with addressing blaring non-issues.'[13]

I do not agree with the writer's conclusion that this could lead to an increasing number of important issues being considered by non-democratic institutions. The public service – which is democratically accountable – has a crucial role in ensuring that this bleak prediction does not come to pass. We in the public service must protect democracy not only through our traditional role of providing advice to ministers, but by creating better mechanisms for engaging with citizens. I don't mean that public servants should have carte blanche; we must all adhere to the code of conduct. I am not suggesting public servants should become involved in partisan political debate. We need to remember the vital importance of remaining impartial and apolitical, and of retaining public and political trust.

That said, the new media holds tremendous potential for creating better ways of engaging with citizens. The internet and social media provide us with tools that have great potential to improve both democratic debate and the way government is conducted. Some of the most valuable and constructive contributions to Australia's policy debate occur on the net – such as *Australian Policy Online* and *The Lowy Interpreter*.

Beyond providing an alternative medium for debate, the new technology gives us in the public service new ways to engage with citizens that could be far-reaching in their impact.

I am optimistic about our ability to respond to these changes. Last year we produced a blueprint for reform the Australian Public Service called *Ahead*

---

13   http://www.economist.com/blogs/democracyinamerica/2011/07/democracy-v-china

of the Game, which aims to respond to the dilemmas Giddens describes. Its overarching goal is to improve the way we deliver services to citizens. Many of the proposals in *Ahead of the Game* are directly focused on this goal, both by improving services, and by finding new ways to collaborate with citizens both before and after decisions are made. In a world where citizens are more demanding than ever, we need to bolster the relationship between government and the community.

Public servants are held in high regard by the public. A recent poll conducted by Roy Morgan Research found that most respondents ranked public sector workers such as nurses, school teachers, police highly for their honesty and ethical standards.[14] The integrity of government in Australia is also ranked very highly in international comparisons. A highly trusted and fully effective public service will engage with citizens in a wide range of ways that reflect changing needs and new technologies.

To engage more effectively we need to make full use of new communications technologies. The report of the Government 2.0 Taskforce makes a compelling case for using the internet and other new technologies to make government more open, accountable, responsive and efficient. It shows how the new tools will give public servants the opportunity to engage with and respond to the community. I am encouraged that almost all the taskforce's recommendations were accepted by government, although there is still a lot more work needed to put them in practice.

As democracy evolves, our conception of democracy must grow

Improving citizen engagement is just one of the ways our conception of democracy can change and grow for the better. Democracy should mean more than just our right to vote in elections every three or four years. Good government has always required effective communication and collaboration between government and citizens.

Going right back to the emergence of the right to petition Parliament, which emerged from the Glorious Revolution, the conversation between government and the citizens has been a crucial feature of democracy. Changes in society and in the economy demand new and better ways for that conversation to occur. Although the explosion in communication media has made that conversation

---

14   Roy Morgan Image of Professionals Survey 2010.

rather noisy, new information technology also provides us with some tools to help constructive dialogue. The Australian Public Service has a key role in facilitating that process.

Notwithstanding the shifts I have described, we have a strong system of checks and balances between various sources of power and influence: through constitutions and conventions, the two chambers of parliament, a professional and impartial public service, political contest, elections, the media, think tanks, universities, courts and tribunals, the federal system, and the participation of citizens.

Our democracy is one of the strongest and most robust in the world. But as in all democracies, there are things we can improve. We should not be afraid of change. The institutions of government will continue to evolve, the balance between the various parts may shift, and the practice of democracy will grow. Our overriding goal should be to ensure that amidst all this change, we keep sight of the central purpose of democracy – to ensure good government, under the authority of the people, to the greatest benefit of the greatest number of people. As public servants we may all be Benthamite utilitarians in practice, but this fits neatly within the constitution, legislation enacted under it and the evolving conventions which give them life.

Appendix: Details of the movement of retiring secretaries since 2004[1]

Name	Department	Date of appointment	Date appointment expires	First appointment as Secretary	Actual date of cessation of appointment
Mr Roger BEALE AO	Environment and Heritage	11 March 2001	10 March 2004	11 March 1996	10 March 2004
	Environment and Heritage / Environment, Sport and Territories / Environment	10 April 1996	10 March 2001		10 March 2001
	Environment, Sport and Territories / Environment	11 March 1996	Not applicable		10 April 1996
Mr David BORTHWICK AO PSM	Environment and Water Resources	11 March 2007	10 March 2010	11 March 2004	2 January 2009
	Environment and Heritage / Environment and Water Resources	11 March 2004	10 March 2007		10 March 2007
Dr Peter BOXALL AO	Resources, Energy and Tourism	3 December 2007	2 December 2012	18 January 1997	1 February 2009
	Employment and Workplace Relations	18 January 2007	17 January 2010		2 December 2007
	Employment and Workplace Relations	18 January 2002	17 January 2007		17 January 2007
	Finance and Administration / Finance	18 January 1997	17 January 2002		17 January 2002
Ms Lynelle BRIGGS PSM	Medicare	17 August 2009	June 2011	6 November 2004	June 2011
	Australian Public Service Commission	6 November 2007	5 November 2010		17 August 2009
		6 November 2004	5 November 2007		5 November 2007

---

1   Including two agency heads, Lynelle Briggs and Dennis Trewin, who held equivalent ranking to a departmental secretary.

Name	Department	Date of appointment	Date appointment expires	First appointment as Secretary	Actual date of cessation of appointment
Mr Robert **CORNALL AO**	Attorney General's	26 October 2007	25 October 2010	24 January 2000	31 August 2008
	Attorney General's	26 October 2004	25 October 2007		25 October 2007
	Attorney General's	24 January 2000	23 January 2005		26 October 2004
Dr Jeffrey **HARMER AO**	Families, Housing, Community Service and Indigenous Affairs	26 October 2008	25 October 2013	10 March 2003	15 April 2011
	Family and Community Services	26 October 2004	25 October 2008		25 October 2008
	Education, Science and Training	10 March 2003	9 March 2006		26 October 2004
Dr Allan **HAWKE AC**	Defence	21 October 1999	20 October 2002	26 April 1994	20 October 2002
	Transport and Regional Development / Transport and Regional Services	11 March 1996	10 March 2001		10 October 1999
	Veterans' Affairs	26 April 1994	26 April 1999		11 March 1996
Dr Kenneth **HENRY AC**	Treasury	27 April 2006	26 April 2011	27 April 2001	27 April 2011
		27 April 2001	26 April 2006		
Ms Joanna **HEWITT AO**	Agriculture, Fisheries and Forestry	26 October 2004	25 October 2007	26 October 2004	4 May 2007
Mr Michael **L'ESTRANGE AO**	Foreign Affairs and Trade	15 January 2009	16 January 2012	17 January 2005	15 December 2009
		17 January 2005			

Name	Department	Date of appointment	Date appointment expires	First appointment as Secretary	Actual date of cessation of appointment
Mr Ken MATTHEWS AO	Transport and Regional Services	5 February 2003	4 February 2008	5 February 1998	26 October 2004
	Transport and Regional Services	1 November 1999	4 February 2003		4 February 2003
	Agriculture, Fisheries and Forestry / Primary Industries and Energy	5 February 1998	4 February 2003		1 November 1999
Mr Terry MORAN AC	Prime Minister and Cabinet	3 March 2008	2 March 2013	3 March 2008	4 September 2011
Mr Andrew PODGER AO	Prime Minister and Cabinet (Associate Secretary)	6 November 2004	30 June 2005	20 December 1993	5 November 2004
	Public Service Commissioner	18 January 2002	17 January 2005		17 January 2002
	Health and Aged Care / Health and Family Services	11 March 2001	10 March 2004		10 March 2001
	Health and Aged Care / Health and Family Services	11 March 1996	10 March 2001		11 March 1996
	Housing and Regional Development	26 April 1994	26 April 1999		26 April 1994
	Administrative Services / Arts and Administrative Services	20 December 1993	Not applicable		26 April 1994
Ms Patricia SCOTT	Broadband, Communications and the Digital Economy	3 December 2007	2 December 2012	26 October 2004	29 August 2009
	Communications, Information Technology and the Arts	7 May 2007	6 May 2010		3 December 2007
	Human Services	26 October 2004	25 October 2007		7 May 2007

Name	Department	Date of appointment	Date appointment expires	First appointment as Secretary	Actual date of cessation of appointment
Dr Peter SHERGOLD AC	Prime Minister and Cabinet	10 February 2003	9 February 2008	25 September 1995 (Public Service Commissioner)	9 February 2008
	Education, Science and Training	18 January 2002	17 January 2007		9 February 2003
	Employment and Workplace Relations / Employment, Workplace Relations and Small Business / Workplace Relations and Small Business	5 February 1998	4 February 2003		17 January 2002
	Public Service Commissioner	25 September 1995	24 September 2000		4 February 1998
Mr Richard SMITH AO	Defence	18 November 2005	17 November 2007	18 November 2002	1 December 2006
		18 November 2002	17 November 2005		
Mr Mark SULLIVAN AO	Veterans' Affairs	26 October 2004	25 October 2008	18 January 2002	11 July 2008
	Family and Community Services	18 January 2002	17 January 2005		26 October 2004
Mr Michael TAYLOR AO	Infrastructure, Transport and Regional Development and Local Government	26 October 2008	25 October 2013	17 January 2000	24 April 2009
	Transport and Regional Services	26 October 2004	25 October 2008		26 October 2004
	Agriculture, Fisheries and Forestry	17 January 2000	16 January 2005		
Mr Dennis TREWIN AO	Australian Bureau of Statistics	1 July 2000	6 January 2007	1 July 2000	6 January 2007

Name	Department	Date of appointment	Date appointment expires	First appointment as Secretary	Actual date of cessation of appointment
Ms Helen **WILLIAMS** **AO**	Human Services	7 May 2007	6 May 2010	17 January 1985	11 September 2009
	Communications, Information Technology and the Arts	26 October 2004	25 October 2007		7 May 2007
	Communications, Information Technology and the Arts	18 January 2002	17 January 2005		26 October 2004
	Public Service Commissioner	16 June 1997	10 March 2001		4 February 1998
	Immigration and Multicultural Affairs	11 March 1996	Not applicable		16 June 1997
	Tourism	14 June 1993	Not applicable		11 March 1996
	Various non-Secretary positions—1987 to 1993	Not applicable	Not applicable		Not applicable
	Education/Education and Youth Affairs	17 January 1985	Not applicable		3 July 1987